IMAGES
*of America*

# CLERMONT

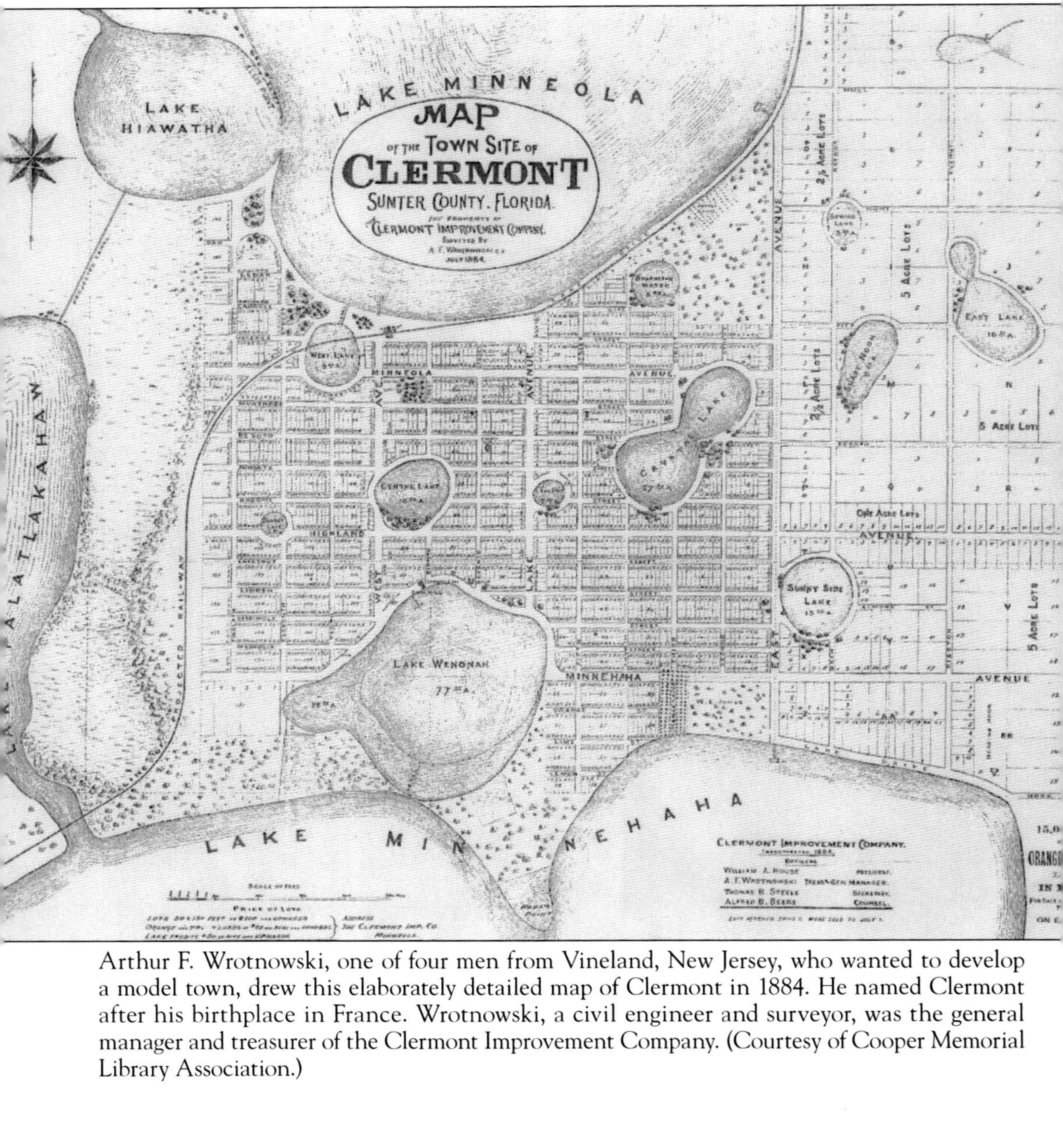


Arthur F. Wrotnowski, one of four men from Vineland, New Jersey, who wanted to develop a model town, drew this elaborately detailed map of Clermont in 1884. He named Clermont after his birthplace in France. Wrotnowski, a civil engineer and surveyor, was the general manager and treasurer of the Clermont Improvement Company. (Courtesy of Cooper Memorial Library Association.)

**On the Cover:** Early Clermont was a hunter's paradise that attracted dignitaries and outdoorsmen from across the country, including those pictured here. Local guide Harry K. Stokes, who ran a hunting and fishing lodge called the Jolly Palms around 1898, shot this 15-foot alligator. Stokes went on to become one of Lake County's most respected leaders. (Courtesy of Cooper Memorial Library Association.)

IMAGES
*of America*

# CLERMONT

Doris Bloodsworth

ARCADIA
PUBLISHING

ISBN 978-0-7385-8586-4

Published by Arcadia Publishing
Charleston, South Carolina

Printed in the United States of America

Library of Congress Control Number: 2009941477

For all general information, please contact Arcadia Publishing:
Telephone 843-853-2070
Fax 843-853-0044
E-mail sales@arcadiapublishing.com
For customer service and orders:
Toll-Free 1-888-313-2665

Visit us on the Internet at www.arcadiapublishing.com

*To my family and supporters of Cooper Memorial Library,
where my love of history and reading found early inspiration*

# Contents

# ACKNOWLEDGMENTS

Clermont's natural beauty captured the imaginations and cameras of visitors from its earliest days. There are more than 200 postcards of the Citrus Tower, alone. But the beautiful vistas only paint part of the picture. The city's real story is its people—visionaries who sought a quality of life for their community and had the tenacity and faith to overcome tough times.

It is impossible to thank everyone who made this book possible. I am especially indebted to Ann Dupee for her insights and photographs and to the board of Cooper Memorial Library Association who generously shared their historical records. My thanks go to the Friends of Cooper Memorial Library and to the library's staff as well as to the South Lake County Historical Society for their enthusiastic support. Others who assisted me include adidas, Cyleta Austin, Richard and Toni Bell, Carle and Wendy Bishop, Clayton Bishop, Phoebe Boychuk, Dennis and Valerie Bronson, Victoria Bucher, Linda Charlton, Jeff Chase, Carol Willard Clark, Clermont High School Alumni, Jody Close, Kim and Jason Couch, Harold Cummings, Barbara Elkins, Joy England, Bonnie Gearhart, Ray Goodgame, Darren Gray, Lucy Hage, Elizabeth Heine, Greg and Ben Homan, Dennis Horton, Kathy Johnson, Brandy Johnson-Scharpf, Daniel Keel, Howard King, Charles Konsler, Nina Kraft, the Lake County Historical Society, Debbie Langley, Dick Langley, Asher Ledwidge, Guy Lillard, Dorothy McGriff, Stan Melnick, Natalie Middleton, Terry Moherek, Steve Monn, Lavonda Morris, the National Hurricane Center, Olivenbaum Insurance, Bonnie Ray, Dr. Dot Richardson, Sanctuary Ridge Golf Club, Ray San Fratello, Glenna Scaife, Leonard and Jo Ann House Seaver, Dennis Smolarek, the *South Lake Press*, the State Archives of Florida, Tracy Swank, Janet Thomas, Carol Tomlinson, Jack and Jackie Ulch, Dolores Gano Walker, Charlie Weatherbee, Jane Williamson, and John Zweifel. Heartfelt admiration goes to Miriam Johnson and Rosemary Young for their exhaustive research, which resulted in *Clermont: Gem of the Hills*. Other helpful references include *About Some Lakes and More in Lake County*, *Boxcars and Candlelight*, *The Citrus Industry in the Sunshine State*, *Florida Hurricanes and Tropical Storms*, *Florida Railroads in the 1920s*, *A History of Florida* (third edition), *Lake County Florida*, and *Through Schoolhouse Doors: A History of Lake County Schools*.

And finally, there is special appreciation for the support of my husband, John, my children, and the Arcadia Publishing production team, including my editor, Lindsay Harris.

# Introduction

Standing on scenic Sugarloaf Mountain or viewing spectacular sunsets across Lake Minnehaha or Lake Minneola, it is easy to see how Clermont became known as "Gem of the Hills" and why it has attracted people for centuries.

Some of the first-known residents of the area were the Timucuan tribes that extended from southeast Georgia to Central Florida. They became extinct through battle fatalities, disease, and assimilation into the Seminole nation.

Clermont's forests and lakes provided food and shelter for those seeking a fresh start. The first permanent white settler was James Anderson, who came from Georgia prior to the Civil War and farmed near Kirkland Lake.

In 1868, Herring and Mary Hooks, along with their 12 children, came from Americus, Georgia, and homesteaded land at nearby Yalaha. Hooks discovered the Clermont area in 1871 during a hunting trip and was taken by the rolling hills and lakes. He bought land for $1 an acre by Lake Minnehaha and built a hunting cabin. The spot was called Hooks Point and is known today as Margaree Gardens, named after Margaree Brantley Cooley.

Hooks and his descendants went on to play major roles in Clermont's history. His son Thomas brokered the land that became the original city limits. Hooks's great-grandson Oakley Seaver was so beloved that he became known as "Mr. Clermont."

In 1878, George Gano and his son Archibald, 21, came from Vineland, New Jersey, a city that would produce Clermont's founding fathers six years later. Archibald Gano made an impact across South Lake County. He was an expert mill operator and the builder responsible for many of the oldest homes in Clermont, Groveland, and Mascotte. He built a tomato-packing plant in Clermont and signed the city's incorporation papers in 1891. His Clermont home, built in 1891, became a boardinghouse and then a bed-and-breakfast inn, before serving as a women-and-children's shelter.

During the 1880s, railroad expansion in Florida ignited a population explosion. The Orange Belt Railway ran from Sanford to St. Petersburg, with a stop in Clermont. A smaller rail line, the Tavares and Gulf Railroad, ran from Tavares to Clermont.

John Compton arrived in 1880. The former Ohio resident planted a citrus grove by Lake Minnehaha and was appointed the first superintendent of public schools after Lake County was formed. Compton held the position for 27 years and also served as a county commissioner.

Clermont's official birthday came in 1884 when four visionary entrepreneurs from Vineland, New Jersey, bought 15,000 acres in a deal brokered by future state legislator Thomas Hooks, son of Herring Hooks.

William House, Arthur Wrotnowski, Thomas Steele, and Alfred Beers formed the Clermont Improvement Company with the dream of creating a model town. The name "Clermont" came from Clermont-Ferrand, France, Wrotnowski's birthplace.

The men brought formidable expertise and had seen a similar idea succeed in their hometown. Vineland was one of the first and most successful planned communities in the country. It was founded in 1861 by visionary Charles Landis, who purchased 20,000 acres in southern New Jersey and advertised to attract settlers.

William House was the president of Clermont Improvement Company. He was a former Pennsylvania senator before moving to Vineland, where he served on New Jersey's supreme court. He and his family moved to Clermont in 1884 and built a five-story house near Lake Minneola.

Arthur Wrotnowski, a civil engineer and surveyor, was the company's general manager and treasurer. He drew an intricate map of the new town that is still amazingly accurate. Company secretary Thomas Steele returned to New Jersey, but his son Charles Steele stayed in Clermont. Judge Alfred Beers served as legal counsel. He returned to Bridgeport, Connecticut.

The company advertised Clermont's charms to Northerners. "It will be our aim not only to make it a model town," one advertisement promised, "but a health resort and educational center."

In 1888, Hattie Daggett, a 23-year-old former nurse from Vineland, visited Clermont while looking for a winter home for her parents. She eventually made Clermont her permanent home and married. She supervised the creation of a canal and built the historic Log House, a popular three-story lodge that stood until 1959.

Some settlers, such as Montgomery Cooper, came from the Midwest. They discovered that the area was ideal for growing tomatoes. By 1890, Clermont had become the tomato capital of Florida. Crate-loads of tomatoes were transported by barge, steamship, and train.

In 1891, twenty-four citizens voted for the city to incorporate under Florida laws. The first mayor was C. H. Goodenough.

A devastating cold snap in 1894–1895, called "the Great Freeze," wiped out the tomato crops and fledgling citrus groves. Many families moved away. Those that stayed survived mostly from the available fish and game. The town charter was abandoned.

Clermont eventually rebounded, however. The community saw major advances in 1913. The town's first newspaper, the *Clermont Clarion*, was published, and Stuart Bowman of Huntington, West Virginia, founded the Lake Highlands Company, developing residential property on the north side of Lake Minnehaha. Bowman and his associates built the Lake Highlands Clubhouse, which included a formal dining room and boathouse. In December 1916, citizens voted to reincorporate the City of Clermont.

The 1920s were heady times for Clermont. Juanita Films opened a movie studio, produced three films using locals as extras, and hosted a world premiere. Property owners witnessed an unprecedented land boom. More than $2.5 million in real estate was sold in one month. Land could change hands several times in one day. On December 27, 1927, the first foursome teed off at Palisades Golf and Country Club. The city started taxing residents and issuing bonds to make improvements. Bond indebtedness rose to almost $1 million until 1929, when the bonding company sued for payment. As the Great Depression lingered, few people could pay taxes. The millage rate went from 11 to 691 mills. In 1939, the city went into bankruptcy, with the highest bond-indebtedness-per-capita rate in the world.

A plan was devised to pay 50¢ on the dollar. By April 1, 1940, citizens had paid 92 percent of the taxes owed.

During World War II, Clermont was home to two military units. After the war, Clermont's population swelled. In 1956, one of the state's oldest man-made tourist attractions was born when the gleaming white Citrus Tower opened to great fanfare. It was Florida's highest observation point, offering a spectacular 360-degree view for miles. A few years later, the attraction would be joined by the Presidents Hall of Fame.

Citrus reigned as the area's main economic driver until triple freezes in the 1980s. The once-lush green groves and citrus blossom–perfumed air were gone forever after the final freeze of 1989 on Christmas Day. The rolling hills became barren.

However, like flowers in the spring, new housing developments rose from the ground, filling the city with new voices. Active retirement and golf communities flourished. In 1993, Clermont High School graduated its last class and South Lake High School opened, uniting the communities of Clermont and Groveland.

In 2009, the city marked its 125th anniversary with a celebration lasting several days. Today Clermont is Lake County's largest city. The Gem of the Hills never sparkled more brightly.

# One

# Early Settlers

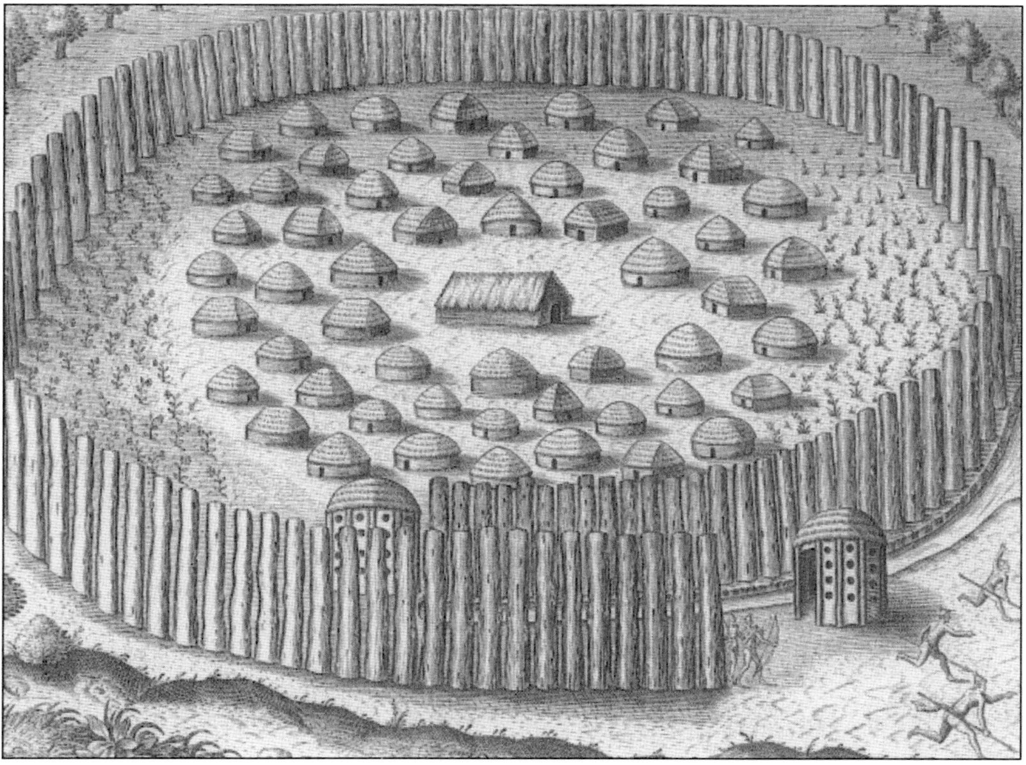

Clermont's lakes and forests provided food and shelter for some of the area's earliest-known inhabitants, the Timucua (pictured here in this *c.* 1564 painting by Jacques le Moyne). Timucuan women tended the crops while the men hunted. They cooked meat by boiling it over an open fire known as the *barbacoa*, the source of the word "barbecue." (Courtesy of the State Archives of Florida.)

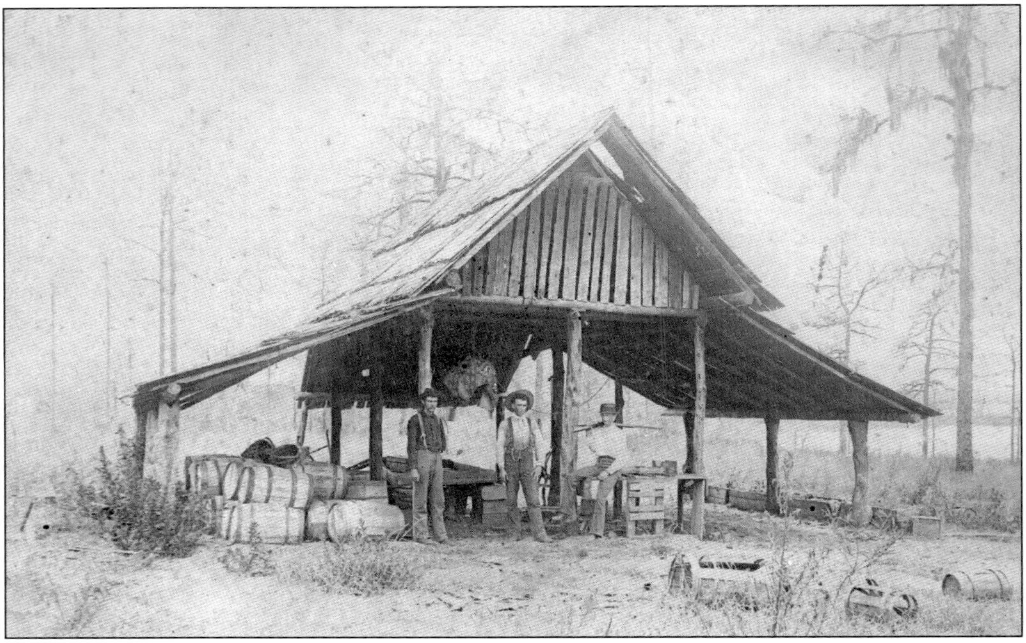

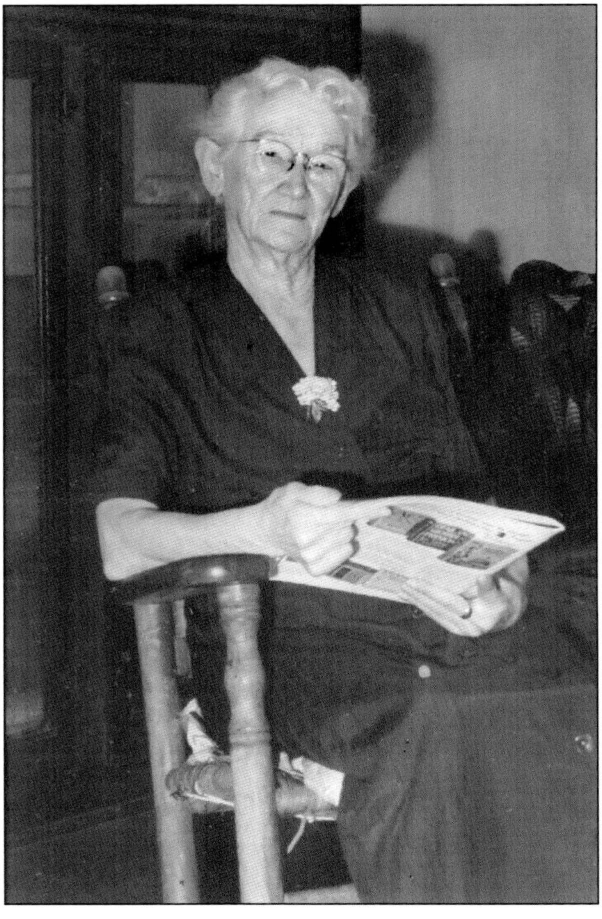

Herring Hooks was homesteading with his family in Yalaha when he discovered the Clermont area in 1874. He and his wife, Mary, purchased land for $1 an acre on Lake Betsy (today's Lake Minnehaha). The spot is called Hooks Point. Herring's camp, seen in this c. 1880 photograph, was located at the present-day intersection of Fifth and Seminole Streets. (Courtesy of Cooper Memorial Library Association.)

Herring and Mary Hooks had 12 children. Their descendants played a major role in Clermont's destiny: Their son Thomas brokered the sale of land that became Clermont's original city limits, and their great-grandson Oakley Seaver was so beloved that he became known as "Mr. Clermont." Pictured here is Oakley's grandmother, Willie Hooks, wife of Herring's son Robert. (Courtesy of Cooper Memorial Library Association.)

In 1875, James Lee and his wife, Lavina, moved their family from Berrien County, Georgia, and homesteaded 160 acres southwest of Lake Minnehaha. The pioneer neighbors helped each other. They took turns once a month getting supplies from Leesburg where they traded alligator and deer hides for staples such as ammunition and coffee. Every two weeks someone went to Webster for mail. (Courtesy of Cyleta Lee Austin.)

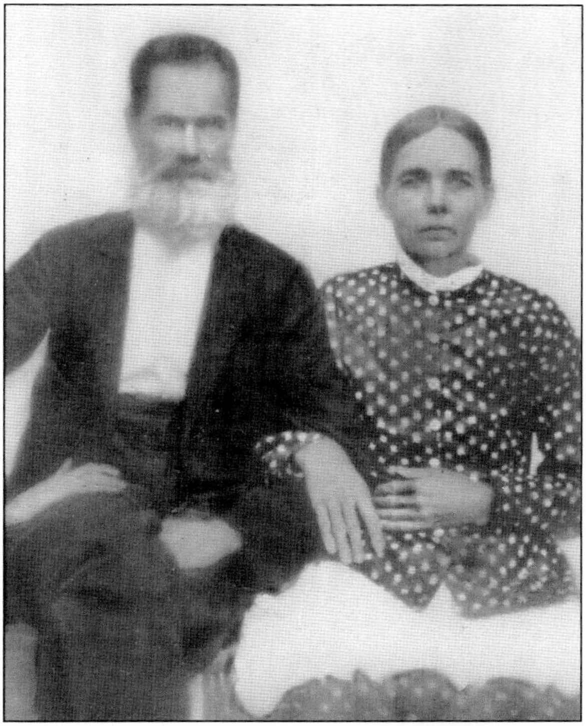

Experienced outdoorsman Lorem Brown lived in Green Swamp with his wife and seven children and served as a tour guide for hunting parties that frequented the Clermont area, as shown in this *c.* 1900 photograph. Years later, during Prohibition, Brown became known as the "Moonshiner of Green Swamp." (Courtesy of the State Archives of Florida.)

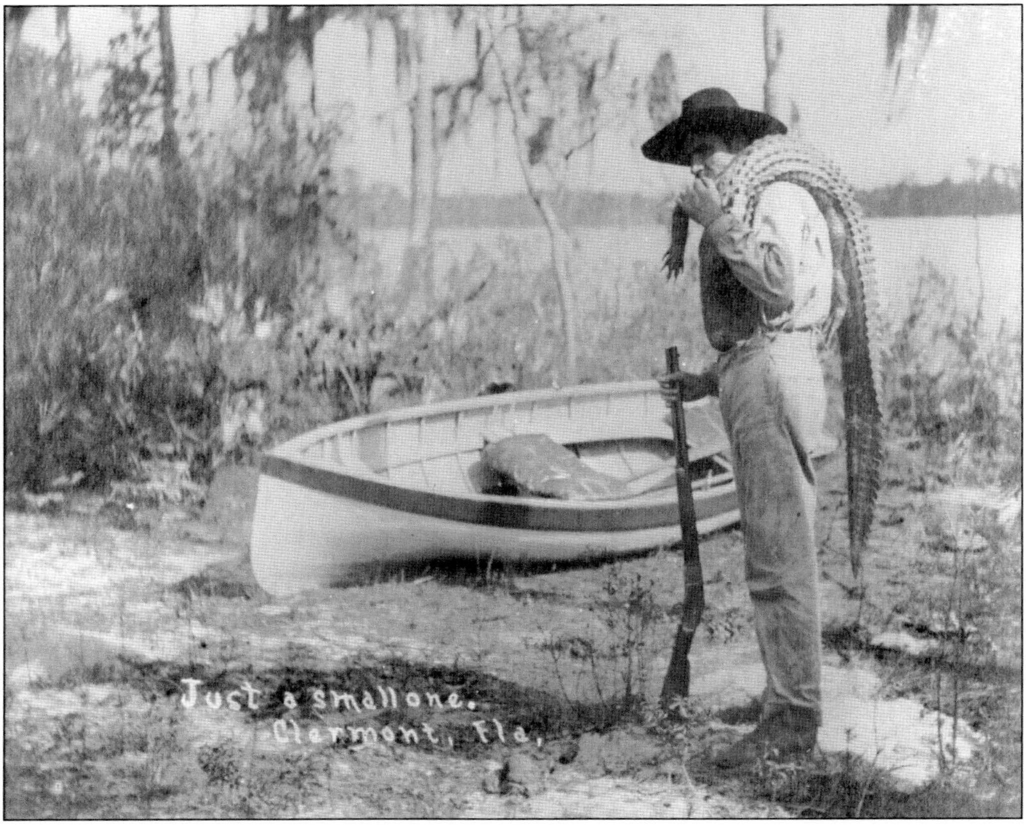

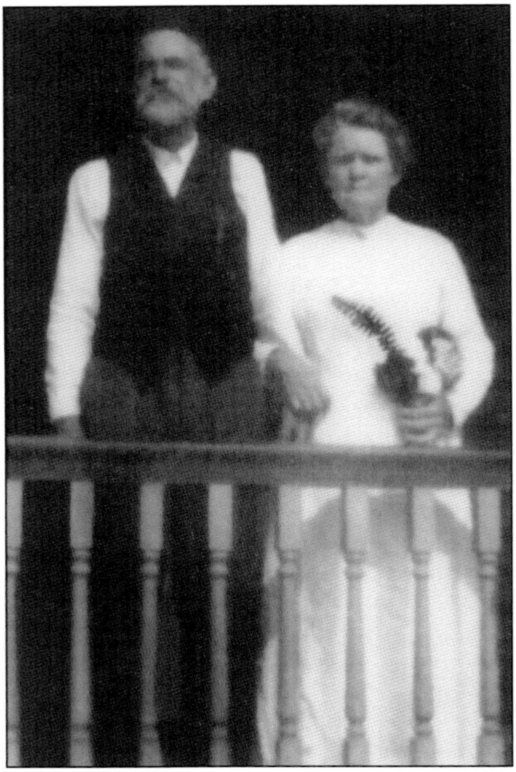

Archibald Gano came to Florida from New Jersey with his father in the 1870s. He and his first wife, Sallie, had 10 sons. He built a packing plant by Lake Minneola essential to Clermont's early tomato industry. He was also an early settler in Villa City, where the dam that helped power his sawmill was dynamited by disgruntled neighbors who blamed the dam for causing the Palatlakaha Creek to flood their property. (Courtesy of Dolores Gano Walker.)

Gano built this home on Minneola Avenue in 1891. C. O. Roe bought the home in 1900 and lived there winters until 1911, when new homeowner Stella Thompson moved the house to the corner of Montrose Street and West Avenue. The home currently serves as a shelter for women and children. (Courtesy of Cooper Memorial Library Association.)

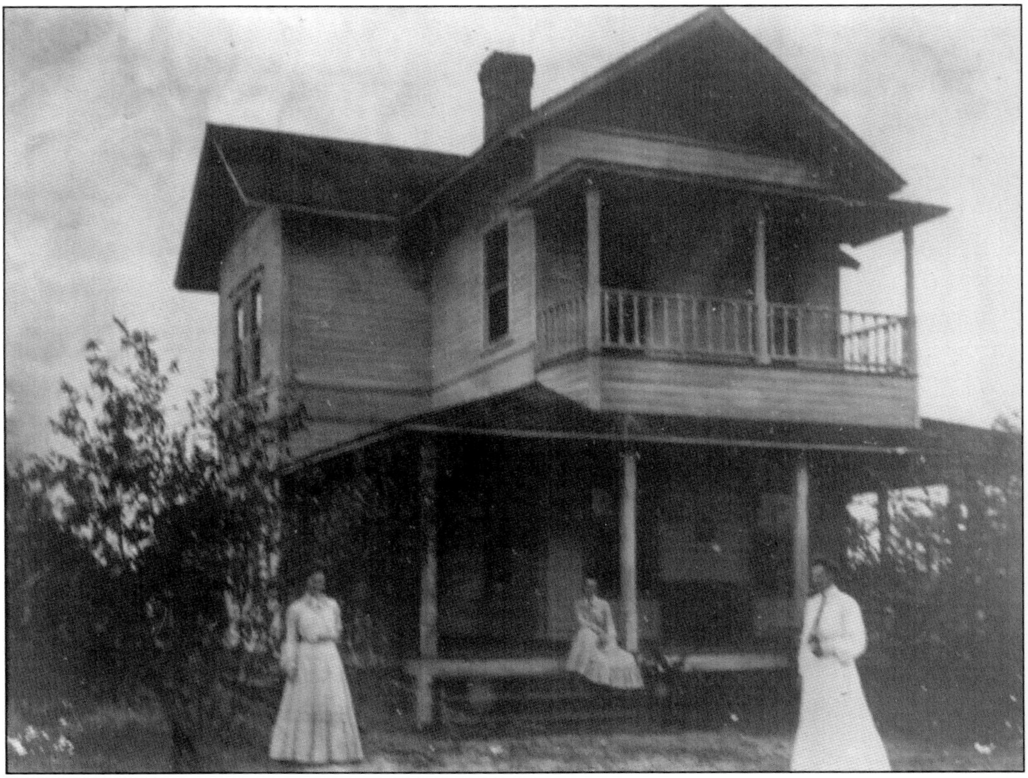

In 1887, Peter Demens extended his Orange Belt Railway from Sanford through Clermont and west to the Gulf Coast. The influence of the former Russian-aristocrat-turned-Florida-land-developer is evident in the Russian architecture of this *c.* 1900 Clermont train depot and in his naming of the destination city, St. Petersburg, which was his childhood hometown in Russia. (Courtesy of the State Archives of Florida.)

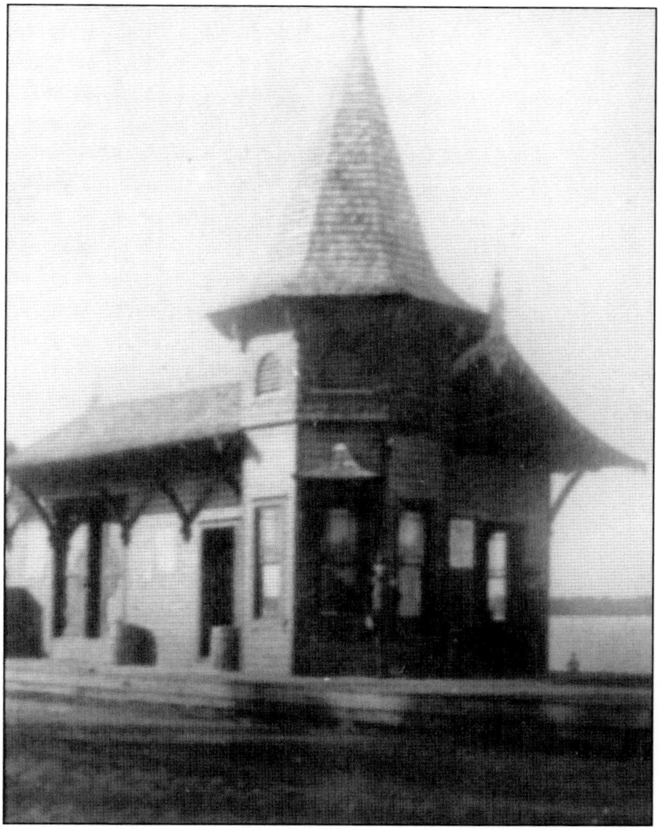

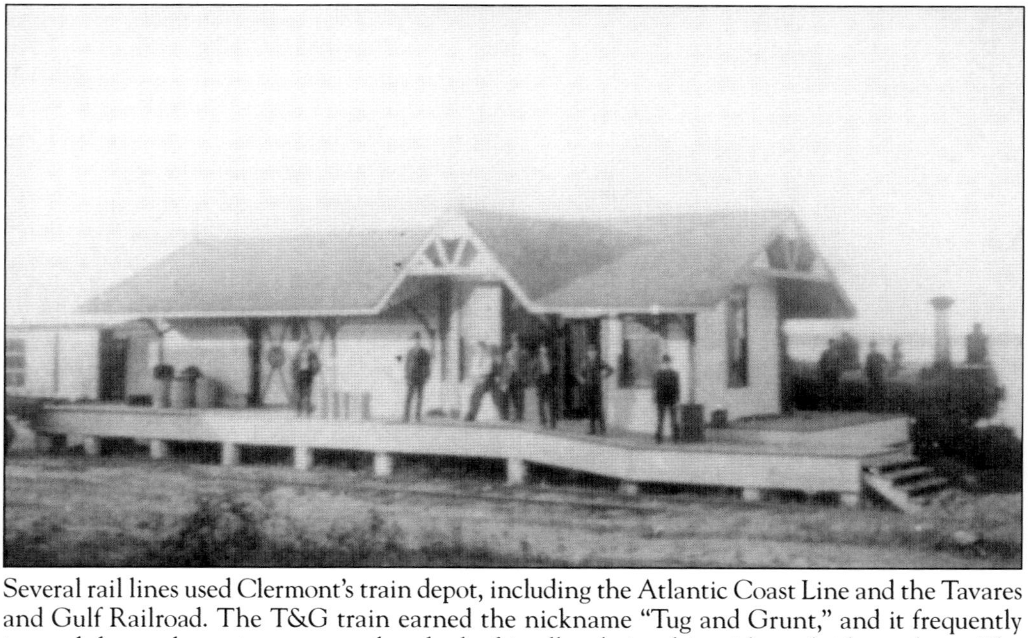

Several rail lines used Clermont's train depot, including the Atlantic Coast Line and the Tavares and Gulf Railroad. The T&G train earned the nickname "Tug and Grunt," and it frequently jumped the track, yet its crew members had a friendly relationship with trackside residents. The engineer played tunes on the whistle and threw teaberry gum to children along the way. (Courtesy of the State Archives of Florida.)

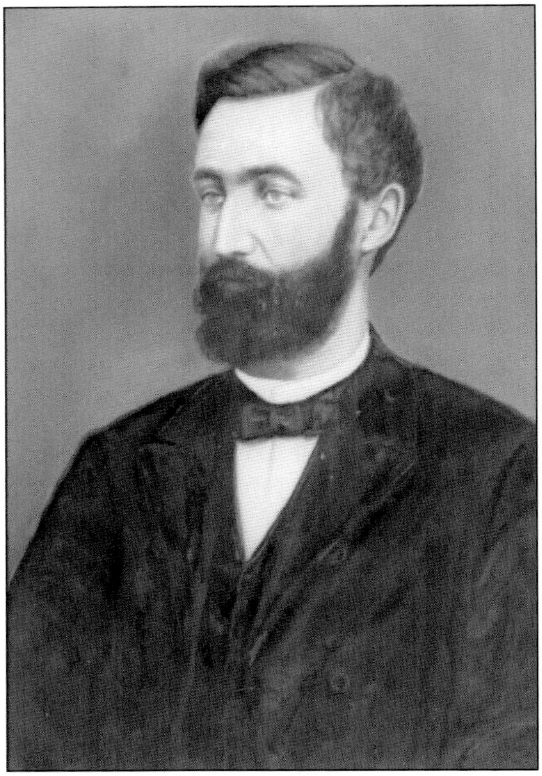

William A. House was one of four men from Vineland, New Jersey, who dreamed of creating a model town. They formed the Clermont Improvement Company in 1884 and purchased 20,000 acres in what became the original city limits. House, president of the company, was a former Pennsylvania senator and New Jersey Supreme Court justice. He and his family moved to Clermont in 1884. He died in 1891. (Courtesy of Cooper Memorial Library Association.)

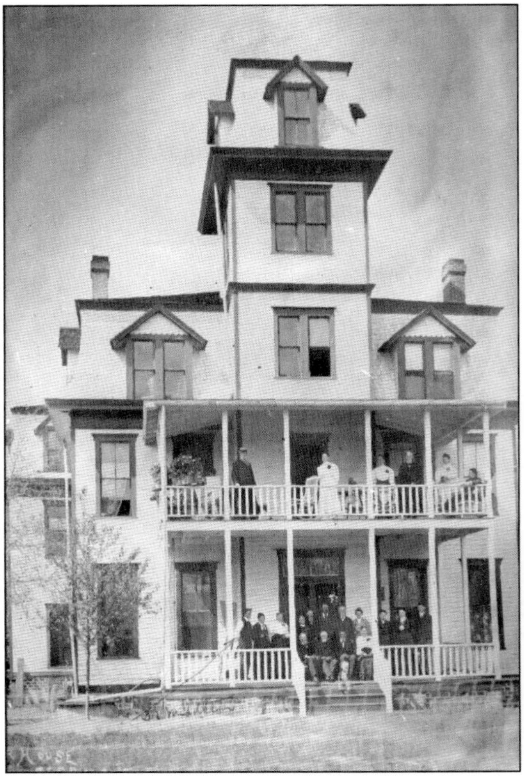

William and Eliza House built this distinctive five-story home around 1885 at the northwest corner of Lake Avenue and Montrose Street. It changed hands several times and was known for years as the Hoobler House, after its owners. Years later, it was remodeled as the Palm Park Hotel. (Courtesy of Cooper Memorial Library Association.)

House and his associates understood the power of advertising. Their hometown, Vineland, New Jersey, was one of the first and most successful planned communities. The founder, a visionary named Charles Landis, advertised in hopes of luring farmers to the settlement. Another advertisement the Clermont Improvement Company published promoted Clermont for winter homes and farms in the "Land of Flowers." (Courtesy of Cooper Memorial Library Association.)

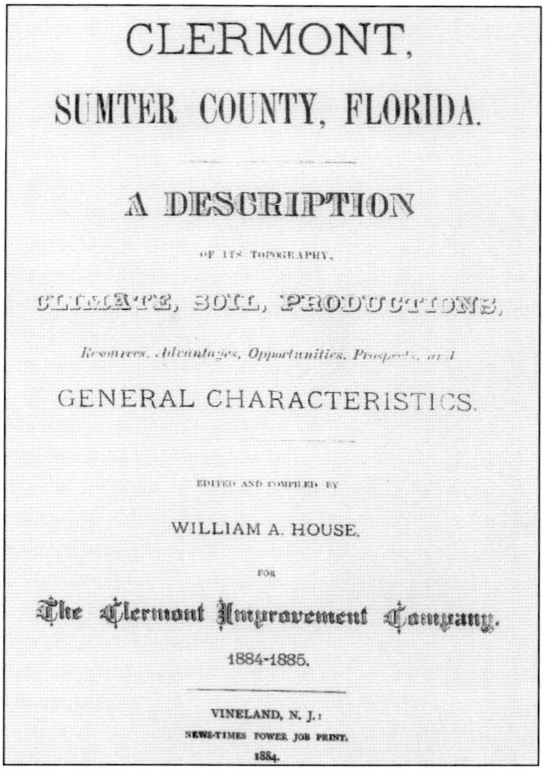

CLERMONT,

SUMTER COUNTY, FLORIDA.

A DESCRIPTION

OF ITS TOPOGRAPHY,

CLIMATE, SOIL, PRODUCTIONS,

*Resources, Advantages, Opportunities, Prospects, and*

GENERAL CHARACTERISTICS.

EDITED AND COMPILED BY

WILLIAM A. HOUSE,

FOR

The Clermont Improvement Company.

1884-1885.

VINELAND, N. J.:
NEWS-TIMES POWER JOB PRINT.
1884.

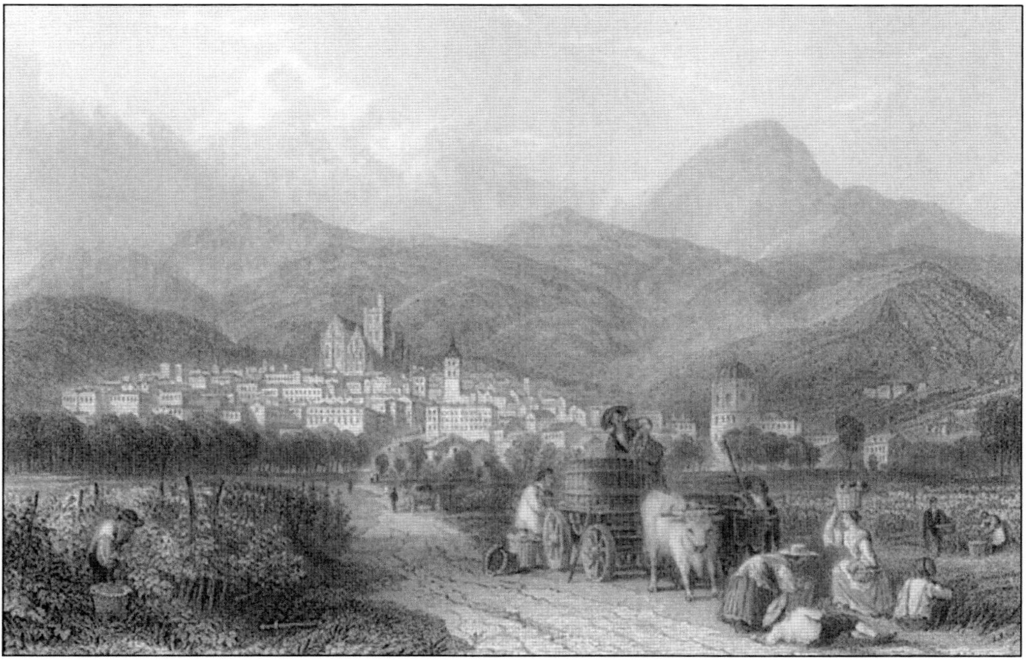

Clermont was named after Clermont-Ferrand, France, the birthplace of the company's general manager and treasurer, Arthur Wrotnowski. This 1879 engraving of the French city was created about 36 years after his birth. When he was 11 years old, Wrotnowski moved with his family to Baton Rouge, Louisiana, where his father ran a sugarcane mill. (Courtesy of Steve Hall.)

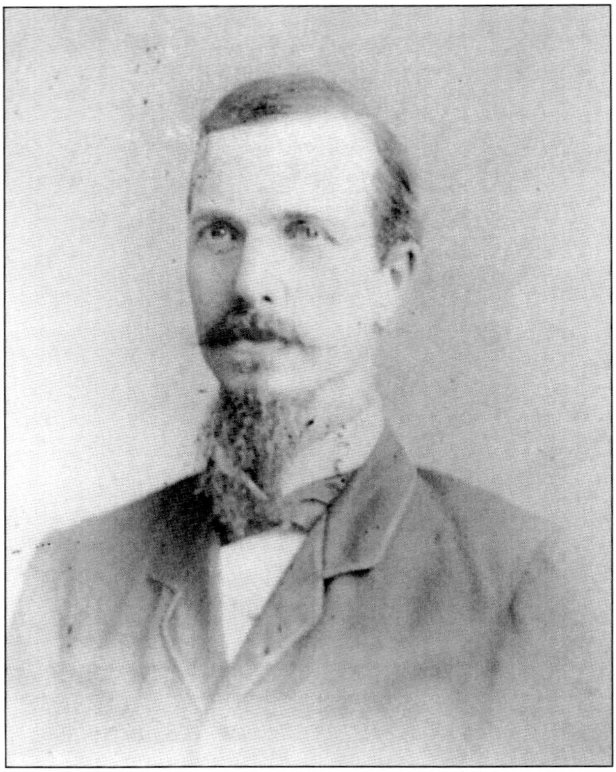

Arthur Wrotnowski was a civil engineer; he surveyed and mapped Clermont in 1884. He served as a lieutenant colonel in the Union Army's Engineering Corps before moving to Clermont in 1884. While living in Clermont, he served as the town's first postmaster and met and married his second wife. In 1889, the Wrotnowskis moved to Mexico and later to New Orleans, where Arthur would oversee engineering projects. He died in Nogales, Arizona, in 1911. (Courtesy of the Lake County Historical Society.)

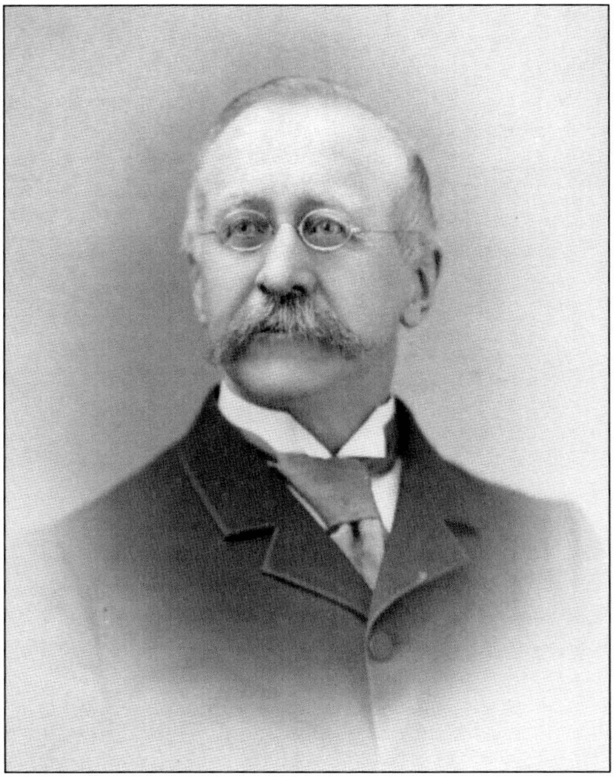

Thomas Steele was the secretary for the Clermont Improvement Company. He came from Vineland, New Jersey, and brought his son Charles to help start Clermont in 1884. Though Thomas returned home, Charles stayed and married Laurette Bishop Pollard. In 1898, the couple had a daughter, Elsie. The family later moved to Daytona Beach and eventually to Seattle. (Courtesy of the Lake County Historical Society.)

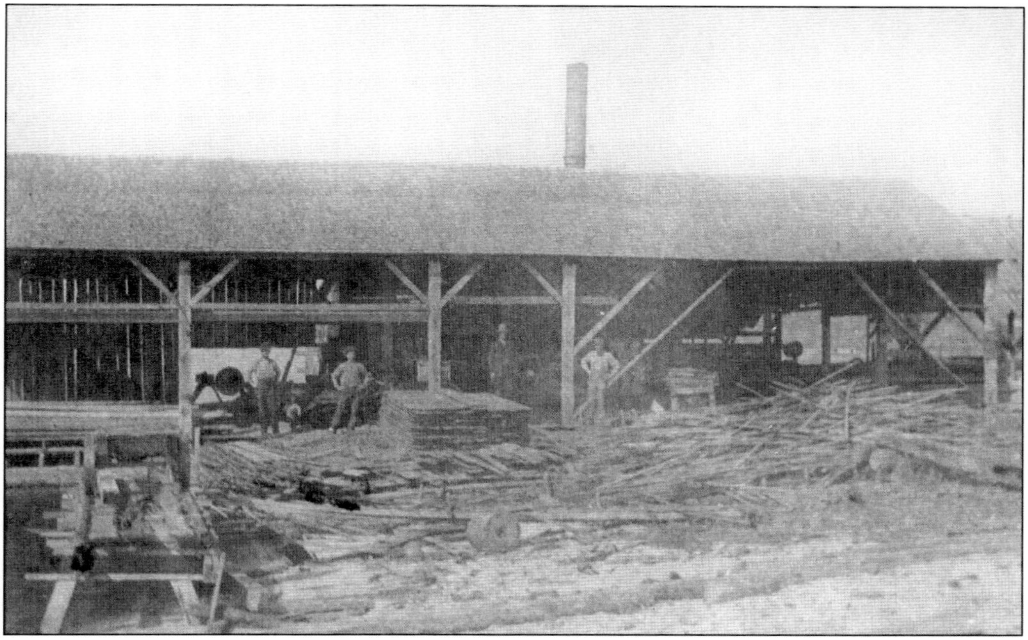

Charles Steele's in-laws, Fernando and Thankful Bishop, also helped settle Clermont in 1884. Fernando Bishop and his business partner, M. P. Godfrey, brought their lumber business from Michigan and built the sawmill pictured here beside Lake Minneola. Heavy equipment came by train to Wildwood, then it was transferred to a 21-mule team, which took six more days to reach the mill. (Courtesy of Cooper Memorial Library Association.)

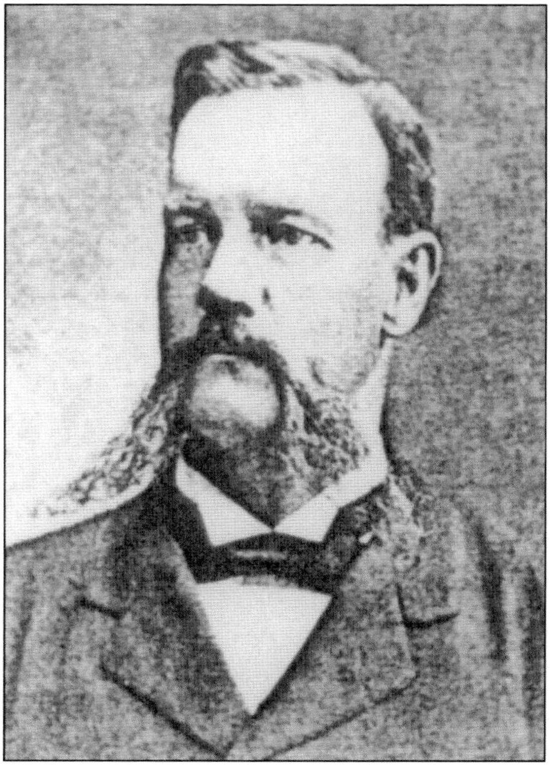

Judge Alfred Beers served as the legal counsel for the Clermont Improvement Company. Afterward, he returned to Bridgeport, Connecticut, where he became active in the Grand Army of the Republic, the fraternal organization of Union veterans that, in 1867, established the annual observance of Decoration Day, now called Memorial Day. (Courtesy of the Lake County Historical Society.)

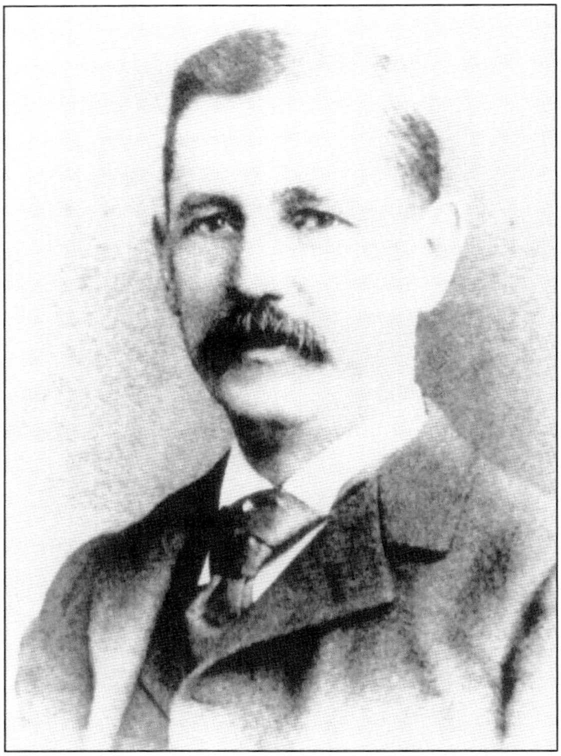

Disston Avenue was named after Hamilton Disston, a real estate developer and son of a successful Pennsylvania saw manufacturer. Disston purchased 4 million acres of Florida land in 1881. This was an area larger than the state of Connecticut and reportedly the biggest land purchase by a single person in world history. Disston pushed to build canals and rail lines and helped create numerous cities across the state. (Courtesy of the State Archives of Florida.)

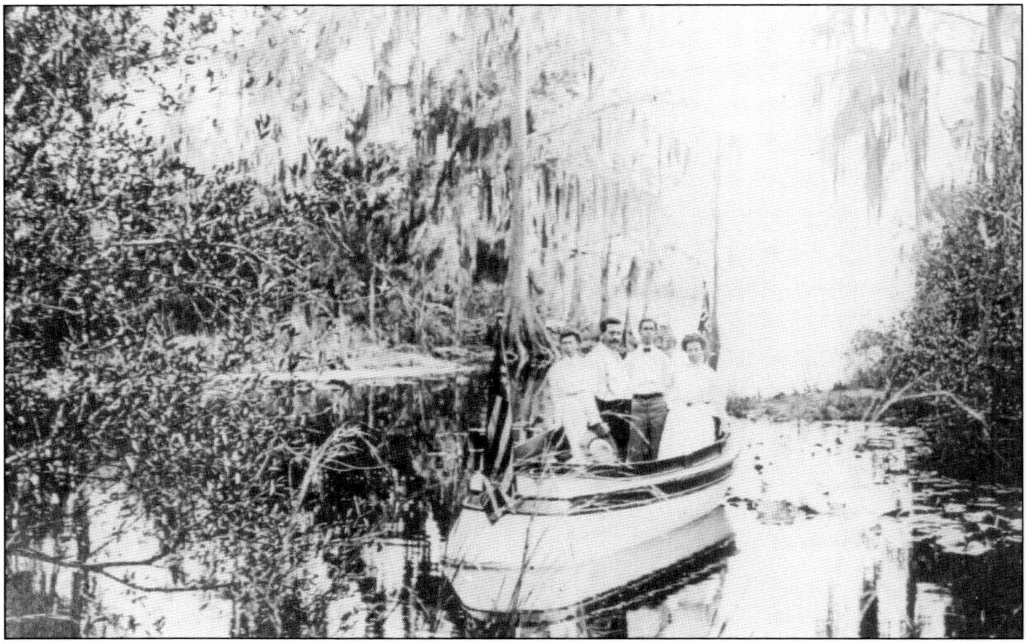

Disston urged the digging of Florida canals to make boat travel easier. Clermont's chain of lakes, connected by the Palatlakaha Creek, provided a major route to obtain supplies and mail. It also afforded picture-perfect afternoons for relaxing, as captured in this c. 1910 photograph. Seen here from left to right are May and A. B. "Tony" McNiece and George Pollard and his mother, Laurette Pollard. (Courtesy of Cooper Memorial Library Association.)

# *Two*

# Clermont, a Model Town

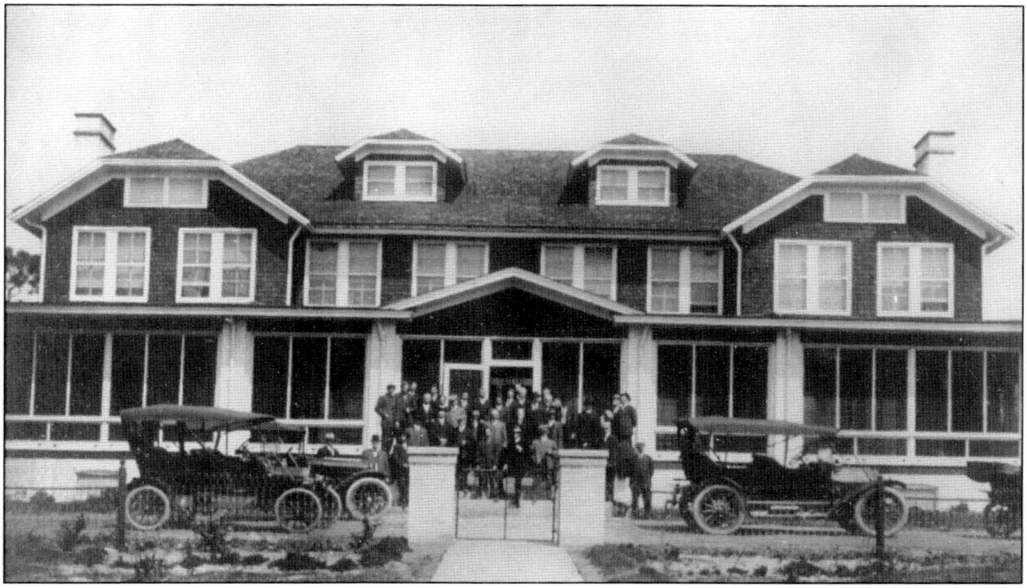

Clermont was designed to be a "model town." A promotional brochure described a community with uniform building standards, shade trees, and sidewalks "securing the beauty and health of the town." The planners dreamed of making Clermont "the most desirable winter resort in America," as realized for those visiting the Lake Highland Clubhouse, pictured here in 1914. The vision included making Clermont an educational center, a "good society free from the contaminating influences" of larger cities. In the decades that followed, residents enjoyed a rare quality of life, but they also endured near financial ruin during the Great Depression. Today the clubhouse serves as Westminster Care of Clermont, a nursing home. (Courtesy of Cooper Memorial Library Association.)

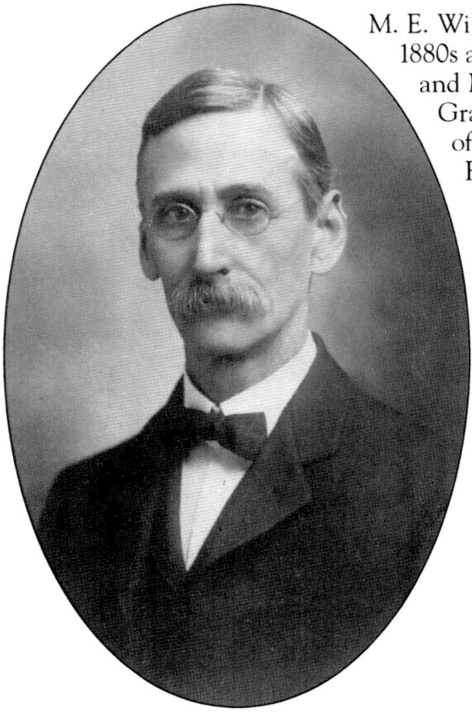

M. E. Wilson moved to Clermont from Philadelphia in the 1880s and opened a general store at the corner of Seventh and Montrose Streets. He was instrumental in starting Grace Baptist Church and also served as the supervisor of the schoolhouse on Broome Street. After the Great Freeze of 1894–1895, he sold his store to Alexander Kern and moved his family to Pensacola. (Courtesy of Cooper Memorial Library Association.)

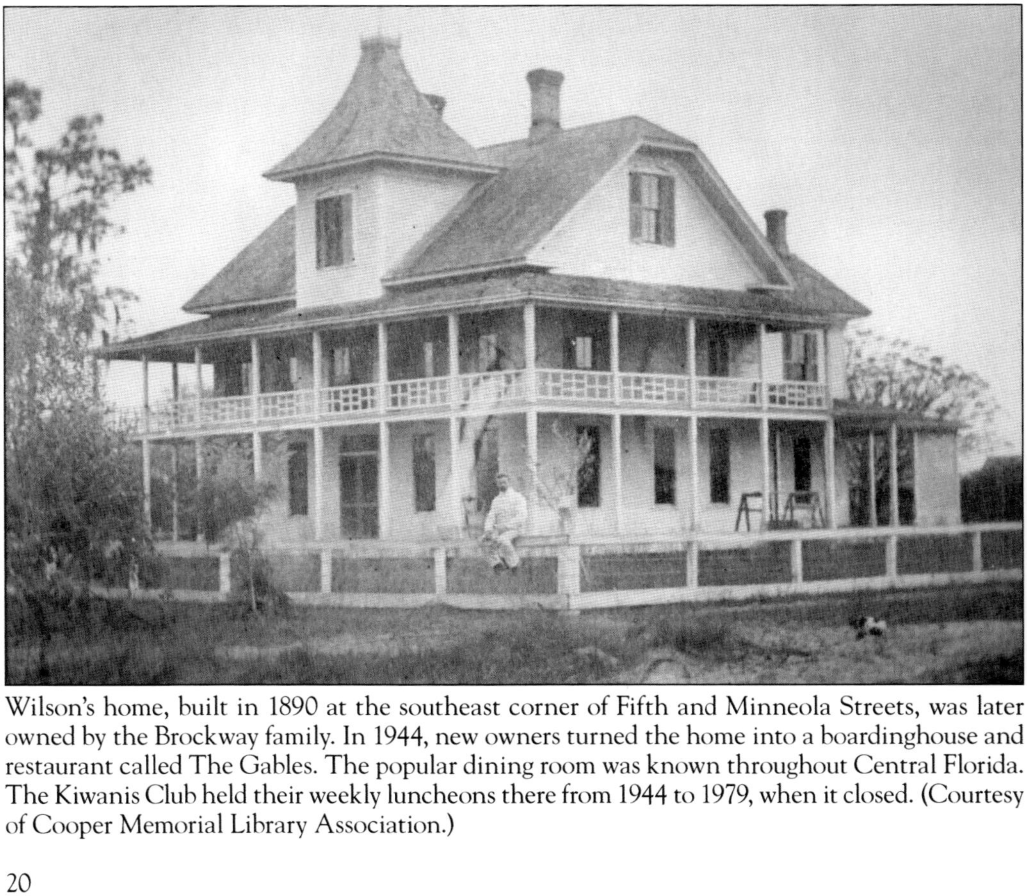

Wilson's home, built in 1890 at the southeast corner of Fifth and Minneola Streets, was later owned by the Brockway family. In 1944, new owners turned the home into a boardinghouse and restaurant called The Gables. The popular dining room was known throughout Central Florida. The Kiwanis Club held their weekly luncheons there from 1944 to 1979, when it closed. (Courtesy of Cooper Memorial Library Association.)

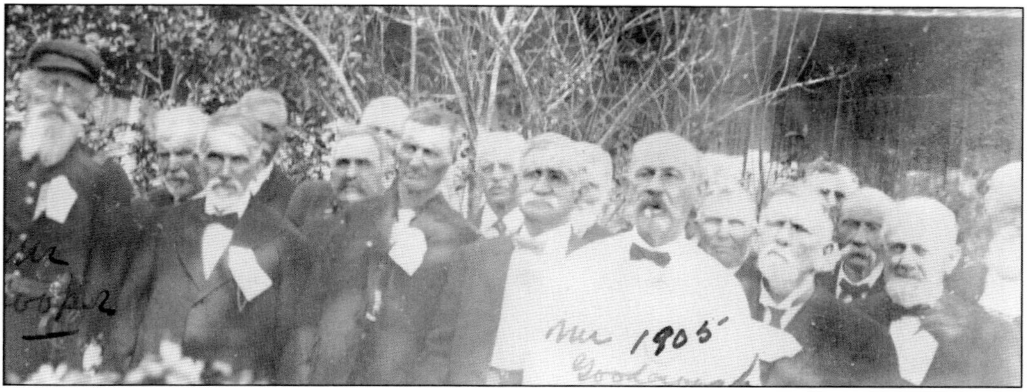

Many of Clermont's early settlers were veterans of the Civil War and included soldiers from both the Union and Confederate Armies. At far left above is Capt. Montgomery Cooper from Washington County, Iowa. The group also included C. H. Goodenough, Clermont's first mayor, who came from Chapel Hill, New Jersey. Confederate veterans included Maj. D. A. Cook and S. M. Ogletree from Georgia. The soldiers' wives (below) also attended this picnic, which has always been a traditional pastime for Clermont residents and a way to bring people from different backgrounds together. For many years, residents gathered every March at Kehlor Park to celebrate the All-States Picnic where each state had a separate space and competed for best decorated table. (Both courtesy of Cooper Memorial Library Association.)

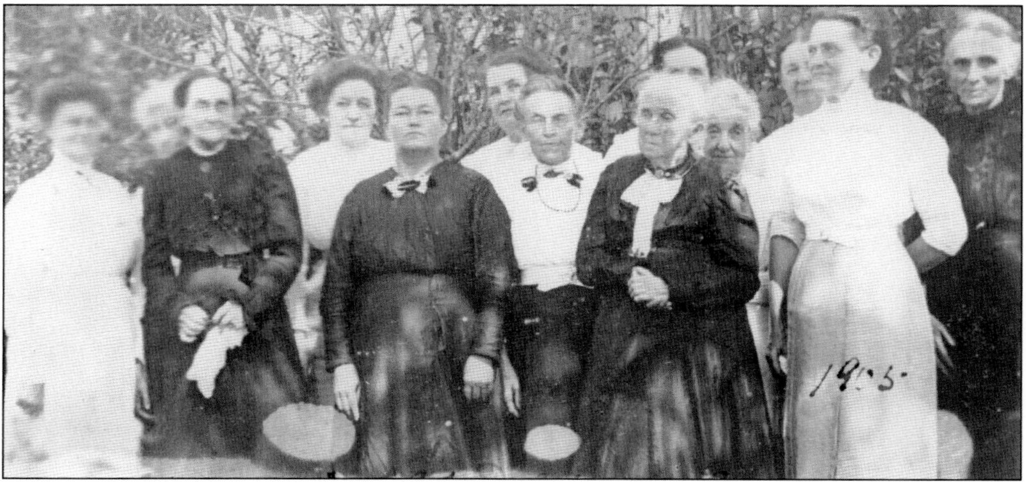

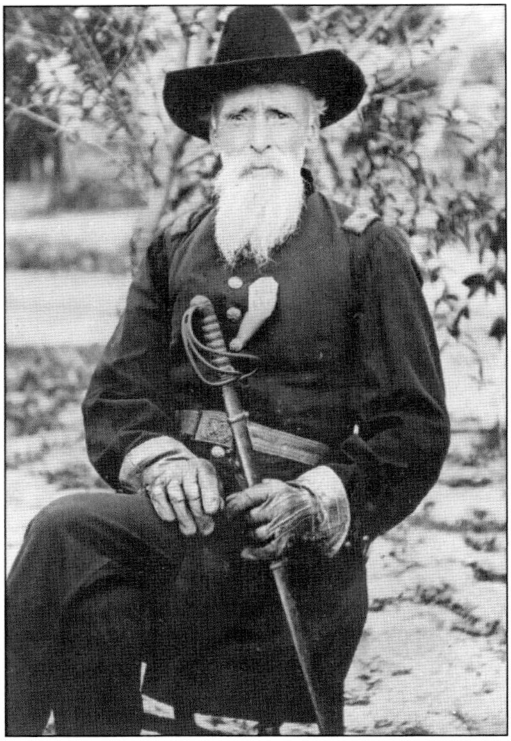

Capt. Montgomery Cooper; his wife, Alice; and their children, Perry, May, and Helen Mar, moved from Iowa to Clermont in 1885. Cooper was a member of the 10th Iowa Infantry, which engaged in many Civil War campaigns, including the capture of Vicksburg, Mississippi. His battle-dented sword is preserved by his great-grandson, Clermont fire chief Carle Bishop. (Courtesy of Cooper Memorial Library Association.)

Cooper is seen here in his wooded backyard, which faced DeSoto Street. He and Alice donated the land in 1914 to build the city's first library, known affectionately today as the "Little Cooper" Memorial Library. Currently, Cooper's backyard serves as the parking lot for Clermont City Hall. (Courtesy of Cooper Memorial Library Association.)

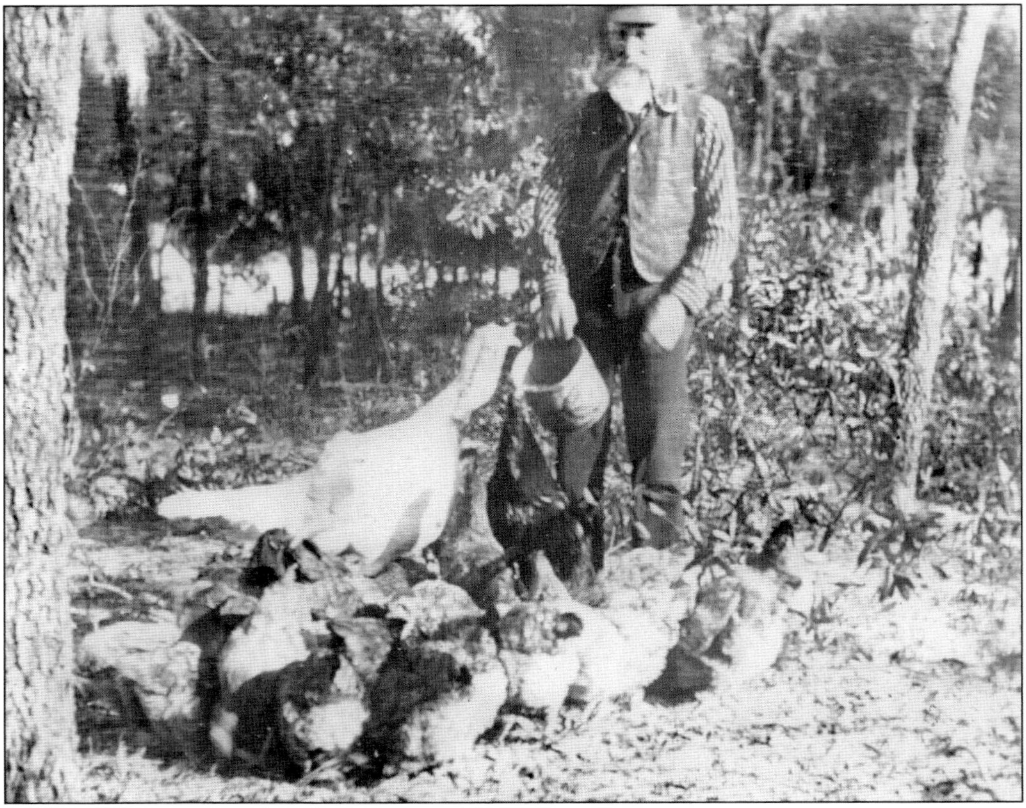

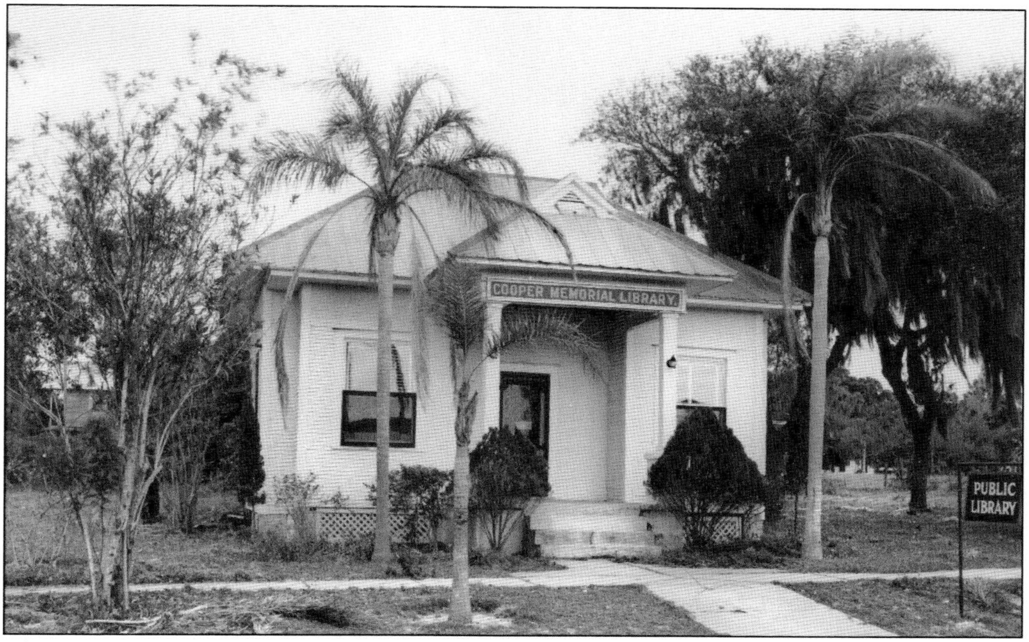


Clermont's Cooper Memorial Library owes its start to a scam. In 1905, a salesman told Tallulah McCain, who ran the Hoobler House, that he would donate books to start a library if she purchased a lecture series. McCain gathered supporters who paid the salesman. A few lectures materialized, but none of the books. The group pursued having a library anyway, and in 1914, Cooper Memorial Library opened. (Courtesy of Cooper Memorial Library Association.)

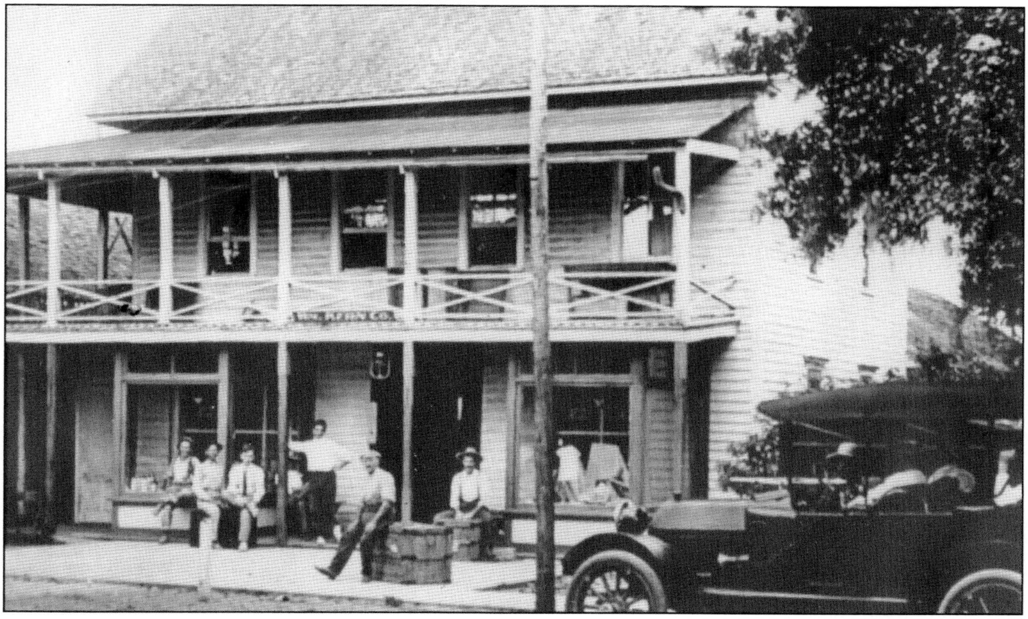

Alexander Kern, of New Jersey, bought the Wilson Store in 1897. Kern's store, later run by his son William, sold groceries, clothing, medicine, farm tools, and ice cream. After working in the fields, men gathered on the porch to whittle, smoke, and swap jokes. Little boys played skin-the-cat around the hitching rack. The Kern family house has been preserved as part of Clermont's Historic Village. (Courtesy of Cooper Memorial Library Association.)

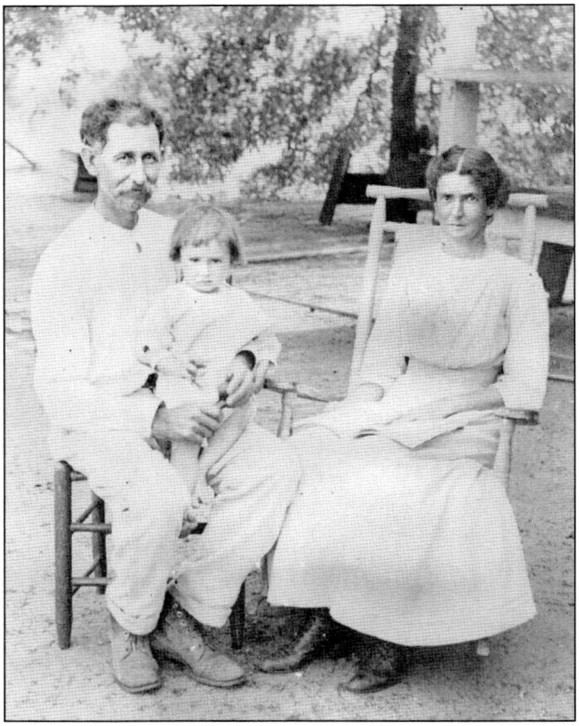

In 1894, Stibbins Brantley, son of a Georgia doctor, moved his wife, Mattie, and daughter, Margaree, to Clermont and found success growing citrus and numerous vegetable crops. He had groves on the southeast side of Lake Minnehaha and on Hooks Point, later named Margaree Gardens. He also helped build a Sunday school, repaired streets, and served on the city council when the town reincorporated in 1916. (Courtesy of Cooper Memorial Library Association.)

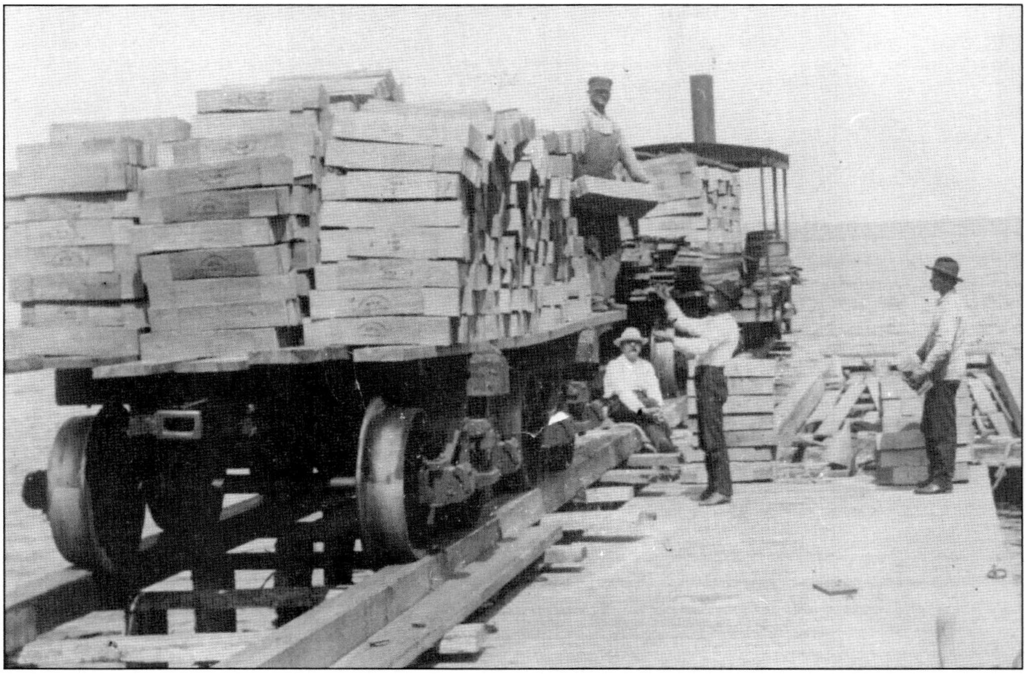

Another 1894 arrival was Jasper Gaines of Vienna, Georgia, who married the sister of his business partner, Jim Jones. In this photograph, Gaines is seen standing on the flatbed, loading bundles of shingles at Hammond's Landing on Lake Louisa. Gaines and Jones operated a small steamer that also carried fruit and railroad ties. The men later went into citrus and truck farming. (Courtesy of Cooper Memorial Library Association.)

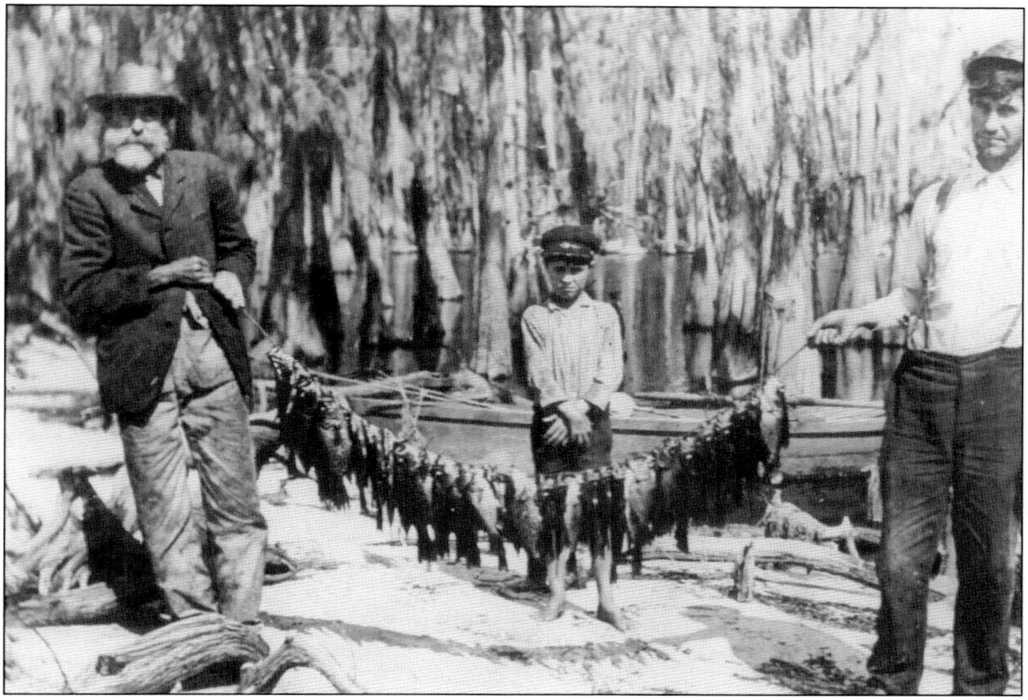

David "Old Mackie" McClendon (above left) and A. L. Cashwell (above right) show off the day's catch of perch while one of Cashwell's eight children watches in the 1880s. Clermont's many lakes were loaded with all kinds of fish, including bass, perch, brim, and catfish. Cashwell came from North Carolina and settled beside Lake Nellie, south of Clermont. The cypress trees in the background line the shores of many Clermont lakes. In the photograph below, McClendon is shown leading an oxcart owned by Ben Patterson. He preferred oxen to horses because they were tougher, especially on hilly terrain. Patterson, of Virginia, had five children. His son Alec became famous as one of the state's best fiddlers. (Both courtesy of Cooper Memorial Library Association.)

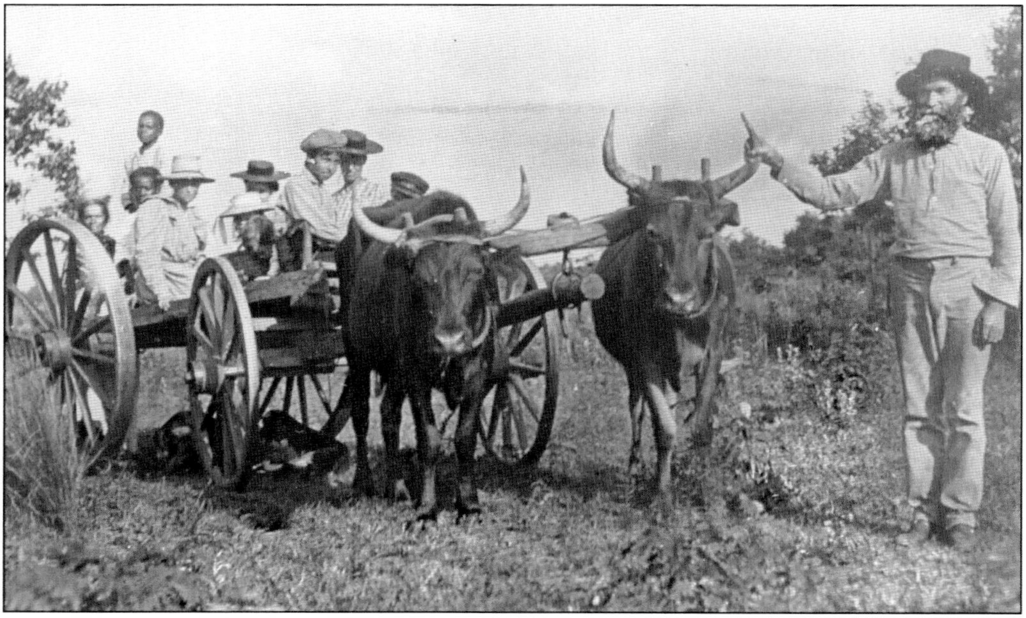

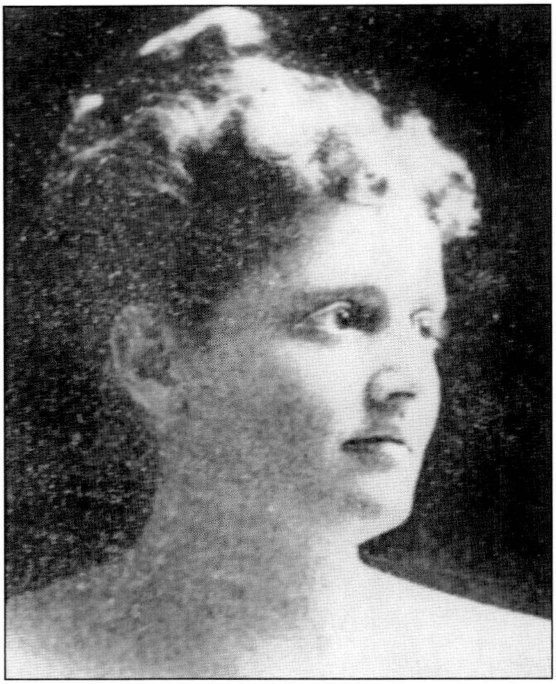

One of Clermont's most fascinating characters was Hattie Daggett Millholland. She was a 23-year-old, single nurse living in Vineland, New Jersey, when she made her first trip in 1888 to look for a suitable location for her invalid father to spend the winter. She eventually moved to south Clermont and bought property near Crescent Lake. She married Capt. Robert Millholland in 1901. (Courtesy of Cooper Memorial Library Association.)

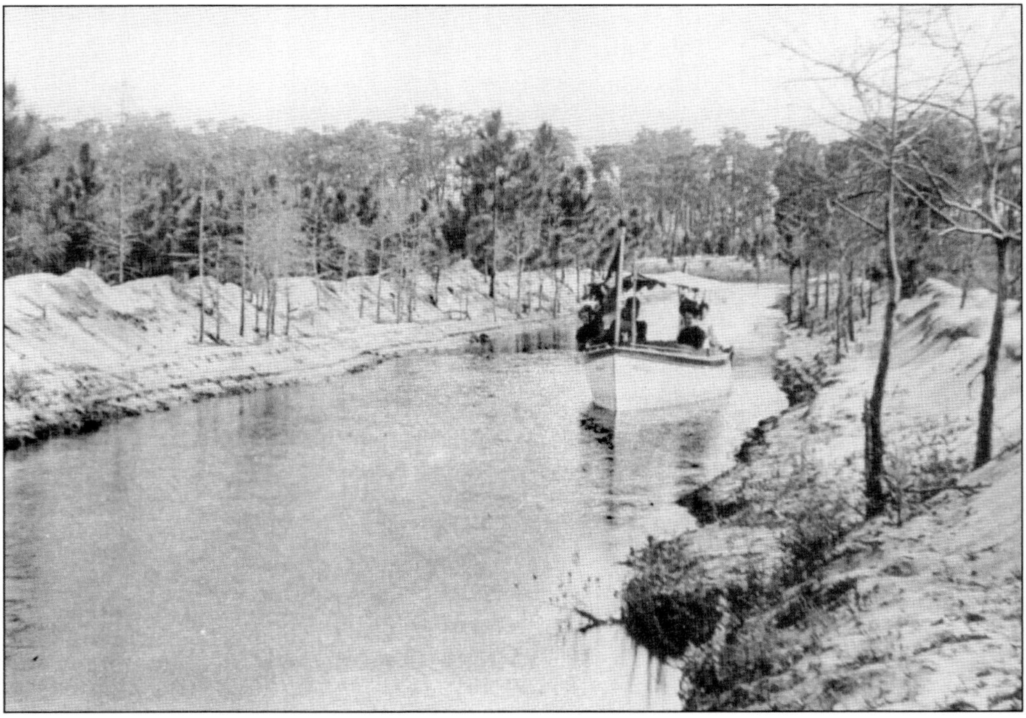

In 1889, Hattie's neighbors asked her to help build a canal that would allow farmers to transport their crops and supplies without having to use the long, hilly sand roads. She had the land surveyed and recruited help from Sanford, then set up a camp. She personally supervised cutting the 30-foot-wide, 6,000-foot-long canal that connected Crescent Lake and Lake Minnehaha. (Courtesy of Cooper Memorial Library Association.)

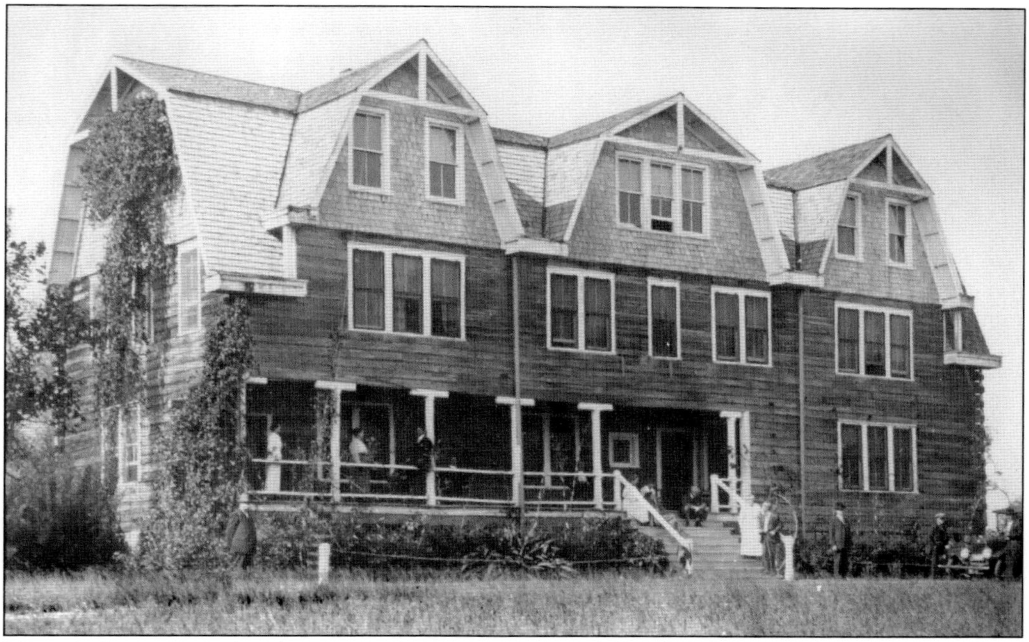

Hattie's dream was the three-story Log House. It took her brother James Daggett, a master builder, nine years to complete. It was 75 feet across, the logs were 5 inches thick, and the roof was made of 47,000 cypress shingles that lasted 34 years. Log House was popular for local entertainment and for hunters' lodging. It was demolished in 1959. (Courtesy of Cooper Memorial Library Association.)

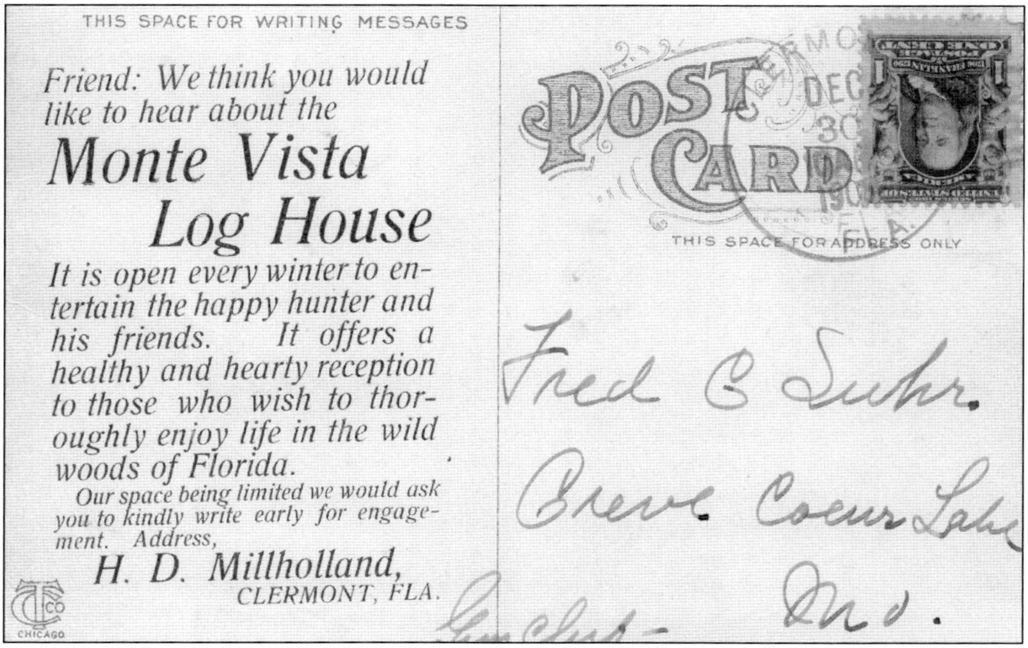


This penny postcard from the early 1900s promoted Hattie Millholland's Log House to hunters and others who enjoyed the "wild woods of Florida." On the opposite side of the postcard is a color photograph of men hunting quail near the Log House. Hattie also advertised in *Field and Stream* and other sports magazines. (Courtesy of Cooper Memorial Library Association.)

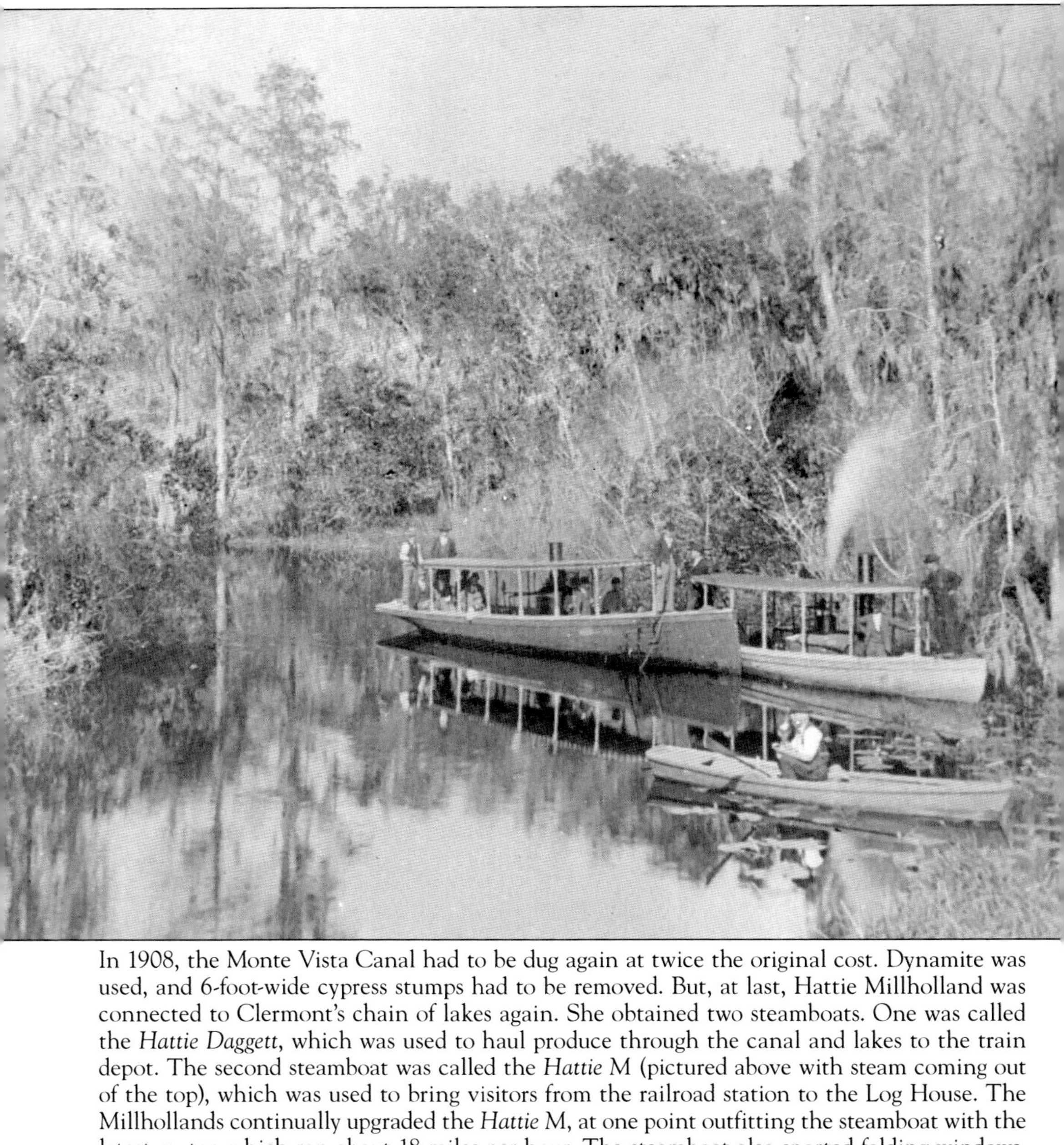

In 1908, the Monte Vista Canal had to be dug again at twice the original cost. Dynamite was used, and 6-foot-wide cypress stumps had to be removed. But, at last, Hattie Millholland was connected to Clermont's chain of lakes again. She obtained two steamboats. One was called the *Hattie Daggett*, which was used to haul produce through the canal and lakes to the train depot. The second steamboat was called the *Hattie* M (pictured above with steam coming out of the top), which was used to bring visitors from the railroad station to the Log House. The Millhollands continually upgraded the *Hattie* M, at one point outfitting the steamboat with the latest motor, which ran about 18 miles per hour. The steamboat also sported folding windows, a stove, refrigerator, and fine upholstery. Eventually the *Hattie* M became a floating chamber of commerce. (Courtesy of Cooper Memorial Library Association.)

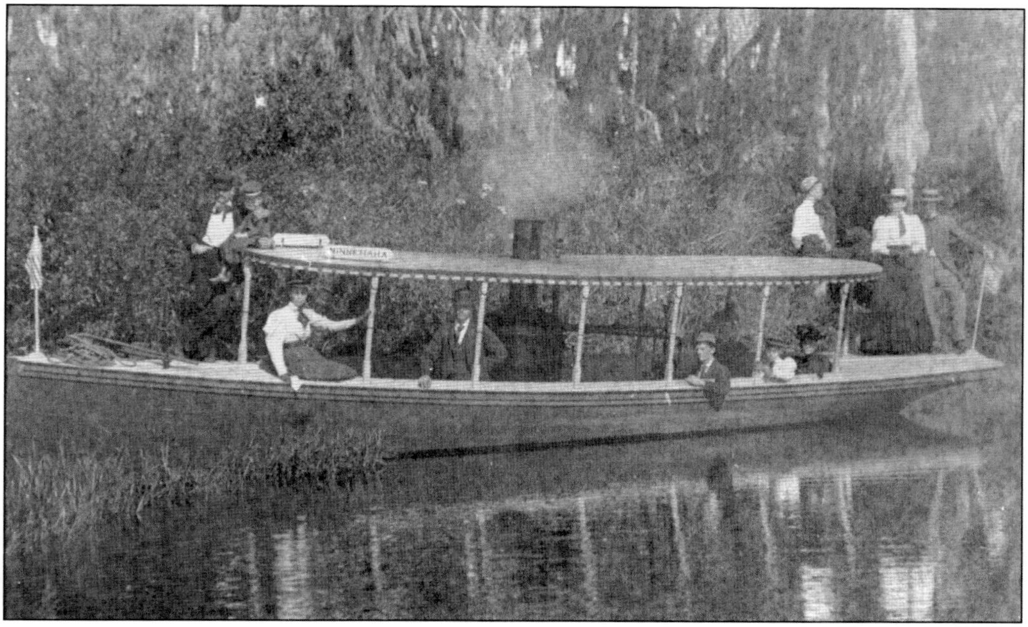


Keeping Clermont's waterways open for large steamboats, such as the *Minnehaha* pictured here, required vigilance. An early chamber of commerce formed a waterways committee that sent weekly crews to remove sunken tree limbs and other obstructions from the canal between Lake Minneola and Lake Minnehaha. (Courtesy of Cooper Memorial Library Association.)

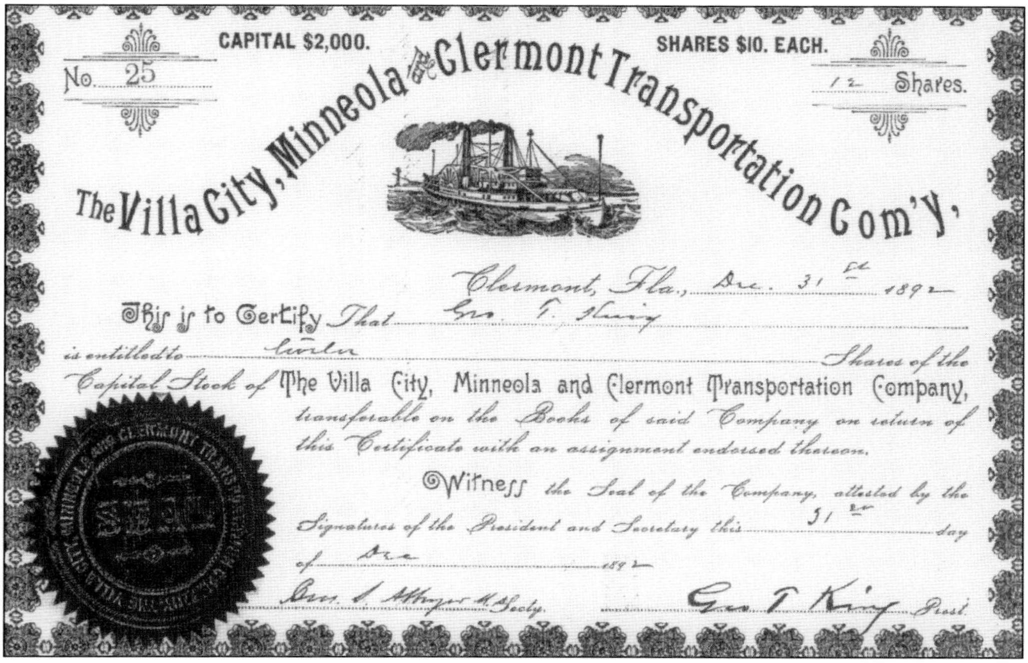
CAPITAL $2,000. SHARES $10. EACH.

No. 25 12 Shares.

The Villa City, Minneola & Clermont Transportation Com'y.

Clermont, Fla., Dec. 31st 1892

This is to Certify That Geo. T. King is entitled to twelve Shares of the Capital Stock of The Villa City, Minneola and Clermont Transportation Company, transferable on the Books of said Company on return of this Certificate with an assignment endorsed thereon.

Witness the Seal of the Company, attested by the Signatures of the President and Secretary this 31st day of Dec 1892

Secty. Geo. T. King Prest.

In 1892, George King, a wealthy Colgate Soap salesman from Baltimore who had founded Villa City, created the Villa City, Minneola, and Clermont Transportation Company and sold shares of stock for $10 each. The enterprise was short lived, however. The Great Freeze of 1894–1895 turned Villa City into a virtual ghost town overnight. King, along with dozens of his neighbors, returned to his northern roots. (Courtesy of Howard King.)

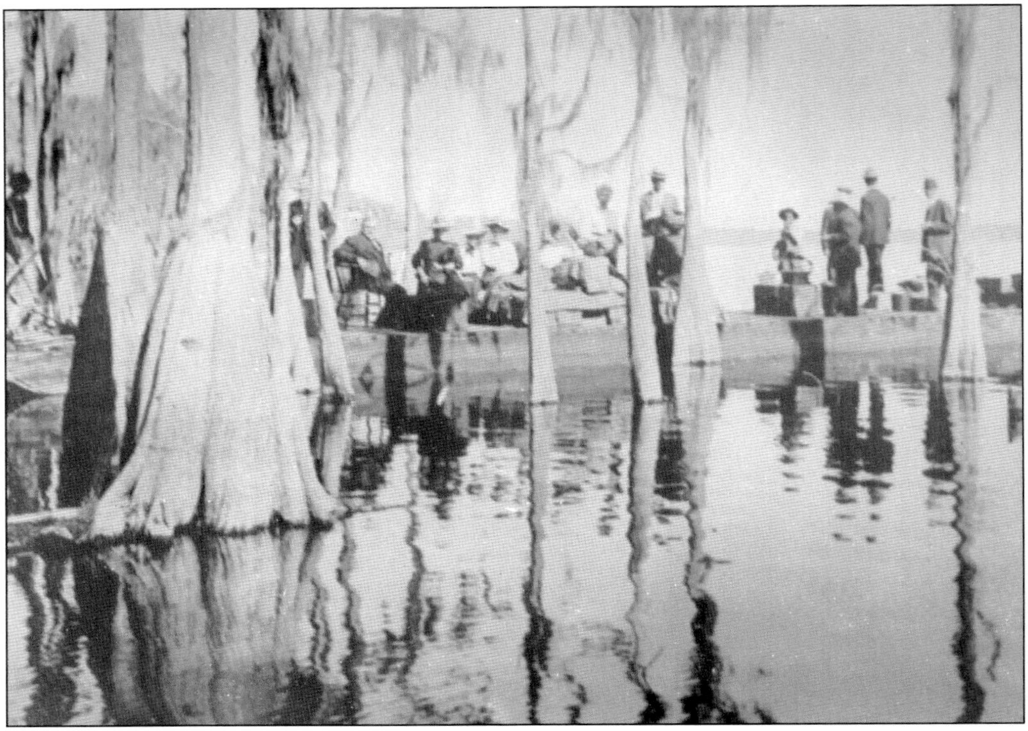

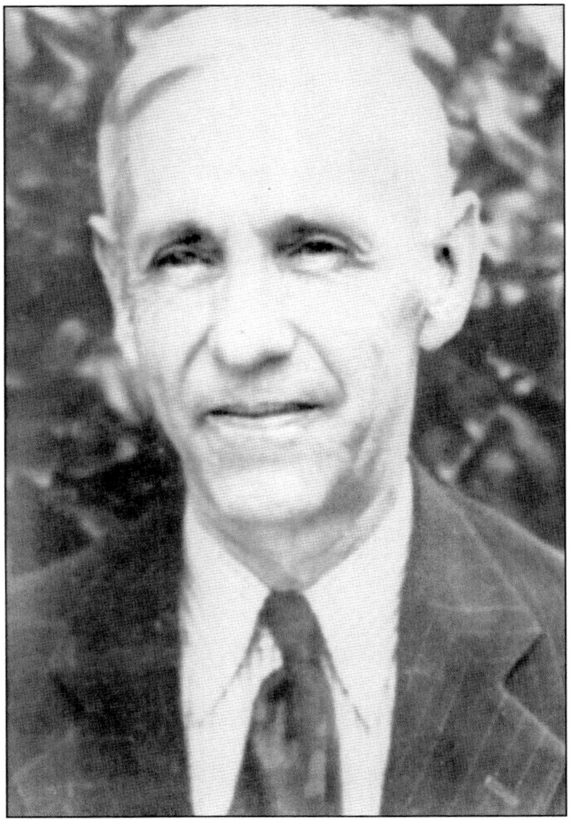

Picnics provided entertainment, gave neighbors a way to share the latest news, and celebrated visitors' arrivals and special occasions. Although most picnics were on land, this one was on a floating barge at Palatlakaha Creek. The lower trunk of the cypress trees shown in this *c.* 1900 photograph are roots called "cypress knees." They once gained popularity as lamp bases. (Courtesy of Cooper Memorial Library Association.)

Harry Stokes, born in 1883, is credited with saving Clermont's natural resources. In 1898, he came to Mohawk, a hunting spot on Clermont's northeast edge, to act as a hunting guide. He served as a county commissioner for almost 30 years and was an ardent defender of the environment. He saved Clermont's marshland and helped direct the location of Highways 27 and 50. (Courtesy of Cooper Memorial Library Association.)

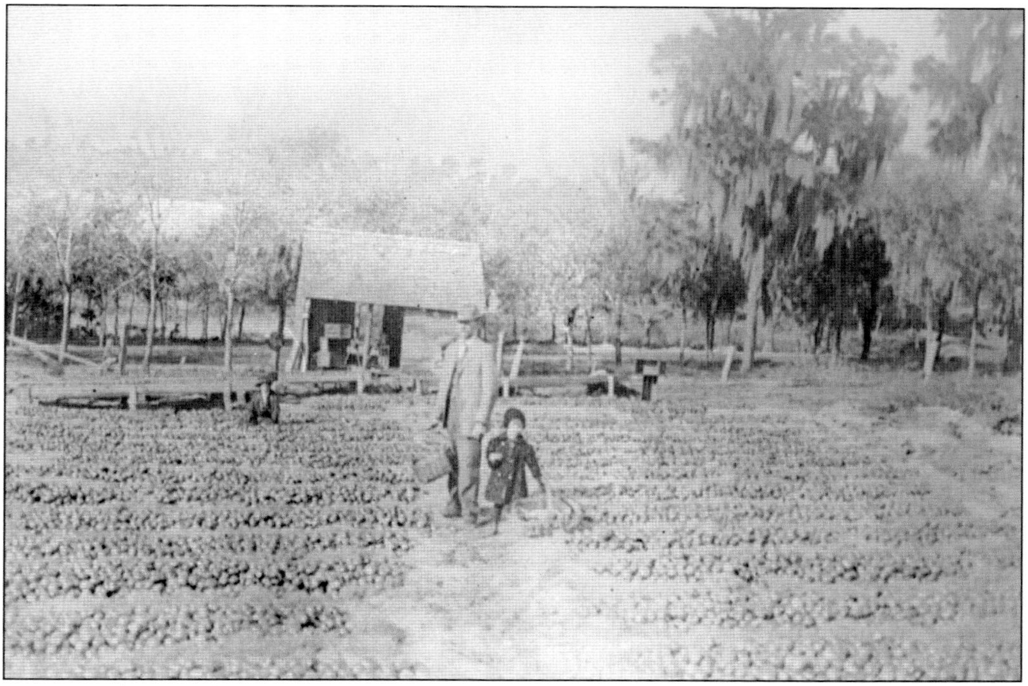

By 1890, Clermont had developed into the largest tomato producer in Florida. Pioneer families, such as the Brantleys, Hooks, and Coopers, were growing 3,000 acres of tomatoes around Clermont. During harvest, 20 carloads were shipped daily. In the foreground, Stibbins Brantley stands by his daughter Margaree while his wife looks on from her seat in the middle of the tomato plants, located at today's Fifth and Seminole Streets. (Courtesy of Cooper Memorial Library Association.)

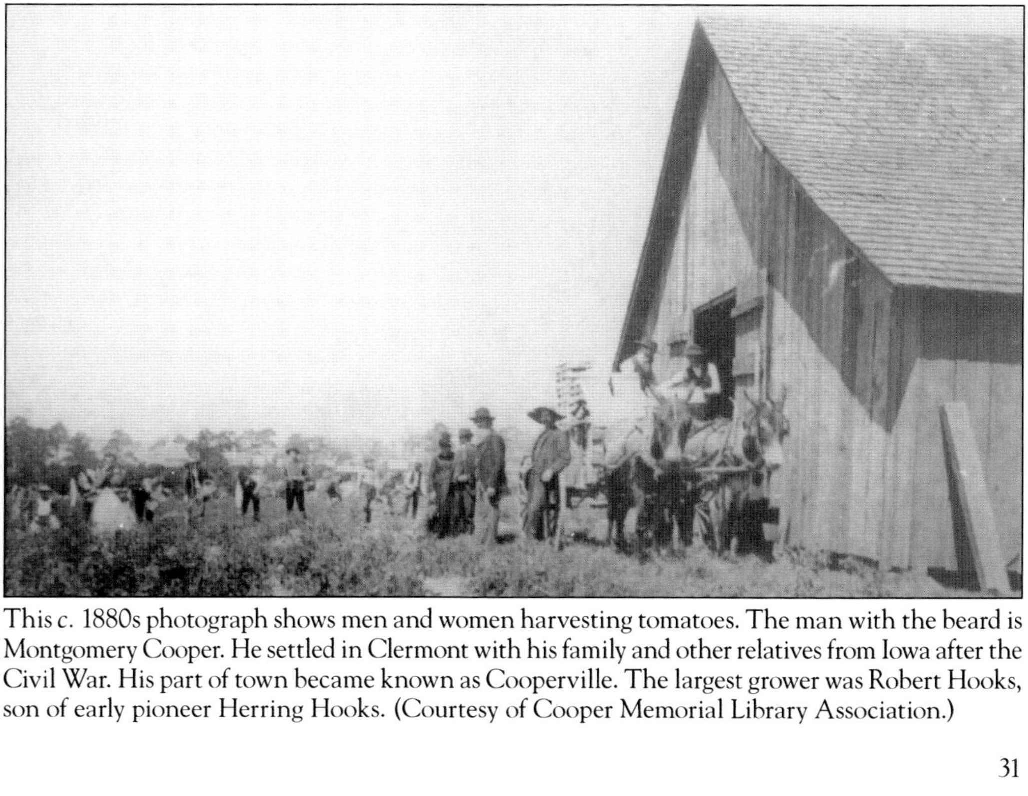

This *c.* 1880s photograph shows men and women harvesting tomatoes. The man with the beard is Montgomery Cooper. He settled in Clermont with his family and other relatives from Iowa after the Civil War. His part of town became known as Cooperville. The largest grower was Robert Hooks, son of early pioneer Herring Hooks. (Courtesy of Cooper Memorial Library Association.)

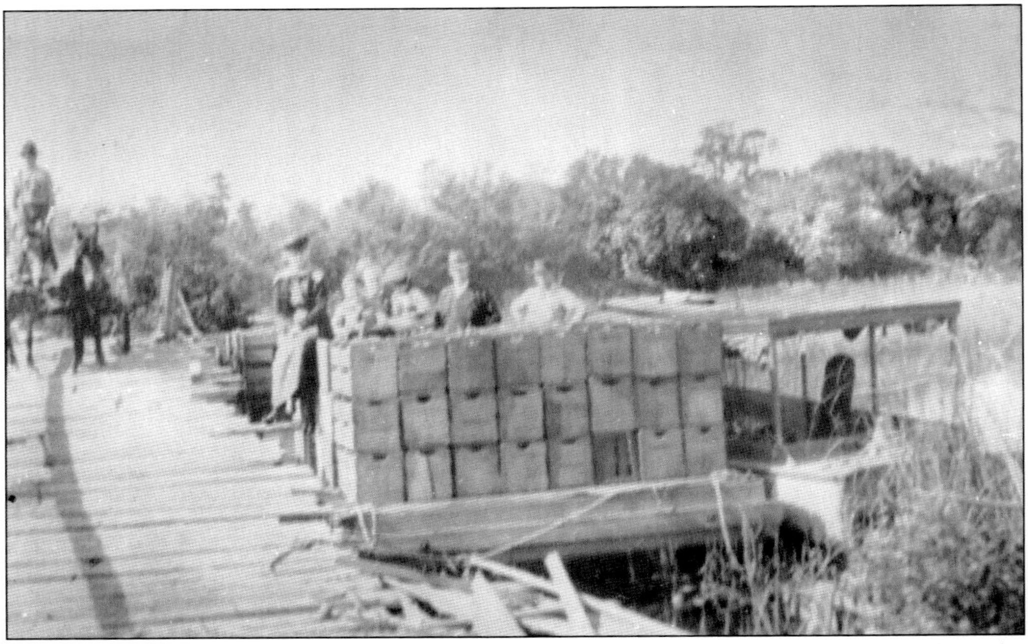

Clermont's canals were the major route used for transporting tomatoes for shipment from the train depot on the south side of Lake Minneola. Archibald Gano, a well-known Clermont sawmill operator, invented the crates used for shipping tomatoes. Two steamboats kept busy transporting tomatoes from the Monte Vista area to the train station. (Courtesy of Cooper Memorial Library Association.)

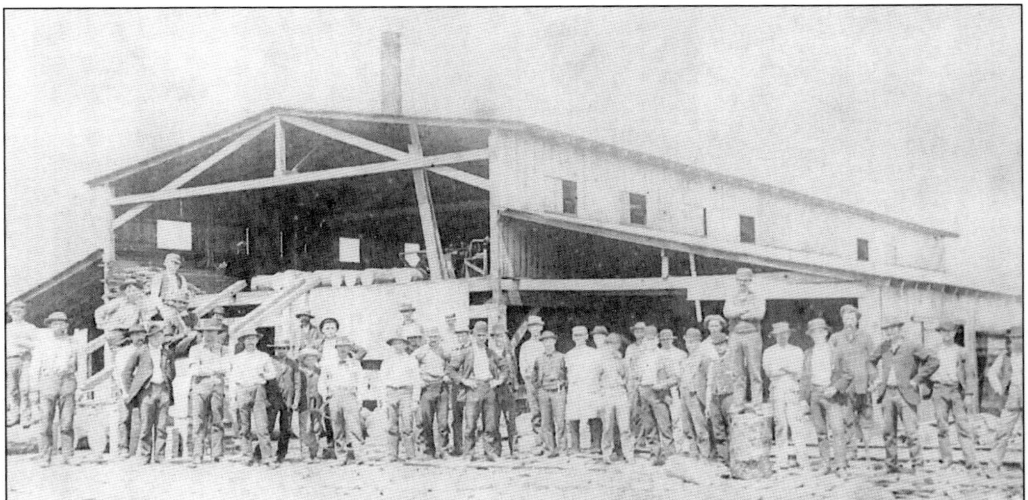

The thriving tomato industry drove Clermont's prosperity in the 1880s and early 1890s and required workers not only for harvesting, but also for building the crates used to transport the tomatoes. Workers seen in this c. 1894 photograph are standing in front of a tomato crate mill that was built by Gano. (Courtesy of Cooper Memorial Library Association.)

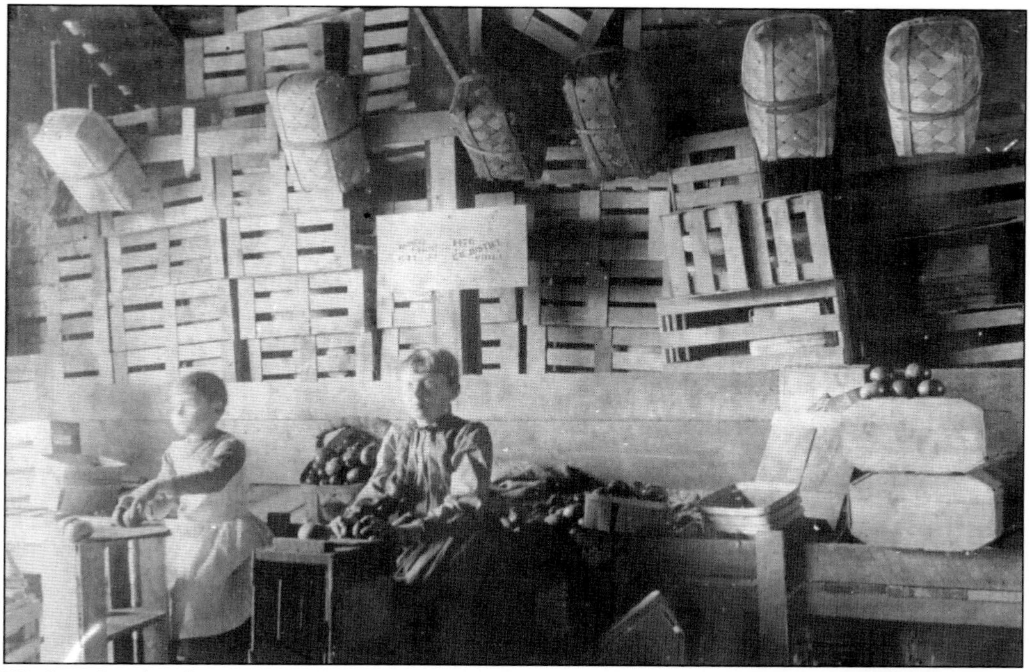

Working hard at the Cooperville tomato packinghouse are Helen Cooper Bishop (left) and her sister May Cooper, the children of Montgomery Cooper. The stamped board above them reads, "C. G. Justice Phila." Justice was one of the managers of the Philadelphia Produce Exchange, where 200 firms organized to buy and sell produce. (Courtesy of Cooper Memorial Library Association.)

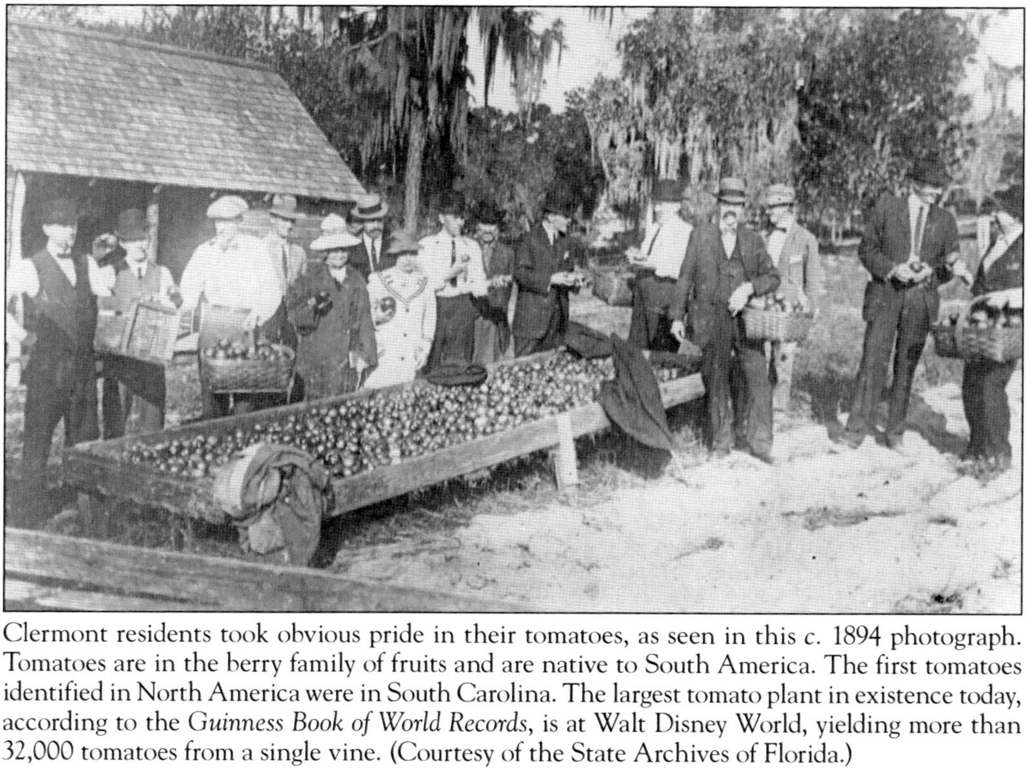

Clermont residents took obvious pride in their tomatoes, as seen in this *c.* 1894 photograph. Tomatoes are in the berry family of fruits and are native to South America. The first tomatoes identified in North America were in South Carolina. The largest tomato plant in existence today, according to the *Guinness Book of World Records*, is at Walt Disney World, yielding more than 32,000 tomatoes from a single vine. (Courtesy of the State Archives of Florida.)

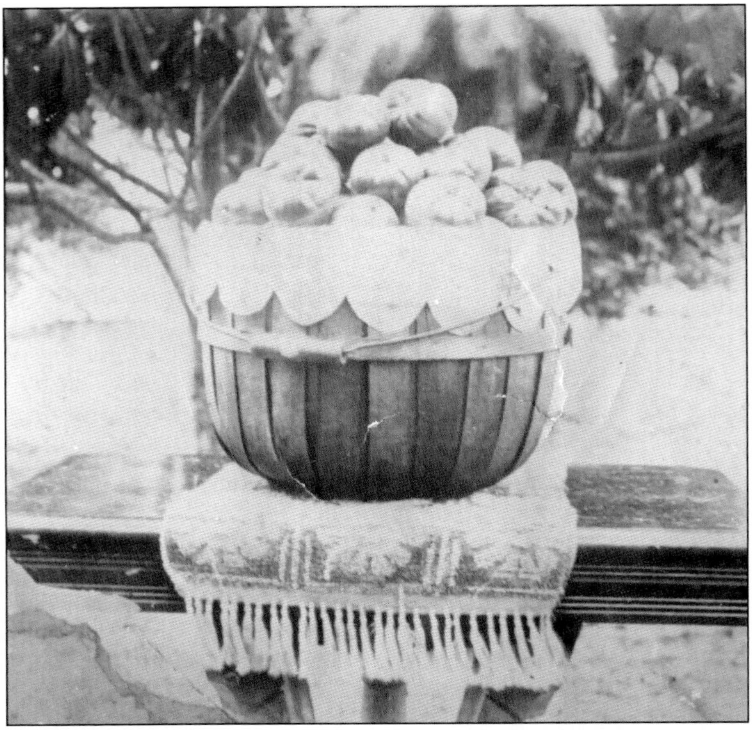

This basket of beauties gives a close-up look at Clermont's tomatoes around 1894. Until the 1820s, tomatoes were considered poisonous. That changed when a Colonel Johnson in New Jersey offered to eat a basketful to prove tomatoes were safe. A doctor warned Johnson would "foam at the mouth" and expose himself to "brain fever." Johnson ate the tomatoes, and they became an American staple. (Courtesy of Cooper Memorial Library Association.)

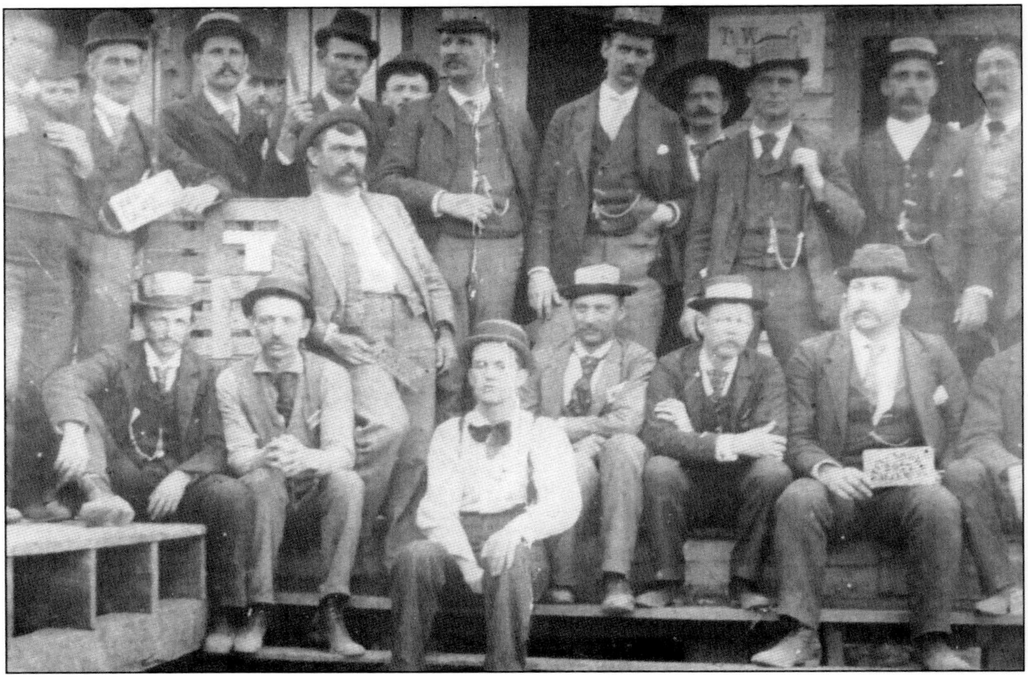

Produce buyers came from across the country to purchase Clermont's tomatoes. On the east side of Eighth Street, from Minneola Avenue to the train station, tents served as packinghouses where teams of buyers would come and go. Clermont households set up cots for the influx of buyers. They often stayed the whole season, visiting the crops and handling shipments for their companies. (Courtesy of Cooper Memorial Library Association.)

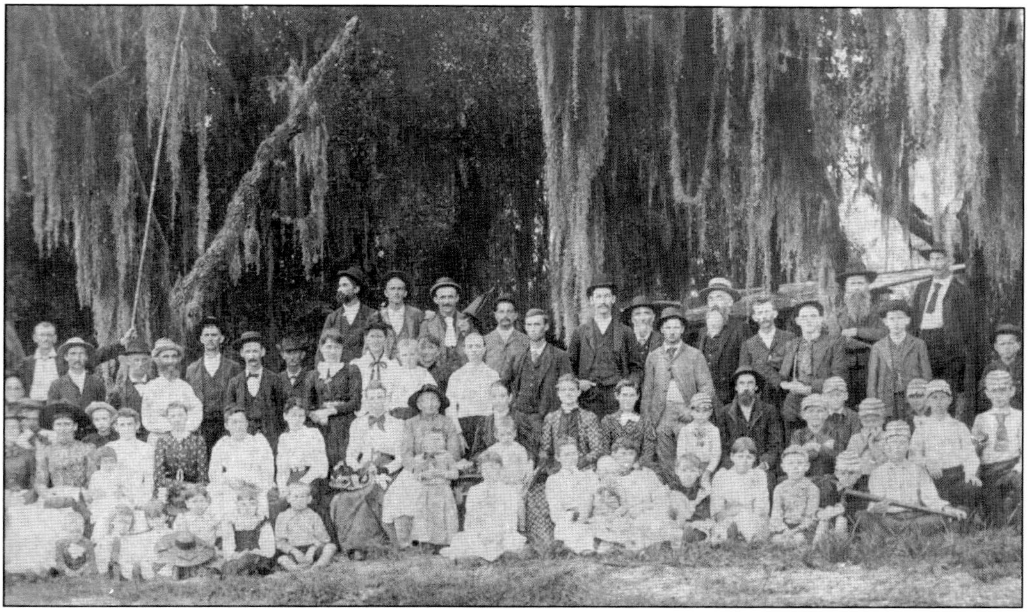

This c. 1894 photograph shows Clermont residents gathered for a picnic at Lake Felter in the waning days of the tomato boom. The oaks are draped in Spanish moss, a gray beard-like plant that is not actually moss but is related to pineapples. Timucuan women used Spanish moss for clothing, and it was used to stuff cushions in the 1940s. (Courtesy of Cooper Memorial Library Association.)

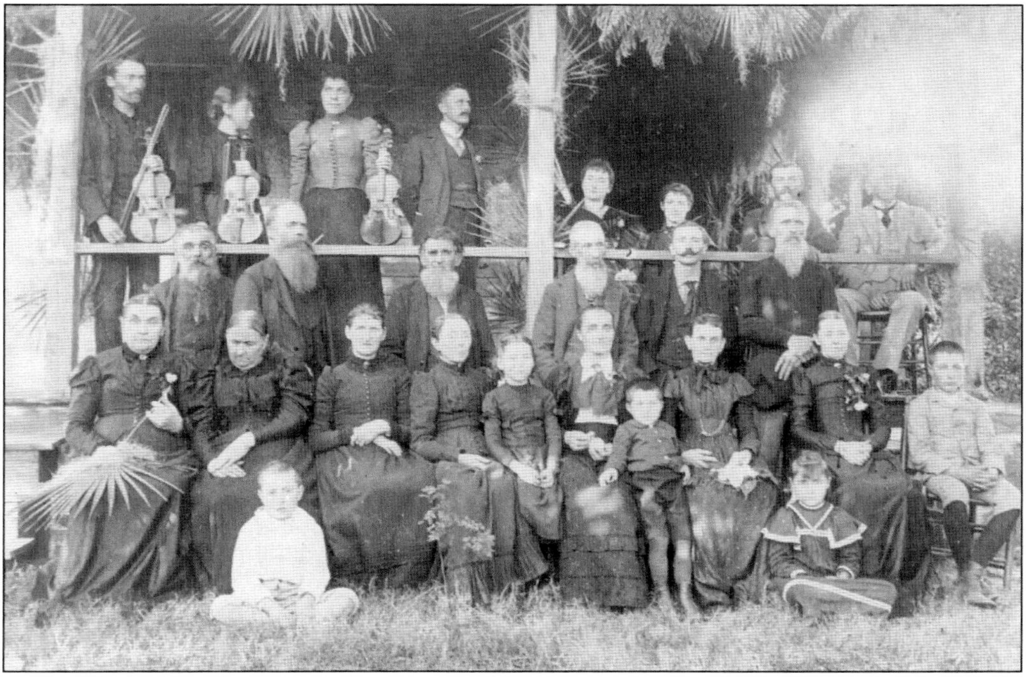

In 1894, the Cooperville Literary Club gathered to celebrate Christmas just five days before the beginning of the Great Freeze of 1894–1895. From the past to present, Clermont residents have always supported the love of literature. Clermont High School's 1927 yearbook featured a school literary club, and today Clermont boasts the largest library in Lake County. (Courtesy of Cooper Memorial Library Association.)

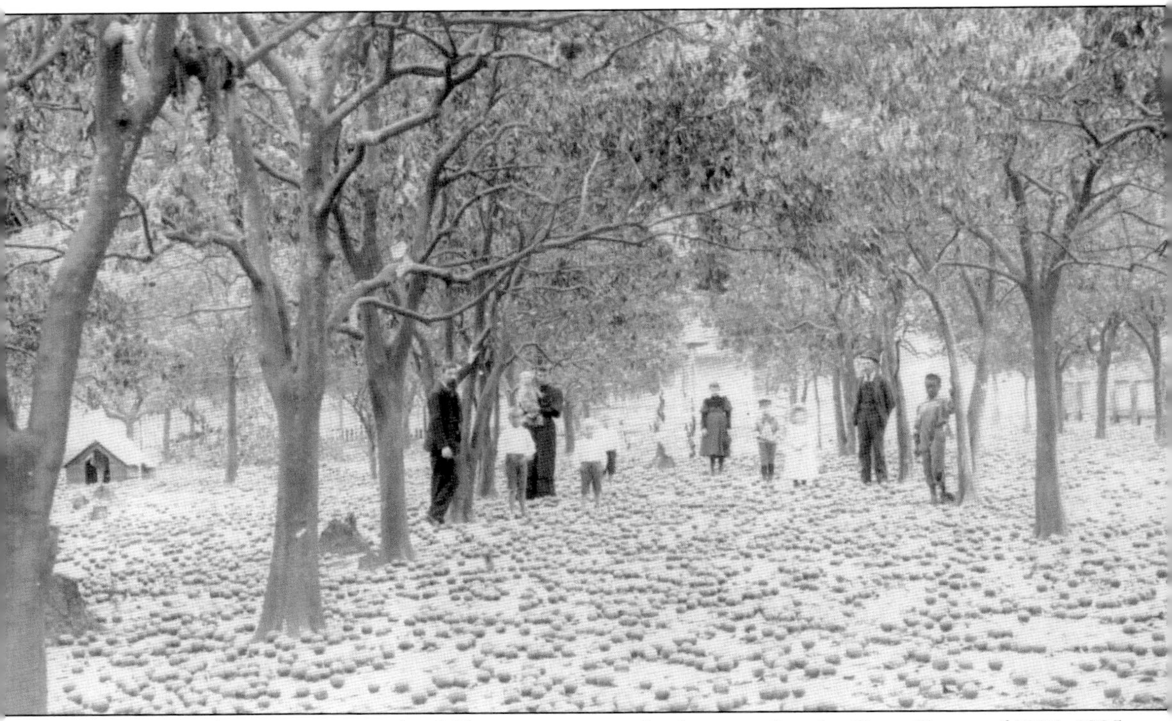

A stunned grove owner south of Clermont surveys the damage after the Great Freeze of 1894–1895, one of Florida's worst natural disasters. On December 29, 1894, the temperature fell to freezing temperatures. This was followed by a warm spell that made the sap rise in citrus trees and caused plants to sprout fresh shoots. A second freeze hit February 7–9, and temperatures dropped to 16 degrees, this time coupled with winds up to 35 miles per hour. Witnesses said the sound of the tree limbs and citrus bursting open sounded like cannon fire. The tomato crops froze and then rotted, bringing on disease that prevented replanting. Florida went from producing 6 million boxes of citrus a year to just 100,000 boxes a year. It would take almost a decade for the citrus industry to recover. The only Clermont grove known to survive was the Compton Grove and a few of the Brantley and Wilson Island trees. Many families moved, merchants closed their businesses, and those that stayed survived off game, fish, and produce they grew in their own gardens. (Courtesy of Department of College Archives and Special Collections, Olin Library, Rollins College, Winter Park, Florida.)

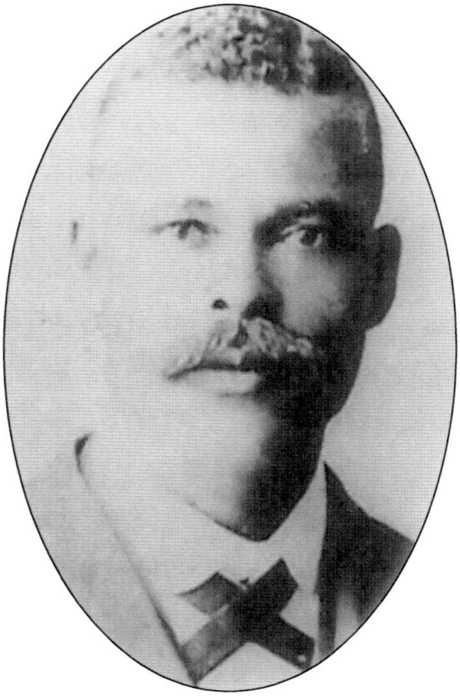

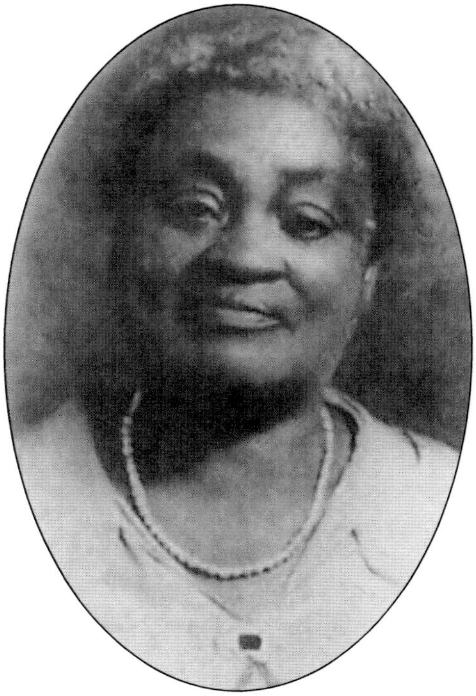

James Townsend and his wife, Sallie, moved from Orlando to Clermont in 1887. They were the town's first African American residents. James farmed, and Sallie took a midwifery course. In 1941, she established a maternity clinic for African American mothers. The couple founded St. Marks African Methodist Episcopal Church and the town's first school for African Americans. (Both courtesy of the South Lake County Historical Society.)

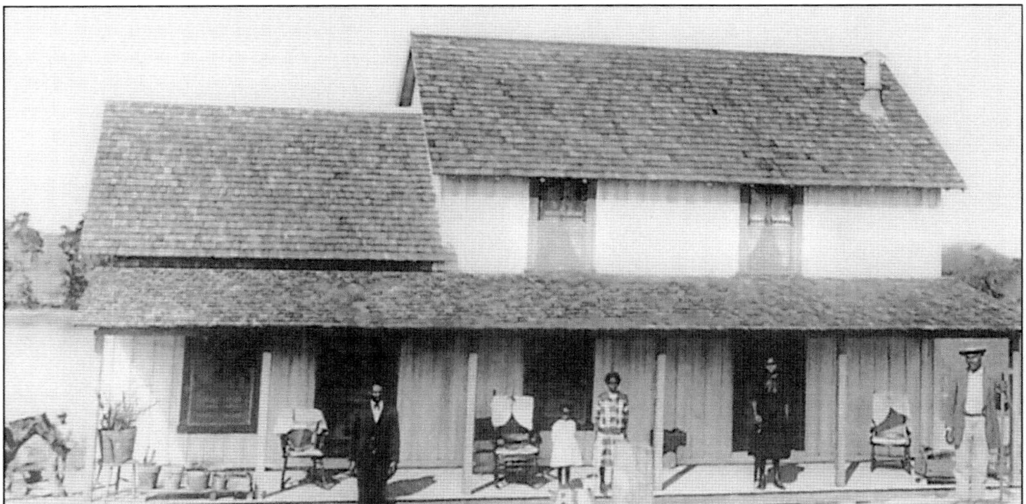

The Townsend home was built from heart pine cut at the Arnold Sawmill and has been preserved at Clermont's Historic Village, originally led by Micki Blackburn. Each year the Townsends' story is recounted on the front porch. Volunteers lead tours through the home, which has been restored with original period artifacts. (Courtesy of the South Lake County Historical Society.)

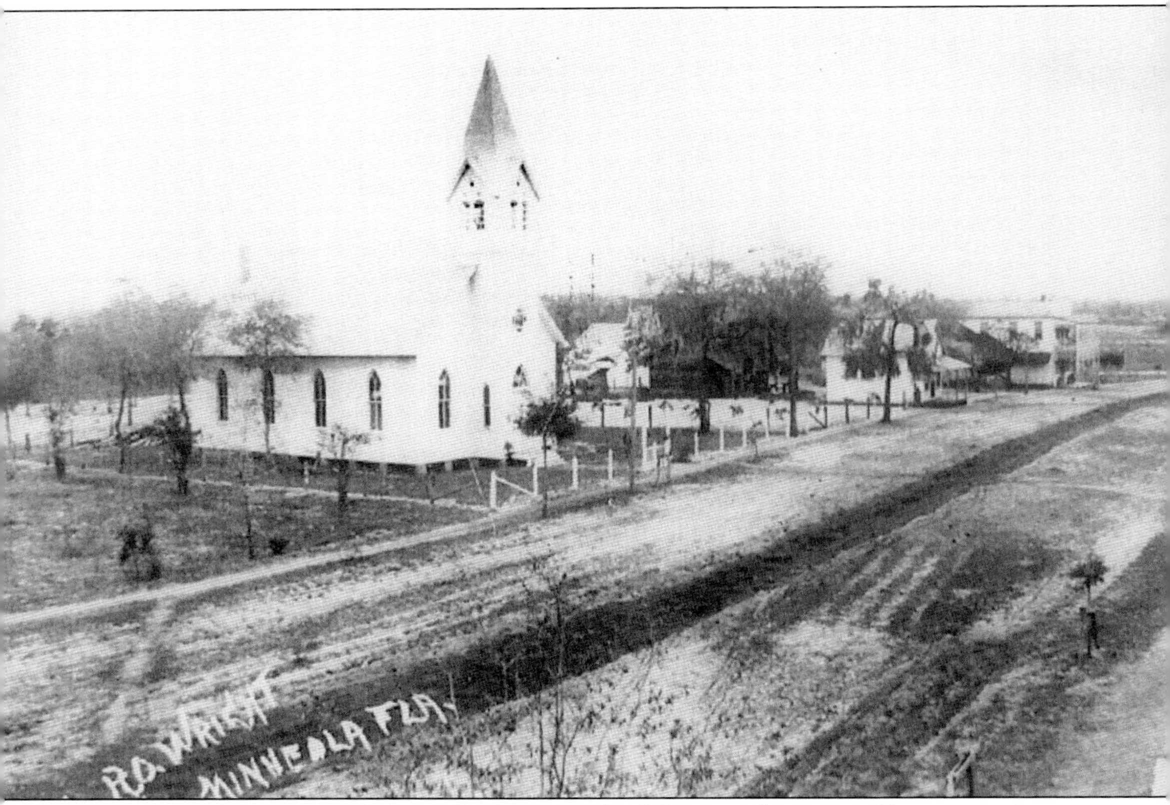


The neighboring city of Minneola shares much of the same history as Clermont and was even platted the same year—1884. Capt. William A. Smith from Georgia settled Minneola around 1870. By 1906, Main Street had a Methodist Church (left), general store, post office, and two railroads. The town was conceived by George Hull, a native Canadian who came by way of Minnesota. His wife, Alice, named the town and the lake it overlooked, which originally had been called Cow

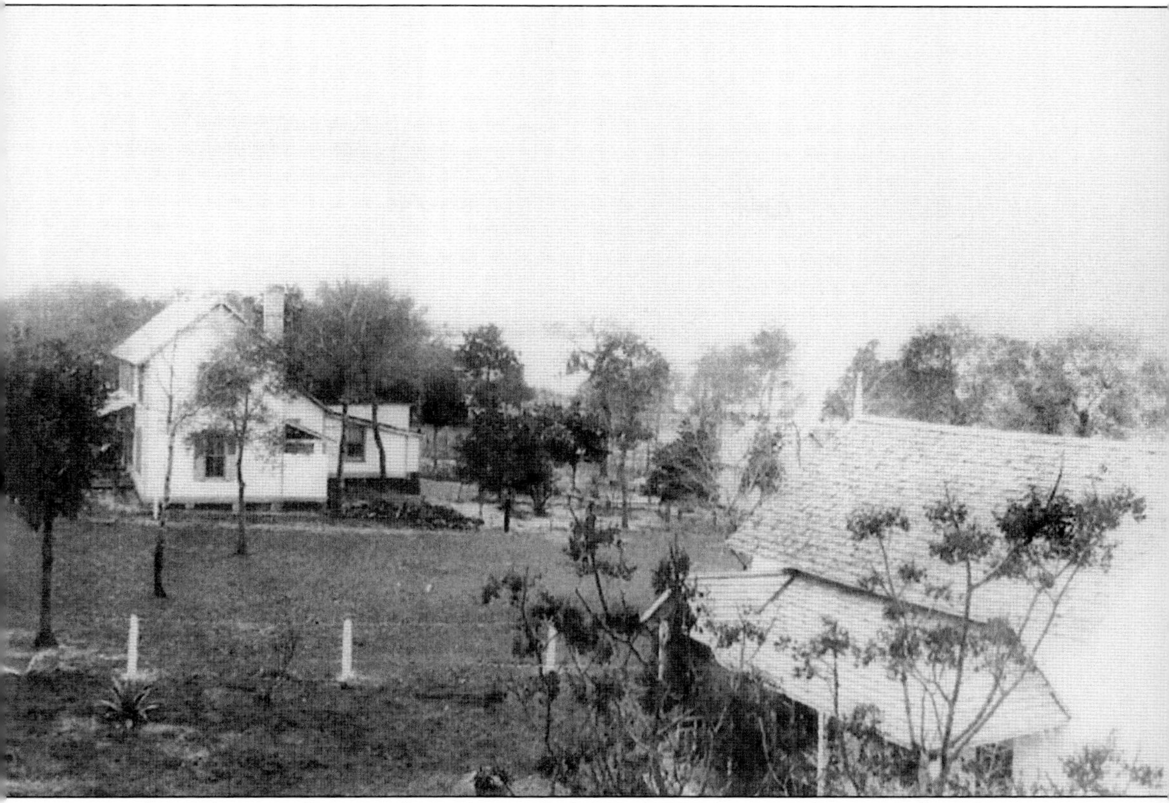

House Lake. Other significant early settlers included Dr. W. N. Reeves, the town's first physician who also built the town's first home; Elizabeth Straker, who operated a popular boardinghouse and served as the first woman mayor; and Fernando Bishop and his business partner, M. P. Godfrey, who brought their sawmill from Michigan. (Courtesy of Cooper Memorial Library Association.)

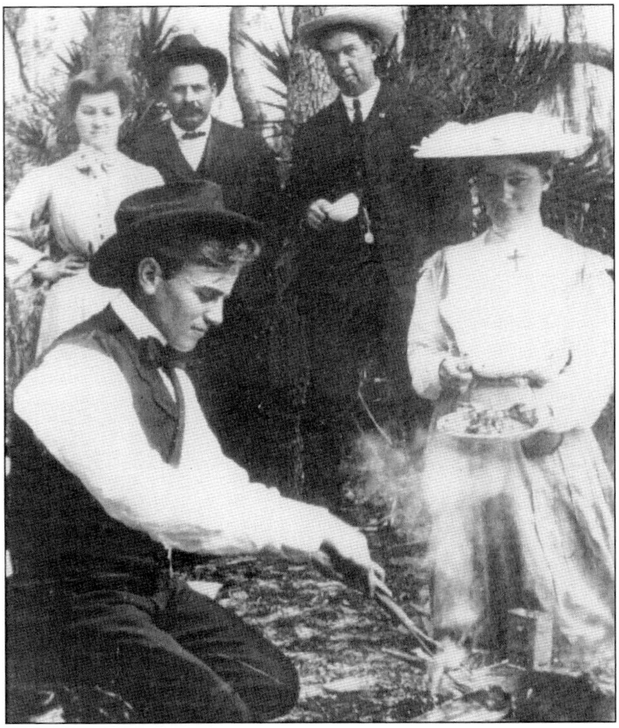

Although many families departed following the Great Freeze of 1894–1895, new arrivals would lead Clermont into more prosperous times. Some of those families are represented in this 1910 photograph of a fish fry. Dr. A. B. Middleton from Illinois, who came to get over pneumonia, is cooking the fish with assistance from an unidentified woman. Waiting in the background for their fish are, from left to right, Bertha Massey, Tony McNiece, and C. O. Roe. (Courtesy of Cooper Memorial Library Association.)

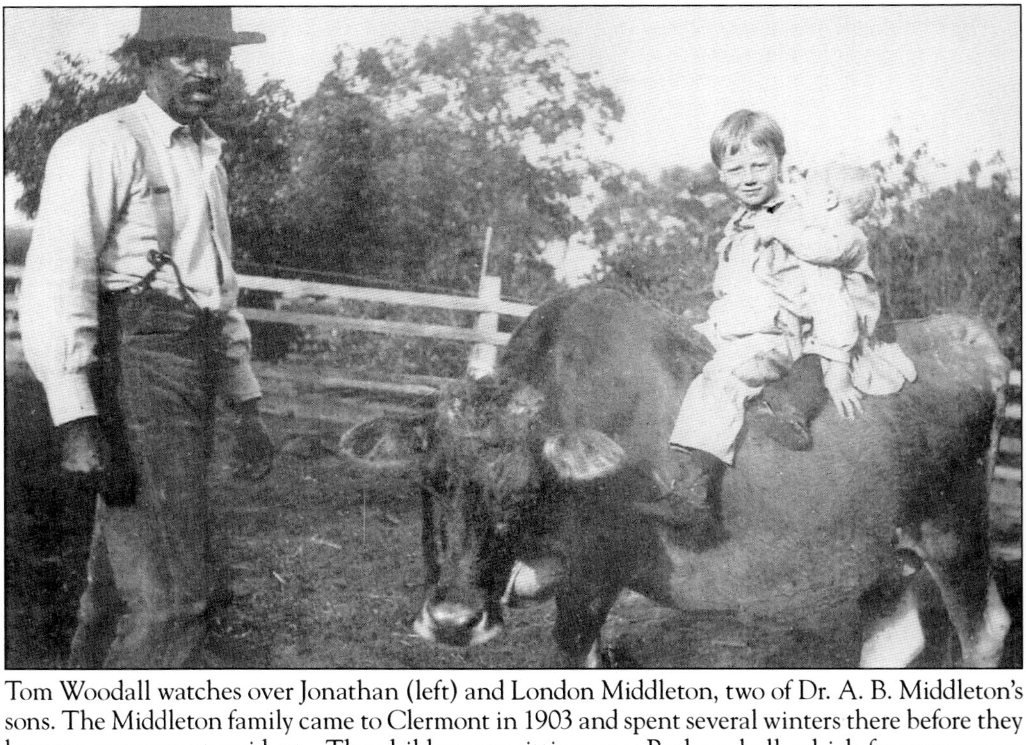

Tom Woodall watches over Jonathan (left) and London Middleton, two of Dr. A. B. Middleton's sons. The Middleton family came to Clermont in 1903 and spent several winters there before they became permanent residents. The children are sitting on a Brahma bull, which for years was a popular docile breed of cattle ideally suited for Florida due to their tolerance to heat and ability to repel insects. (Courtesy of Cooper Memorial Library Association.)

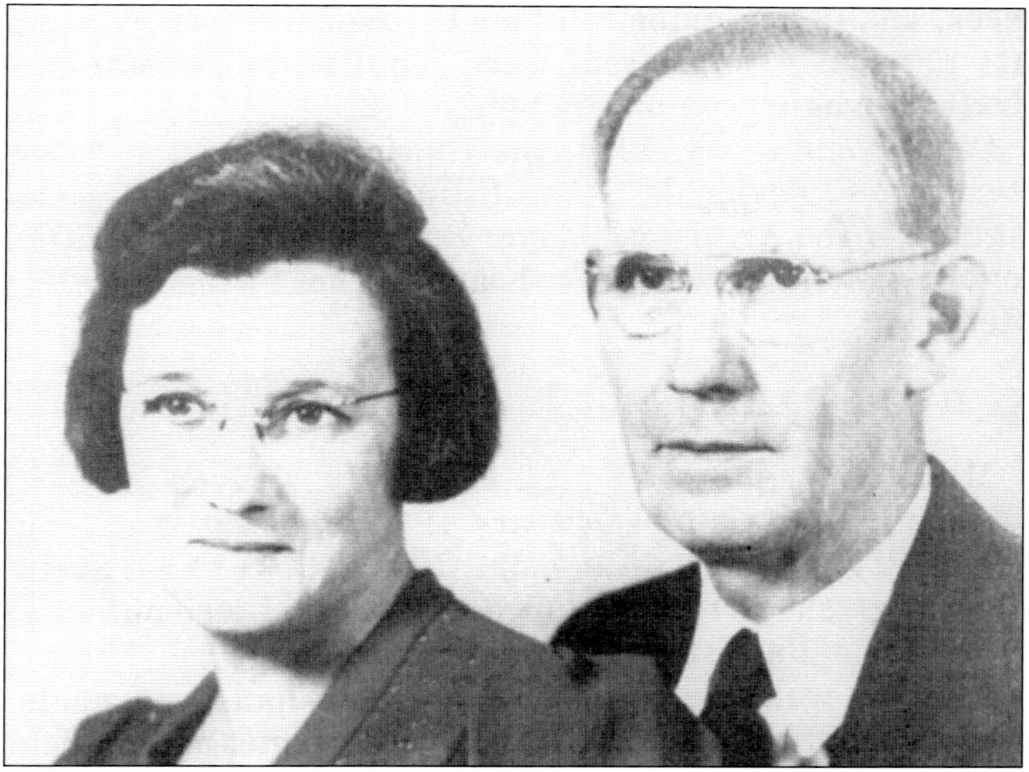

Percy Seaver and his wife, Winnie Hooks Seaver, had deep roots in Clermont. She descended from Herring Hooks and lived on Montrose Street for 92 years. Their son Oakley Seaver became known as "Mr. Clermont" for his community involvement. Percy was best known for his Montrose Street barbershop, which opened in 1913 and remains open today under Mike Hoskinson. (Courtesy of Cooper Memorial Library Association.)

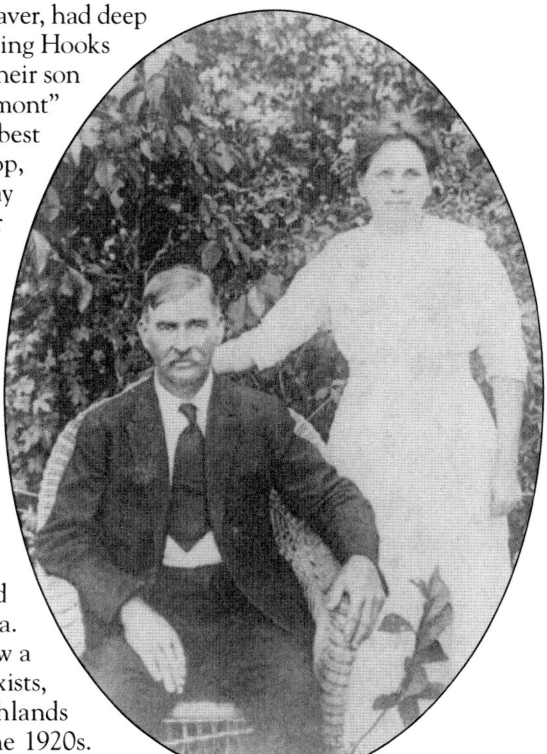

Capt. Daniel Westbrook and his wife, Jessie, moved to Villa City in the late 1890s before moving to Lake Nellie. They later relocated to the Palatlakaha Creek near Lake Louisa. Jessie became the postmistress of Albert, now a ghost town near Monte Vista that no longer exists, and Daniel planted citrus for the Lake Highlands Company and was a city councilman in the 1920s. (Courtesy of Cooper Memorial Library Association.)

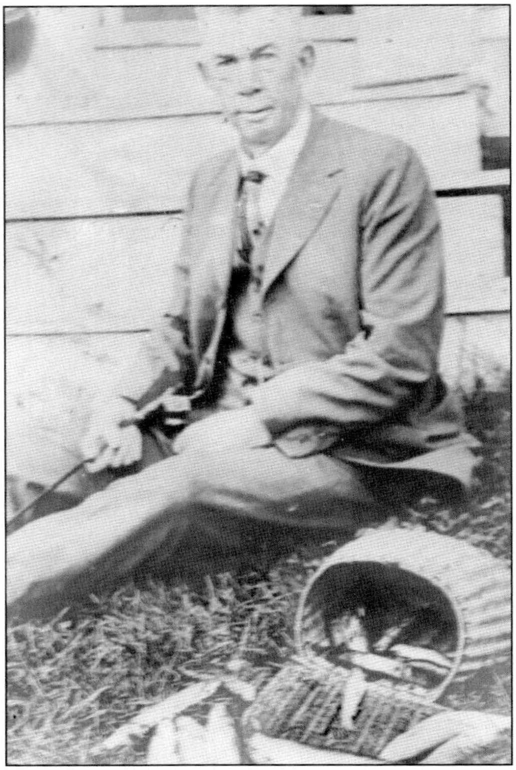

C. O. Roe and his wife, Belle Maxham Roe, visited Clermont in 1899. They inherited the Hotel Maxham, bought Archibald Gano's house, and became winter visitors. They later moved to Clermont permanently. He and his cousin C. W. Roe founded First State Bank and erected the brick home for it on the northeast corner of Montrose and Eighth Streets. The building still stands today. (Courtesy of Cooper Memorial Library Association.)

By 1912, Clermont had rebounded from the Great Freeze. C. O. Roe (right) and his cousin C. W. Roe (left) founded First State Bank, housed in a brick building where Jones General Store had been. The bank opened on March 1, 1913. The nearest competition was in Tavares. C. O. Roe served on the board of directors when the bank merged to form Citizens Bank of Clermont. (Courtesy of Cooper Memorial Library Association.)

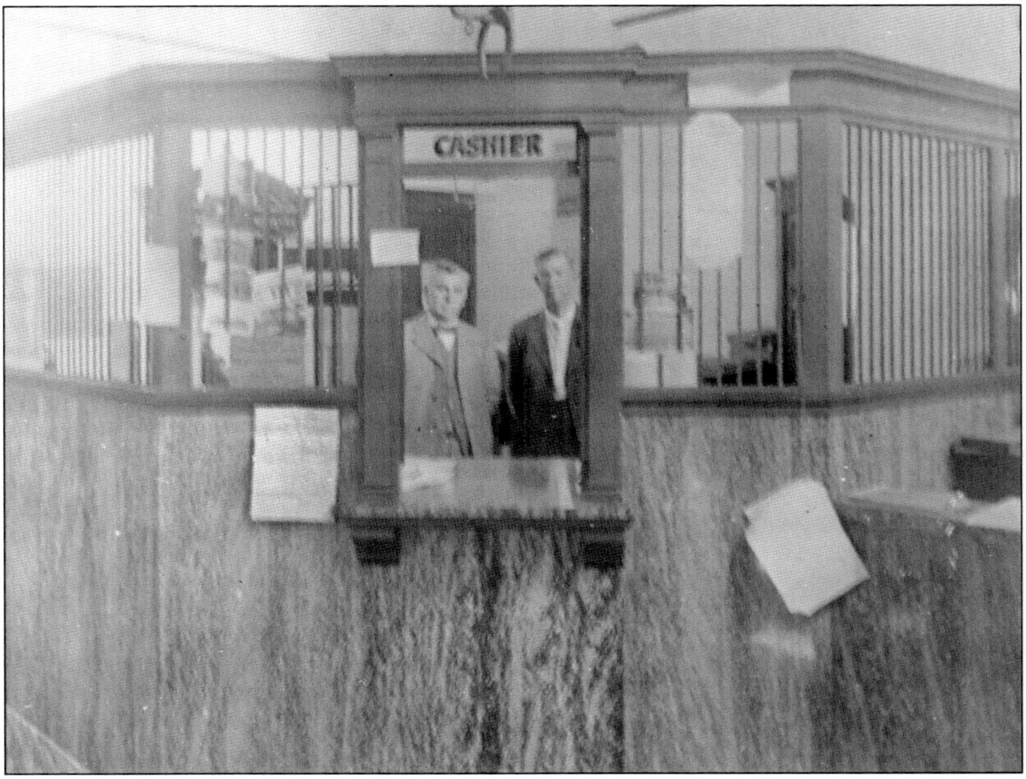

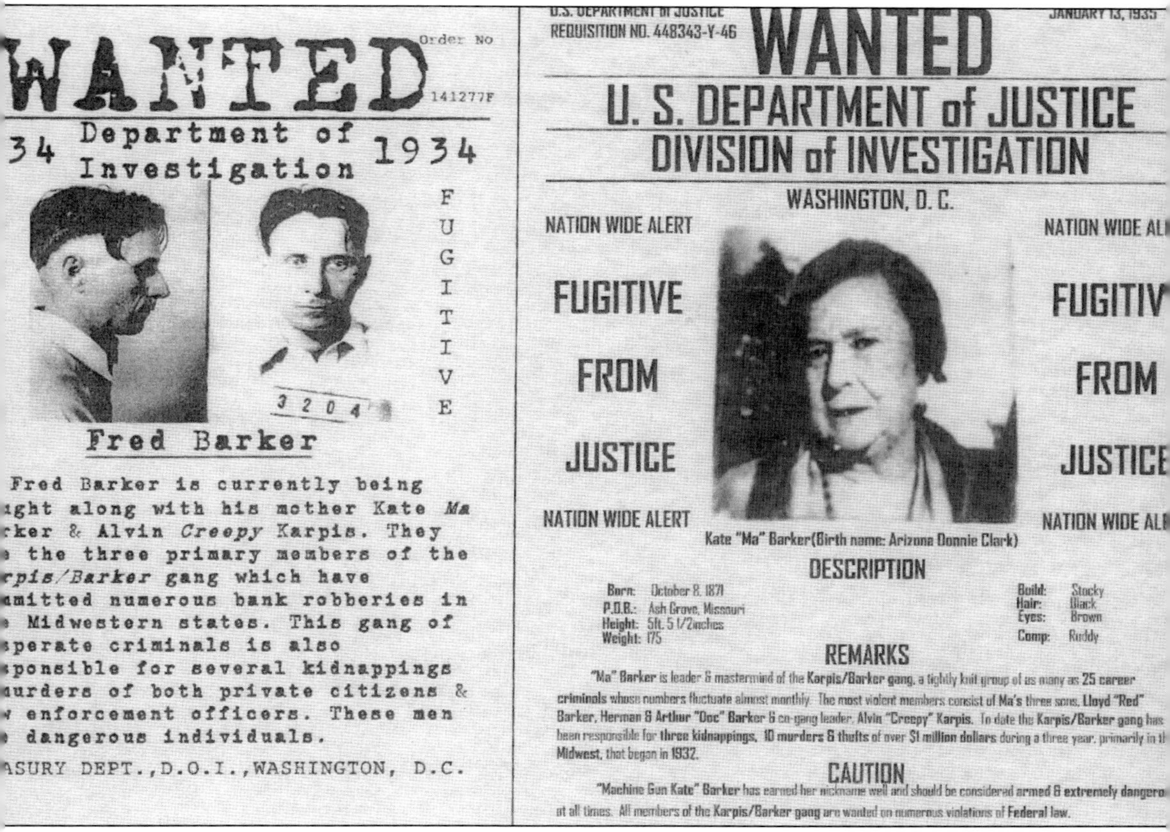


During an era of gangsters that gripped the nation, Citizens Bank was robbed. Assistant cashier George Brady identified the man in the second robbery as Fred Barker, youngest son of Kate "Ma" Barker. According to Brady, he, Harry Stokes, and Paul Settle were at the bank on June 16, 1931, when two men entered at closing time. The men closed the door, pulled the shades, drew their guns, and marched the bank employees into the vault. The robbers were not wearing disguises. One was hefty; the other was young, fair-skinned, and slightly built. The robbers tied up the bankers, taped their fingers, and made them lie on the floor. About $5,000 was stolen; none of it was recovered. Forty miles away, Ma Barker and her gang were hiding out in a rental at Ocklawaha in south Marion County. In an early morning raid, the FBI shot and killed the gangster mother and her youngest son, Fred. Some Clermont residents, including Brady, visited the morgue. He immediately recognized Fred Barker as the young robber. (Courtesy of Most Wanted Posters, Inc.)

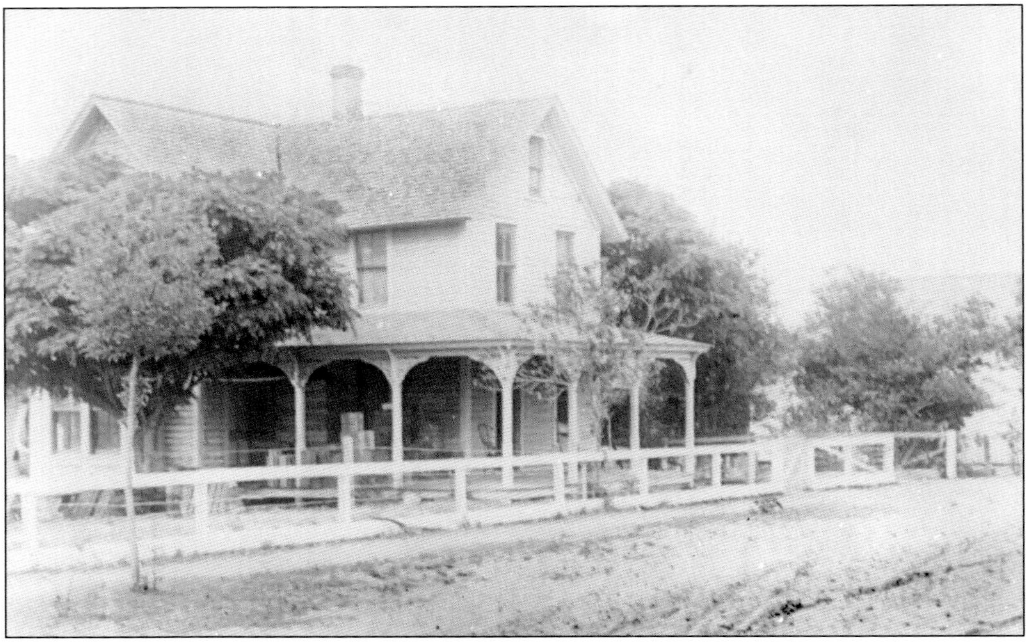

The Clermont post office is pictured in this 1904 photograph. It served the town from 1899 to 1912. The building was later moved west and now houses an insurance company. The city's first postmaster was one of the founders, Arthur Wrotnowski. Residential mail delivery began in 1953. (Courtesy of Cooper Memorial Library Association.)

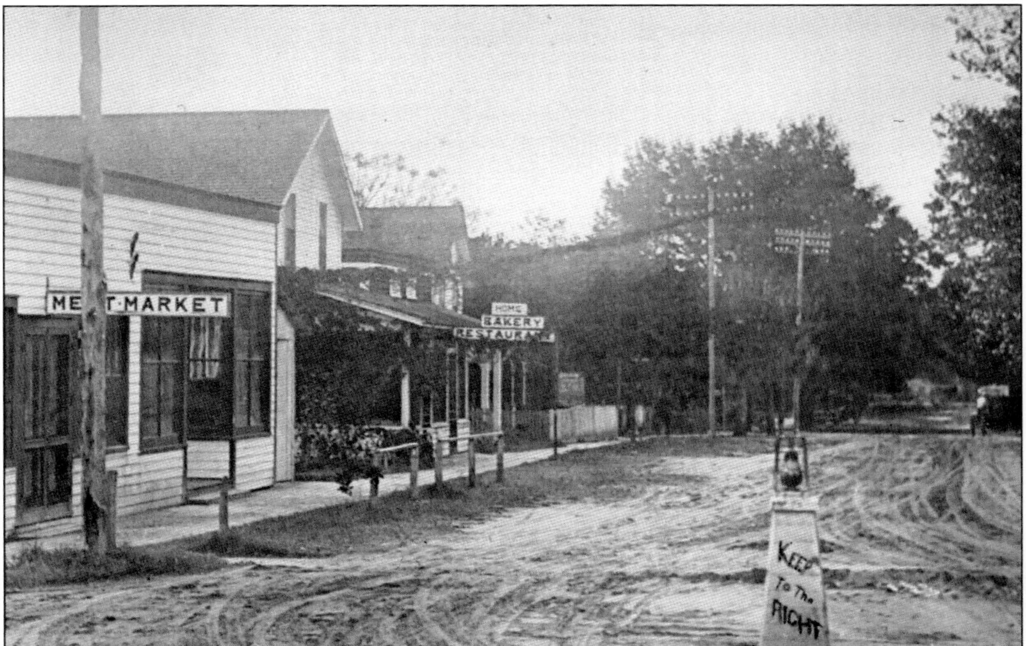


In 1908, downtown Clermont received its first traffic signal—the lantern seen on the stand with a sign that reads, "Keep to the Right." In the early days of automobiles, it was not unusual to see cattle and hogs sharing the dirt streets. Howard and Nannie Bailey owned the bakery and meat market pictured at left on Montrose Street. (Courtesy of the State Archives of Florida.)

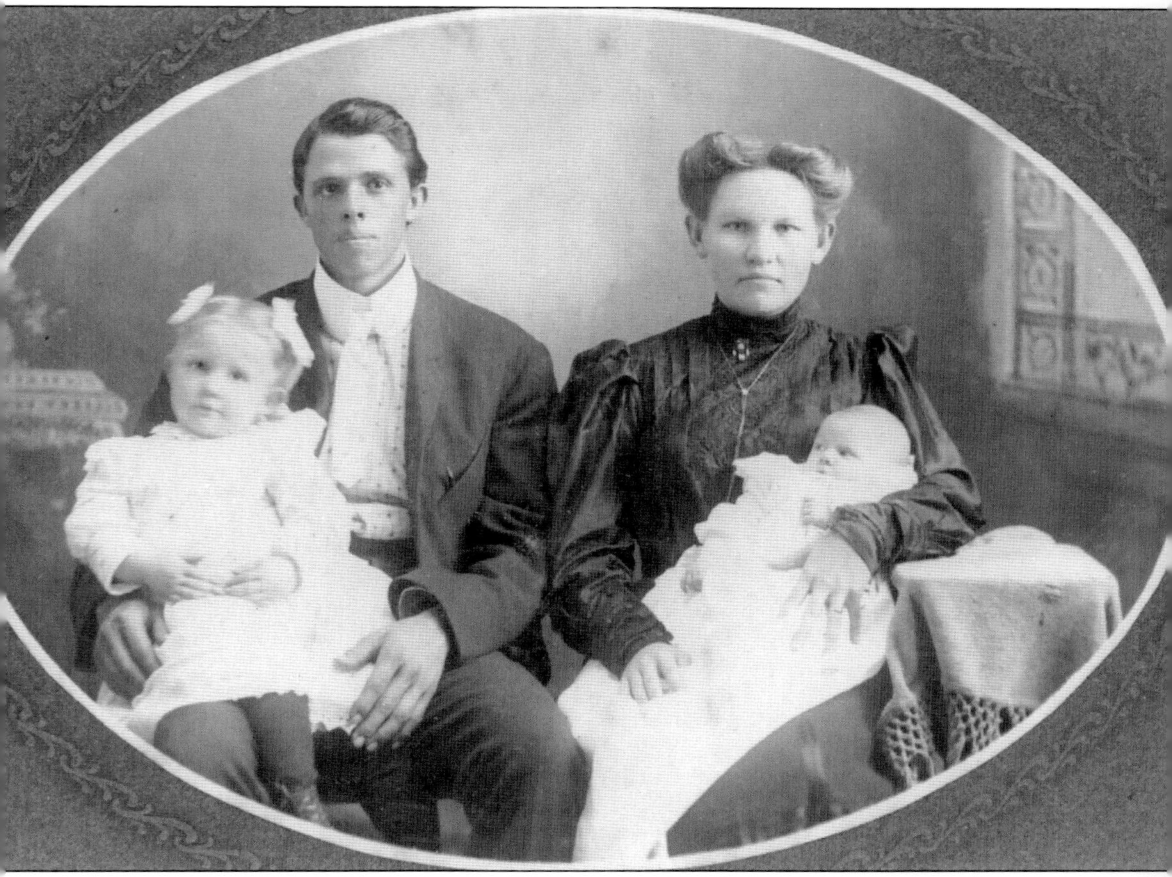

Around 1900, the Hammond family set up headquarters south of the Lake County line and purchased 20,000 acres in Lake and Polk Counties. They operated a sawmill and also manufactured lumber, shingles, and staves—the thin slats used in barrels. They hauled their products 10 miles to Lake Louisa, to a spot called Hammond's Landing, where the lumber and other products could continue by barge through the lakes and canal to the Clermont train station. The forests were filled with longleaf pine trees, which were tapped for turpentine in the late 1890s by the Taylor brothers and D. G. Crenshaw. Pictured above are John William Hammond, holding daughter Mollie, and wife Louise Hammond, holding daughter Ruby. Other Hammond family members included William Hammond; his wife, Maggie; and their children, Percy, Lonnie, Frances, Ernest, and William. (Courtesy of Frankie Hammond, Alfred Hammond Jr., and the Lake County Historical Society.)

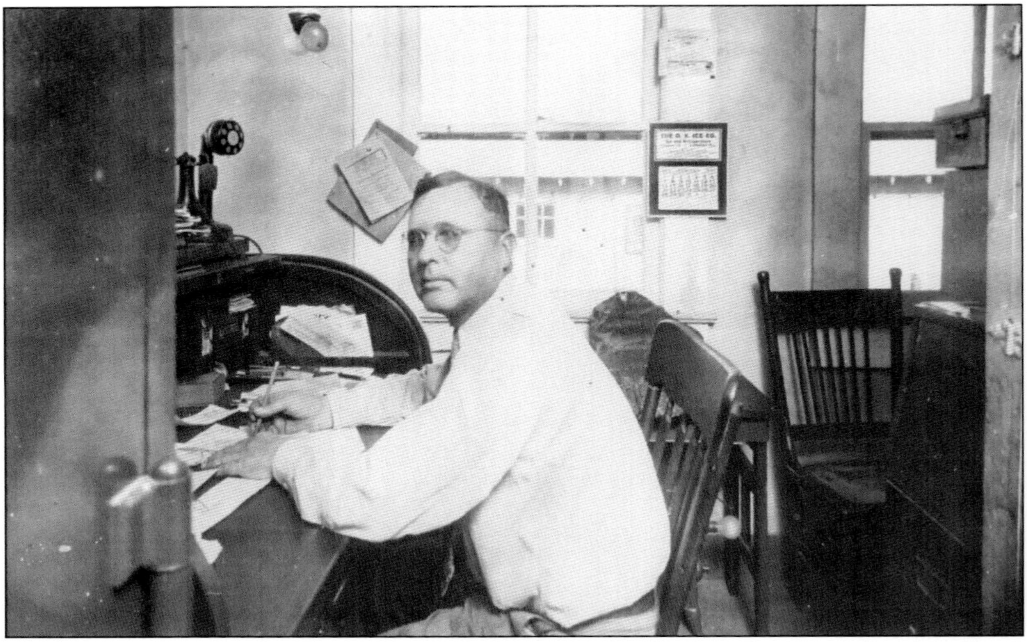

Fred Kreider was a rare breed for Clermont—a native Floridian. He had moved to Cleveland, Ohio, but moved back in 1917 and bought the O. K. Ice Plant that sat at the north end of West Avenue overlooking Lake Minneola. In 1922, Kreider built a new plant on the same site. He sold it in 1945. (Courtesy of Cooper Memorial Library Association.)

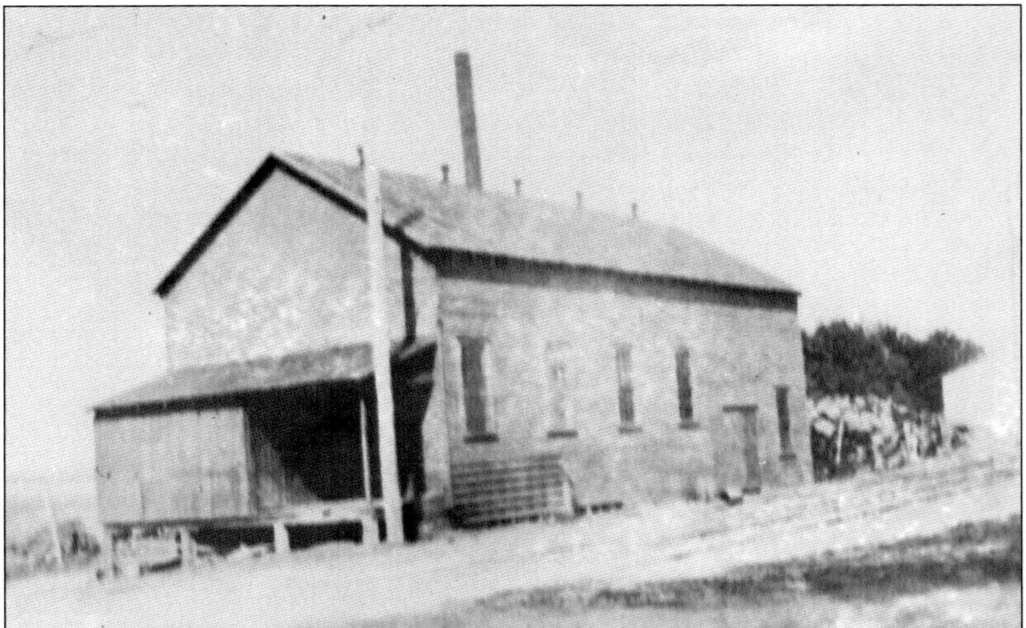

The O. K. Ice Plant is pictured as it looked around 1913. The plant started in 1907 mainly to serve the truck farmers who needed the ice to ship their produce by rail. The plant, located near the train depot, changed hands several times. Fred Kreider sold the plant in 1945 to Bert Willis, who operated it until 1954. At that time, the plant was producing 12 tons of ice a day. (Courtesy of the State Archives of Florida.)

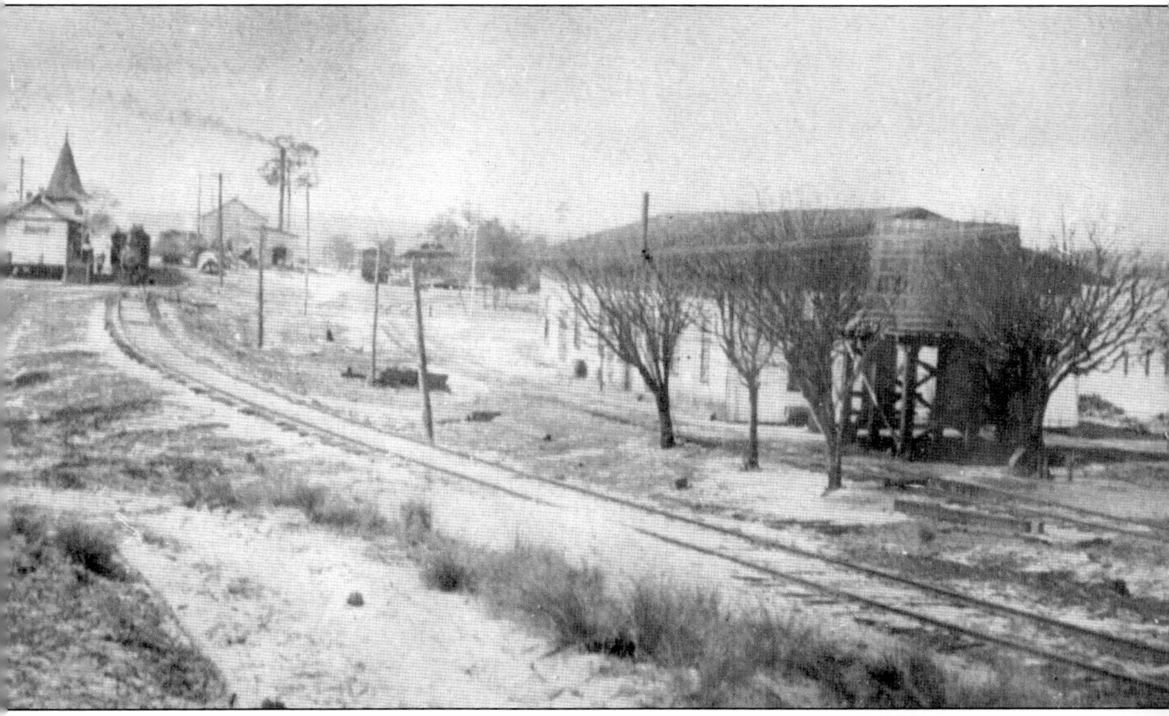

This rare *c.* 1900 photograph shows the proximity of the ice plant and a packinghouse to the rail lines and Lake Minneola. At far left is the train depot used by the Orange Belt Railway. Right beside it, on the other side of the train track, is the O. K. Ice Plant. In the foreground at right is a packinghouse, with Lake Minneola to the right side. Farmers and lumber companies used Clermont's chain of lakes to get their products to the train depot. Having the ice plant close by made it convenient for farmers to keep their produce cool for shipment to distant markets. Several packinghouses made their homes beside the tracks, including Blue Goose and Gem of the Hills. Tavares and Gulf, another railway running beside Lake Minneola, was one of the country's smallest but most lucrative rail lines and was featured at the 1933 Chicago World's Fair. (Courtesy of Cooper Memorial Library Association.)

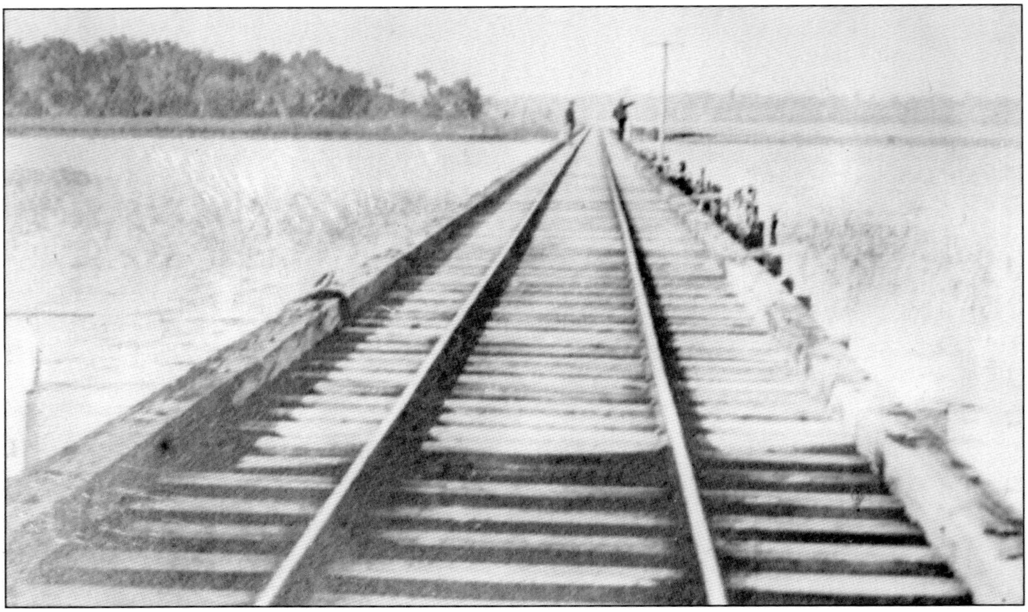

This railroad trestle extended across the west end of Lake Minneola for trains headed west to Trilby, a Pasco County town created at the beginning of the 20th century as a junction for four rail lines. In the early 1900s, one train went off the tracks, broke through the trestle, and landed in the lake. (Courtesy of Cooper Memorial Library Association.)

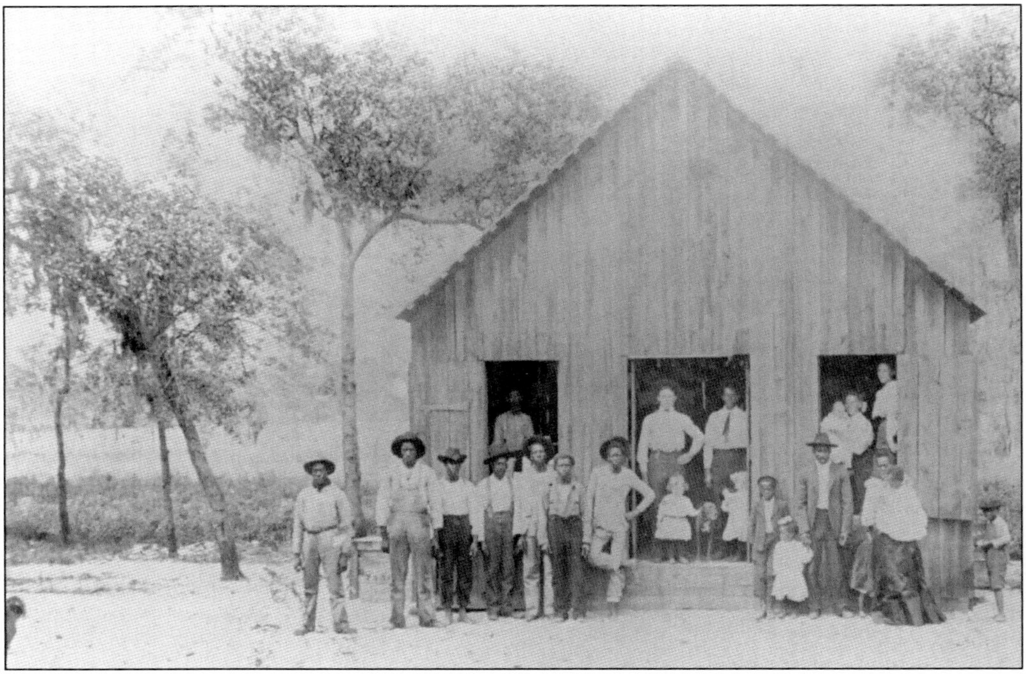

This 1906 photograph shows the commissary at Hammond Sawmill on the south side of Lake Louisa, with John Hammond standing in the doorway and Louise Hammond standing in the window holding a baby. The lake, originally called Lake Louise, was reportedly named after the young mother. In 1973, the state bought the property and turned it into a park. (Courtesy of Frankie and Alfred Hammond Jr.)

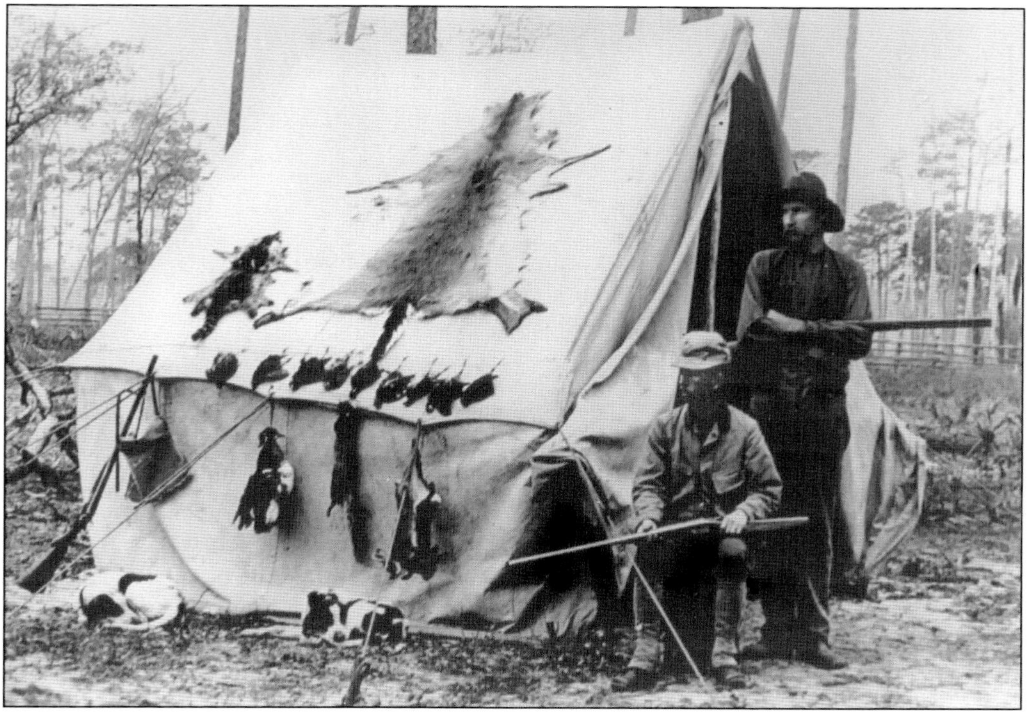

While *c.* 1910 Clermont developed a downtown, industrial business, and citrus industry, the town continued to draw avid hunters. Available game included deer, raccoon, duck, squirrel, and quail. Good hunting dogs, such as those seen here curled up by the tent, were prized assets. Lorem Brown, standing in the rear with a dark hat, was one of the area's most sought-after guides. (Courtesy of the State Archives of Florida.)

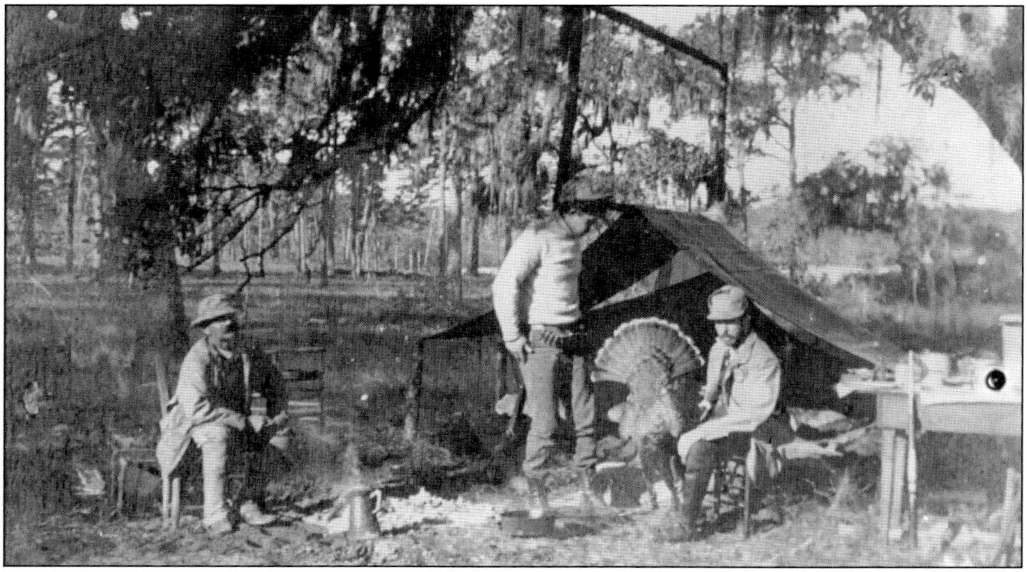

More photographs from the early 1900s show turkey hunters and a good view of the landscape. The tall longleaf pines and wiregrass gave unobstructed views of much of the Clermont woodlands. Florida still offers some of the best turkey hunting in the nation. The two main subspecies are wild turkeys and Osceolas. (Courtesy of the State Archives of Florida.)

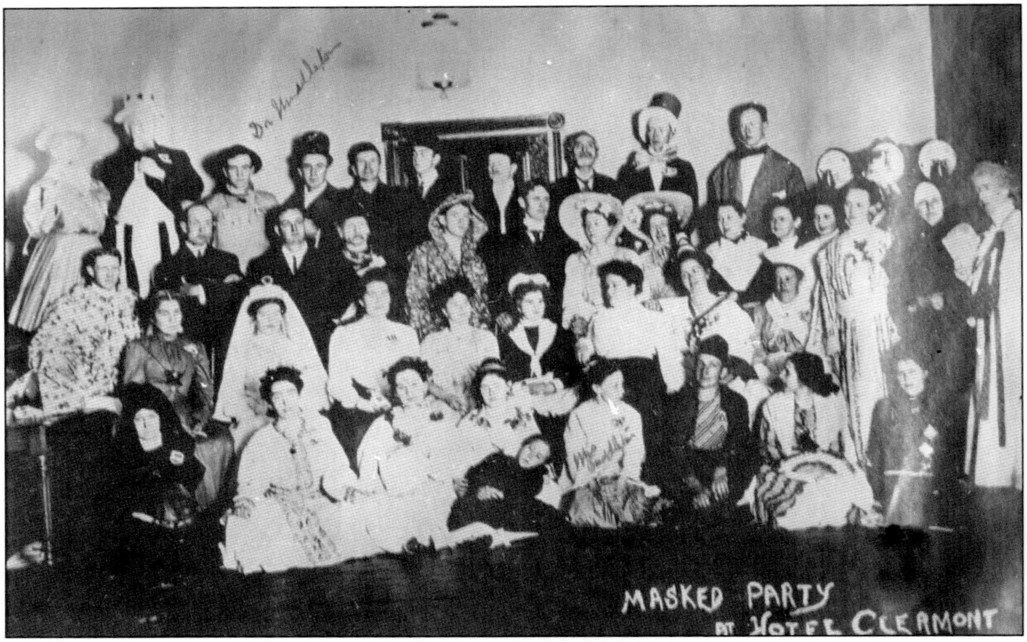


Hotel Clermont was a popular destination for winter visitors. It was also used for local entertaining, as evidenced in this 1906 photograph of a masked party that included Dr. A. B. Middleton (fourth row, third from left) who first visited the town in the winter of 1903–1904. He and his wife, Lillian, and their children, Jonathon, London, and Glenn, eventually moved to the city. (Courtesy of Cooper Memorial Library Association.)

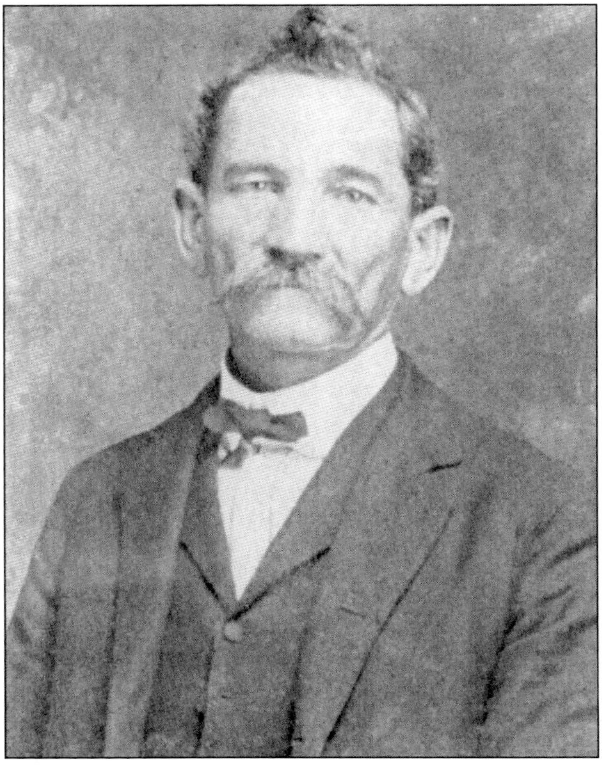

William Brinson Driggers was elected town marshal in December 1918, along with mayor William Kern and councilmen C. H. Wilson and C. H. Goodenough. That same year, the previous city council passed an ordinance requiring citizens to work on street maintenance two days a year or pay $2. (Courtesy of Frankie and Alfred Hammond Jr.)

The dream of Clermont as a model town had not died with the Great Freeze. New developers promoted the town nationally, such as this ad that called the city "a Scarsdale in the Making." The ad bragged that Clermont had the lowest death rate of any city in the nation, attributed to the climate and healthy environment, and had more paved streets per capita than any city in Florida. (Courtesy of Clermont Hill and Lake Company.)

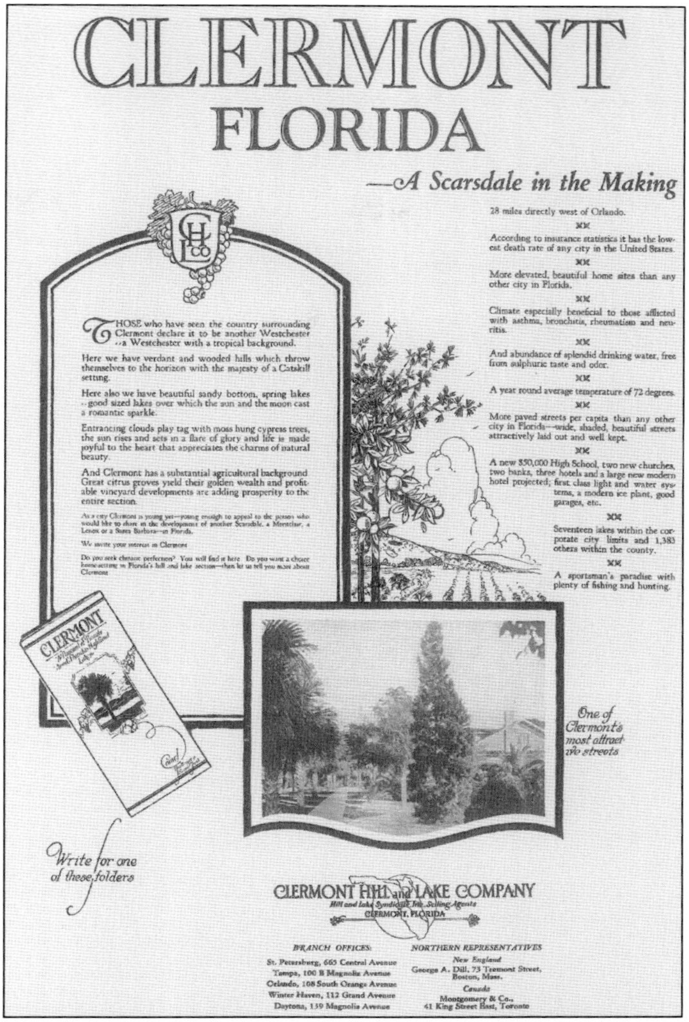


The hustle and bustle of the daily train's arrivals in the early 1900s provided entertainment for the curious settlers. As one eyewitness commented about the 1902 scene (below) of passengers arriving in Minneola, seeing "if anyone came or left was one of the [local residents'] recreations." (Courtesy of Cooper Memorial Library Association.)

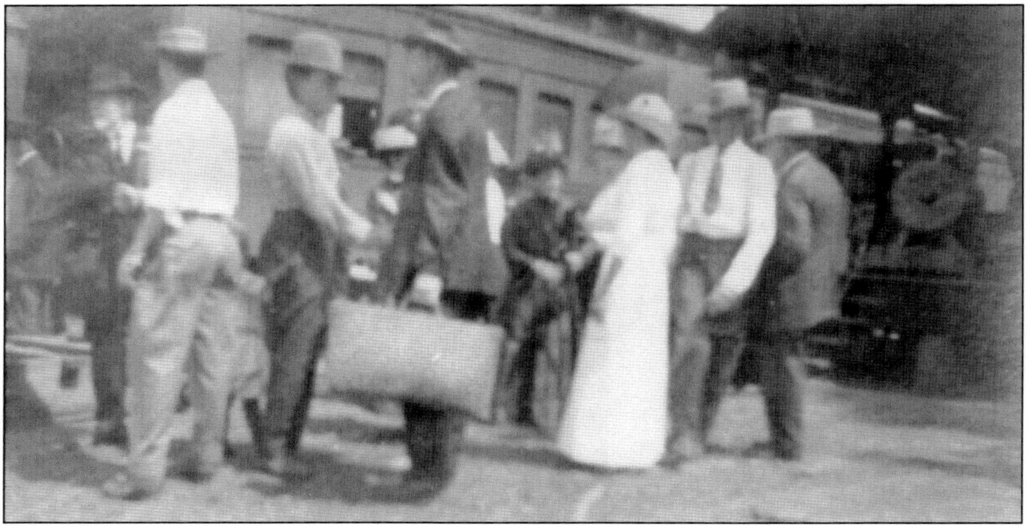

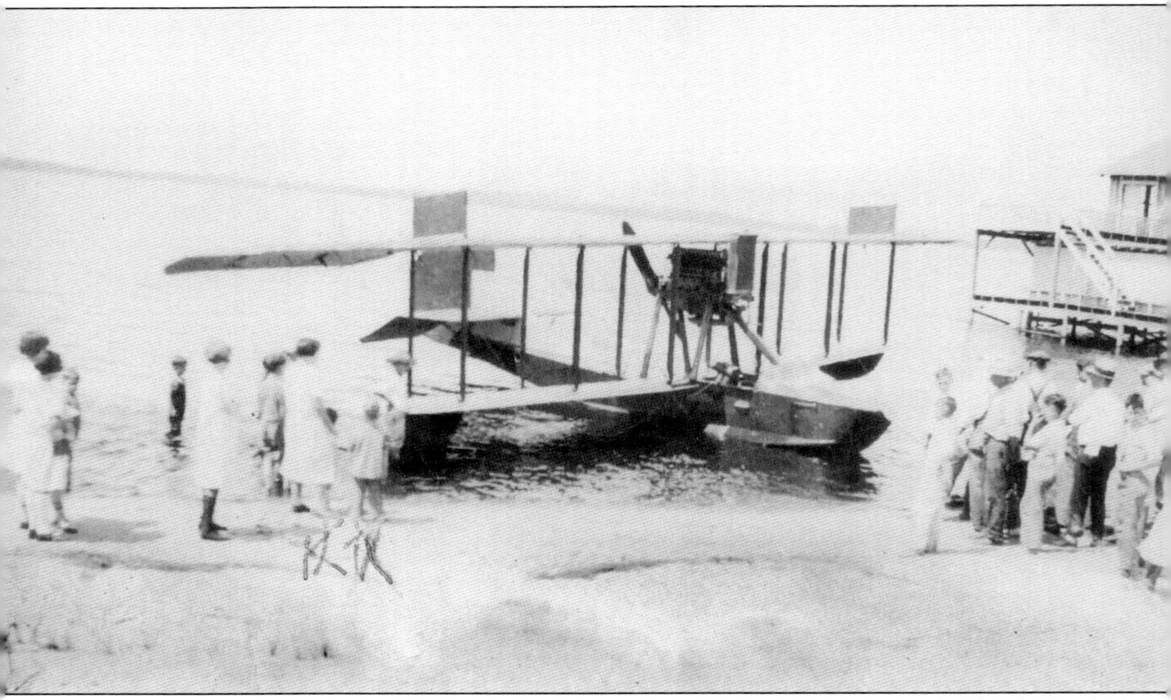

Curiosity also drew a big crowd to Lake Minneola's beach when Thomas Barr of Orlando, head of the Florida Photographic Flyers, landed his hydroplane beside the American Legion Pavilion at the foot of Eighth Street. Barr had been snapping aerial pictures of the city prior to this c. 1925 photograph. He gave several people rides after he finished his photographic assignment. One of the eyewitnesses on the beach was five-year-old Edith Brady, sister of Citizens Bank assistant cashier George Brady. Several other Clermont residents got their first airplane ride in 1921 when another Orlando aviator, Jimmy Johnson, dropped advertising fliers from the air to announce the opening of First State Bank and invited some local guests to accompany him. (Courtesy of the Lake County Historical Society.)

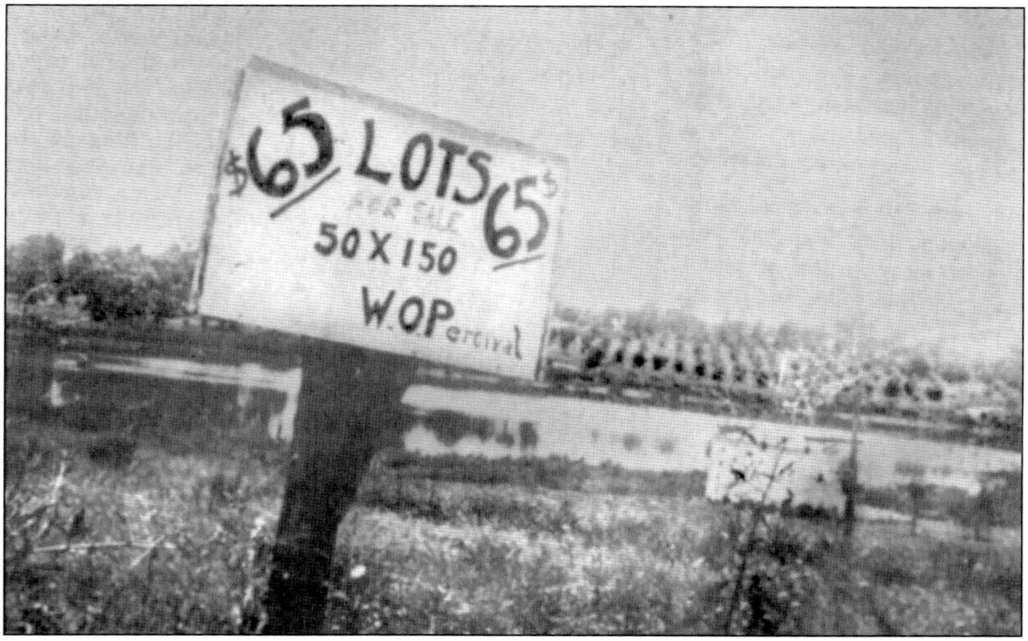


In Clermont's early development, lakeside lots were less desirable than those on higher ground, since elevated homes afforded better cross ventilation. W. O. Percival, the landowner displaying this sign, was a former West Virginia coal operator who built a home and planted a grove on 160 acres in east Clermont. He donated the lot for Clermont's first clinic, which evolved into South Lake Hospital. (Courtesy of Cooper Memorial Library Association.)

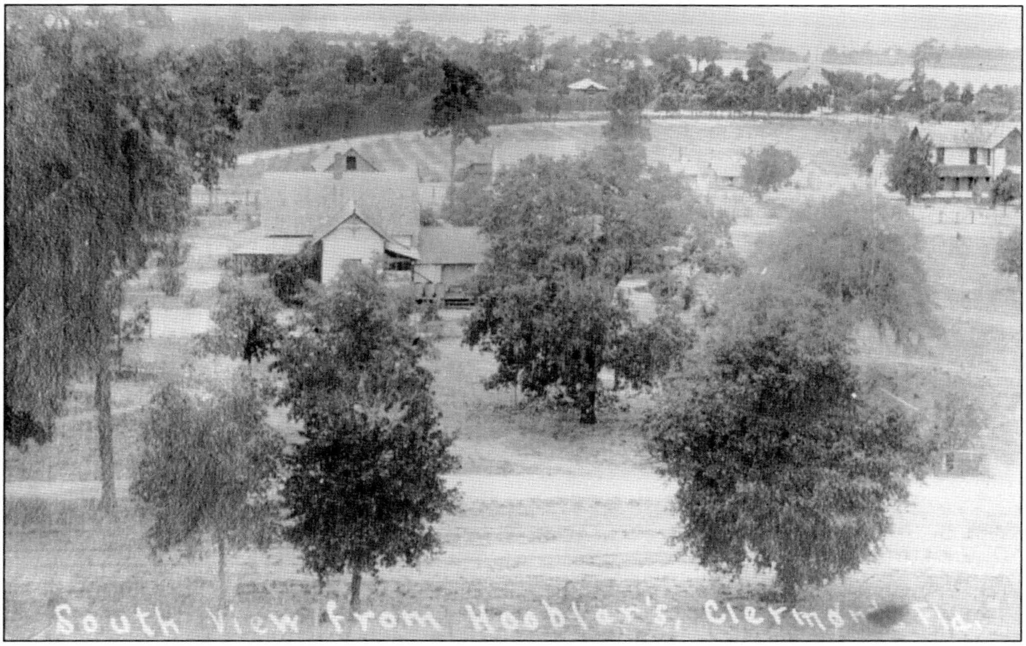


This southern view from the Hoobler House in the early 1900s confirms that many of the early settlers preferred living near the lake but not beside it. The Hoobler House was originally built for William House, one of the founding fathers. The nearby Twin Pines house has been owned by the Schopmeyer family since 1936. (Courtesy of Cooper Memorial Library Association.)

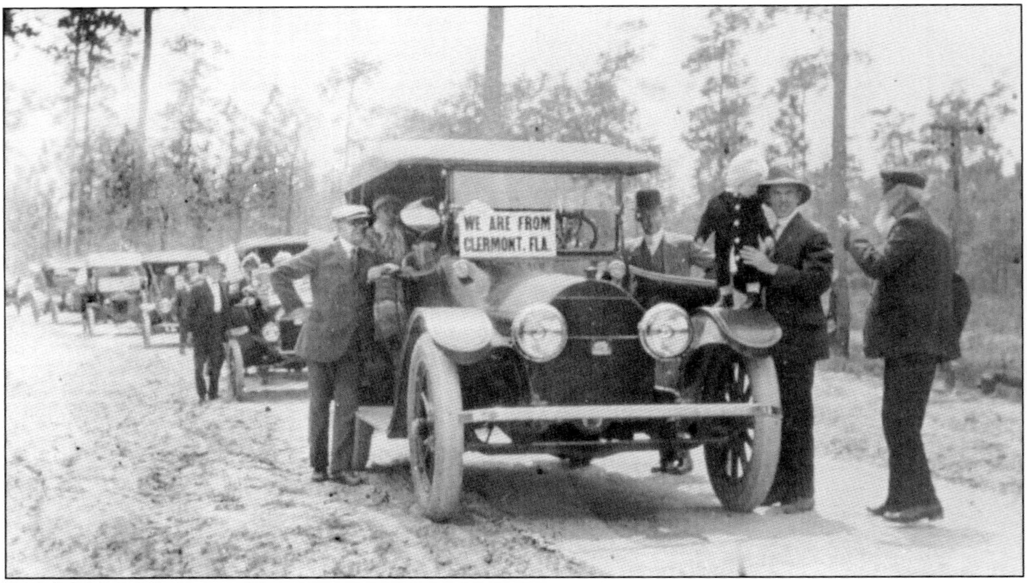


Clermont's first motorcade started March 13, 1916, and was planned by the town's board of trade. C. O. Roe's Cadillac was the pacemaker; there were 20 cars and 96 passengers. They started at the bank and ended in Orlando. Floyd Roe holds his son Charles on the fender. Capt. Montgomery Cooper, for whom Cooper Memorial Library is named, is at far right. (Courtesy of the State Archives of Florida.)

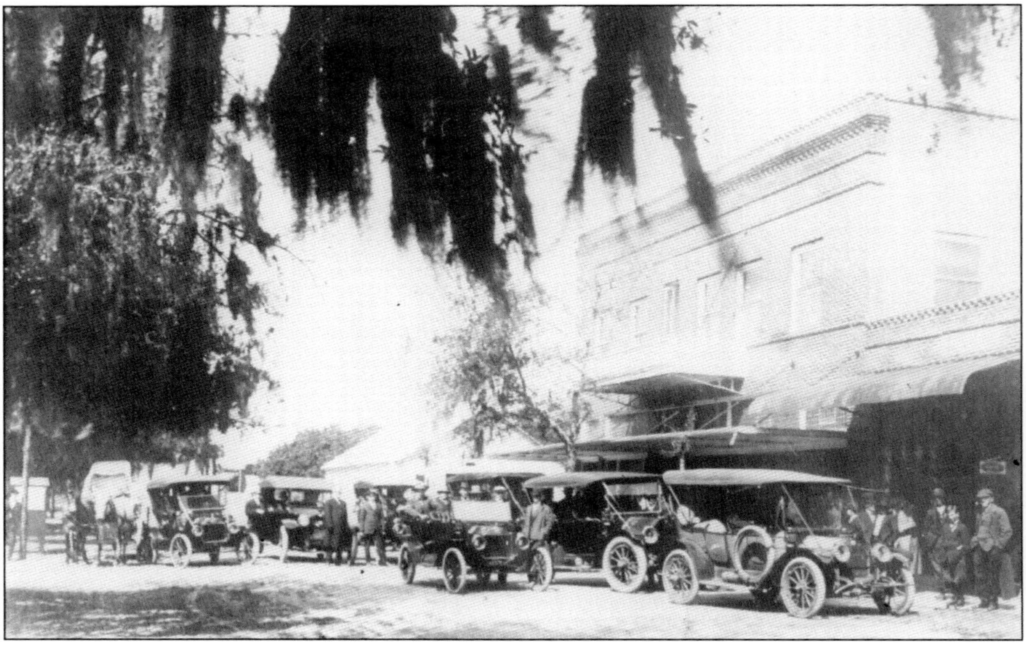

Horse and buggies were outnumbered in this *c.* 1915 photograph looking west at the intersection of Montrose and Eighth Streets. The brick building at right is First State Bank, erected by cousins C. O. and C. W. Roe. The popularity of automobiles drove new businesses, including garages, dealerships, and gas stations. (Courtesy of Cooper Memorial Library Association.)

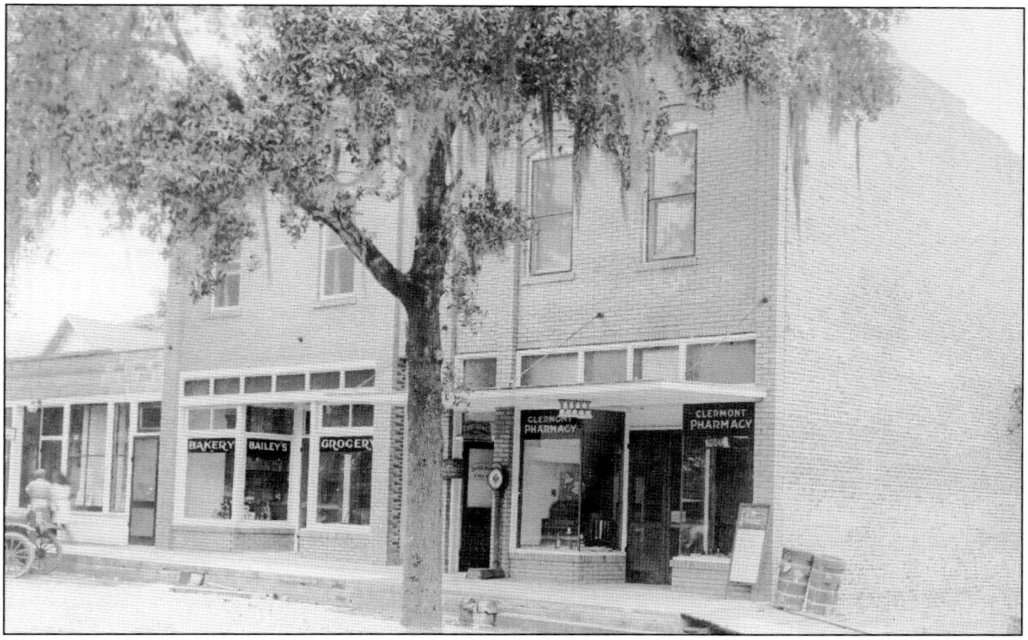


As Clermont thrived, so did its downtown, as pictured here at the southeast corner of Montrose and Eighth Streets. The businesses included Bailey's Bakery and Grocery, Dr. Arthur Izlar, and the Clermont Pharmacy. Izlar, of Ocala, purchased the Clermont Pharmacy around 1919. He was the chamber of commerce's first president. In 1943, the pharmacy became the Hilltop Stationery store. (Courtesy of Cooper Memorial Library Association.)

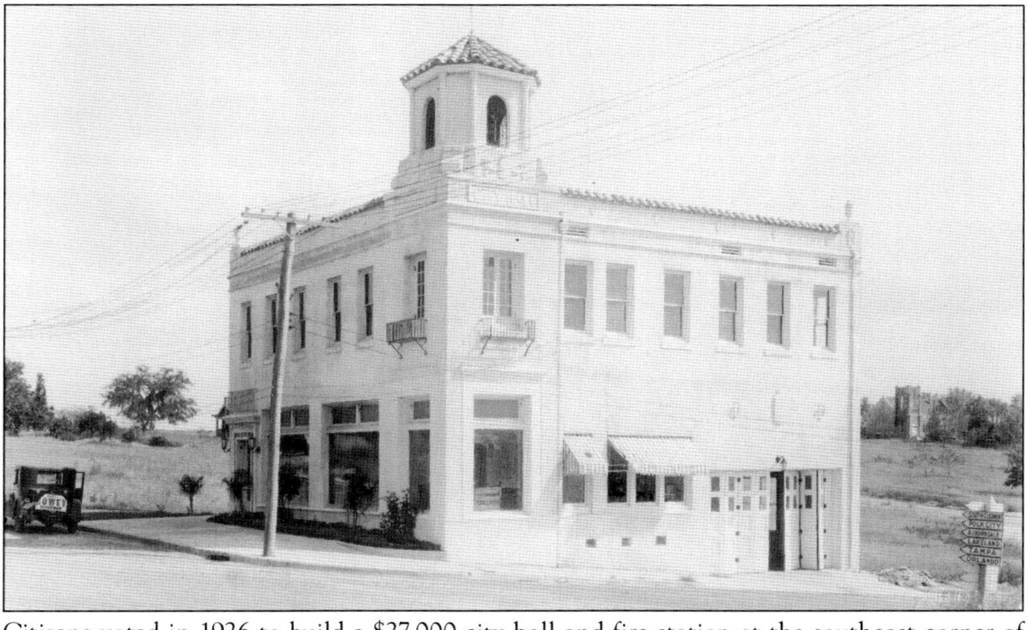


Citizens voted in 1926 to build a $27,000 city hall and fire station at the southeast corner of Eighth Street and DeSoto Avenue. The basement contained a fire truck, police headquarters, and a jail. The city clerk and chamber of commerce occupied the first floor. The second floor held the council chamber and fire chief's living quarters. Note the "Howey for Governor" campaign sign. (Courtesy of the Lake County Historical Society.)

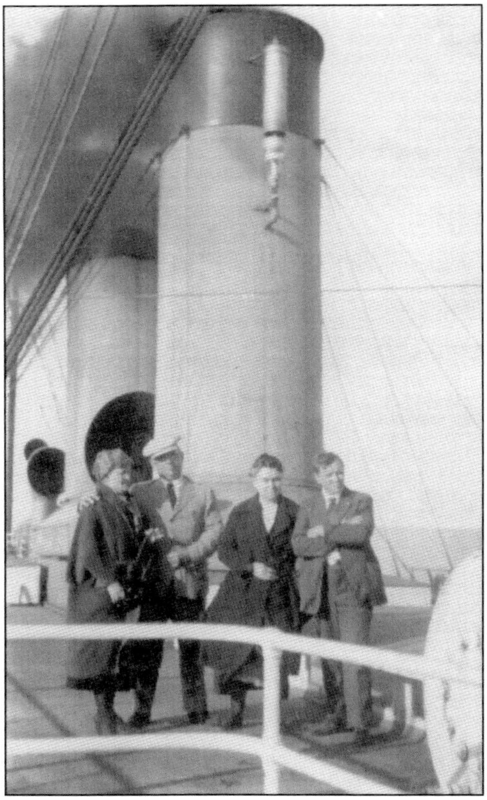

In the early 1920s, Clermont's land boom was fueled partly by W. J. Howey, who bought 60,000 acres in southern Lake County and conducted extravagant promotions. Prospects enjoyed dinner and lodging at Minneola's Straker House, a tour of Clermont grove land, a bus trip to Miami, and a cruise to Cuba, as captured in this 1920 photograph of two Oklahoma families. (Courtesy of Carol Willard Clark.)

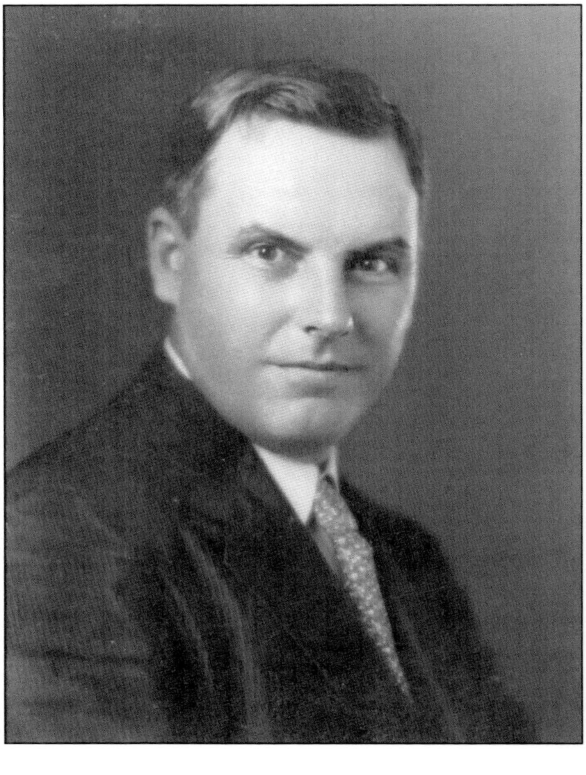

George F. Westbrook served in the Florida House of Representatives from 1928 to 1936 and in the Senate from 1936 to 1941. He was legal counsel for the cities of Clermont, Minneola, and Astatula and was the Postal Colony Company's general manager. He helped save Citizens Bank by securing a $10,000 loan during the Great Depression. (Courtesy of the State Archives of Florida.)

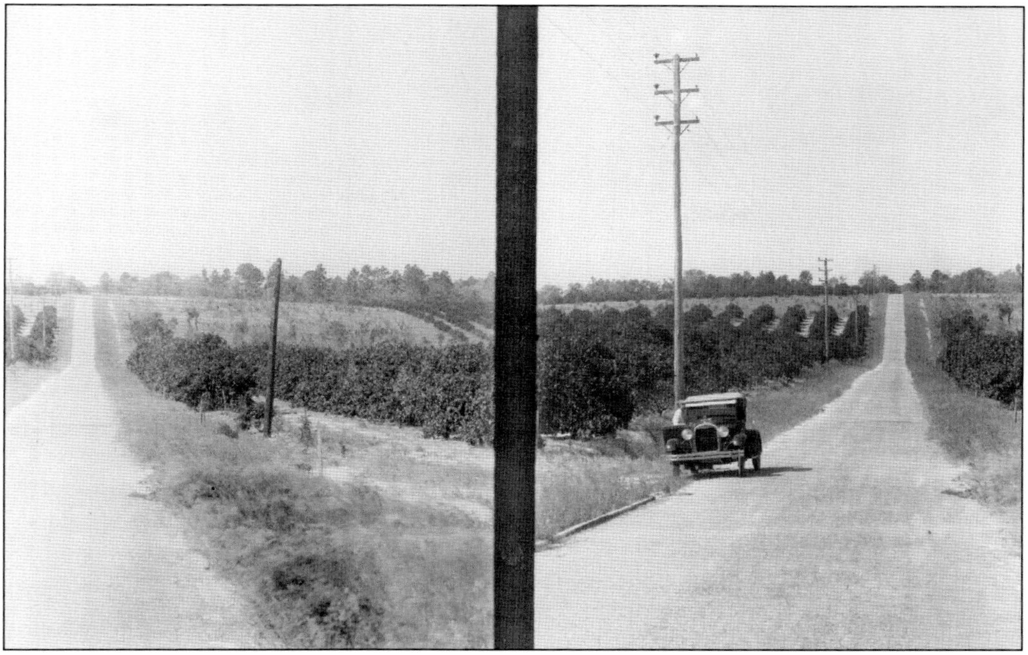

During the 1920s, the roadways in and around Clermont saw great improvements. One of them was the "Roller Coaster Road," which stretched from the end of Minnehaha Avenue, east to the Orange County line. It was completed in 1927. The name was given to this stretch of road after it was built because of its high hills and deep valleys, which made driving it a thrill. (Courtesy of the Lake County Historical Society.)

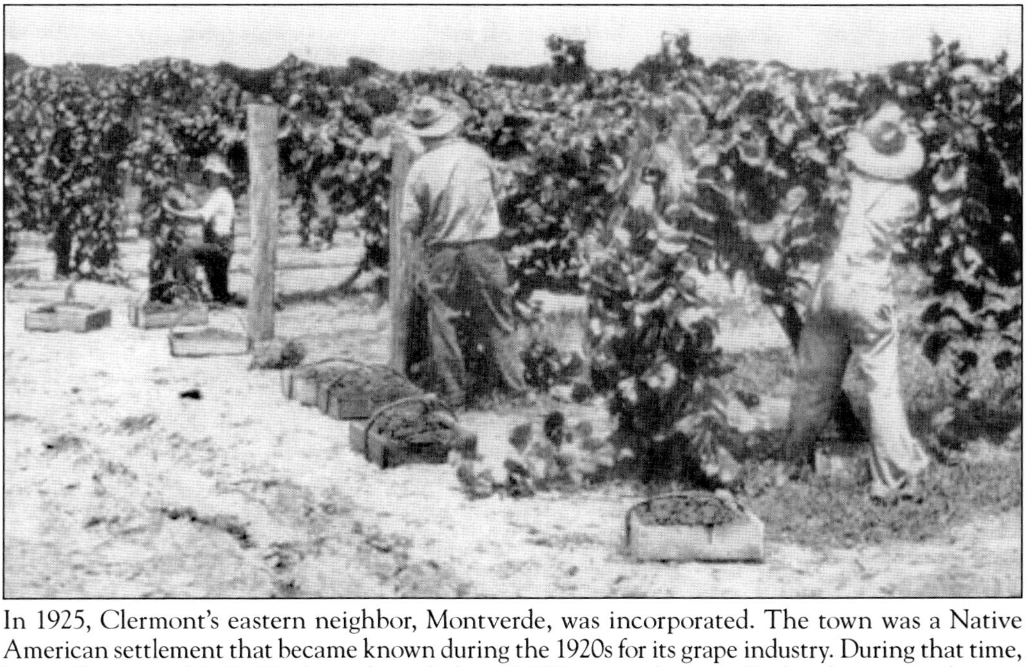

In 1925, Clermont's eastern neighbor, Montverde, was incorporated. The town was a Native American settlement that became known during the 1920s for its grape industry. During that time, Loren Stover and E. E. Truskett planted about 1,200 acres of grapes. Today the town is known better as the place where Snappin' Turtle lawn mowers were invented and as the home of the internationally recognized Montverde Academy. (Courtesy of the State Archives of Florida.)

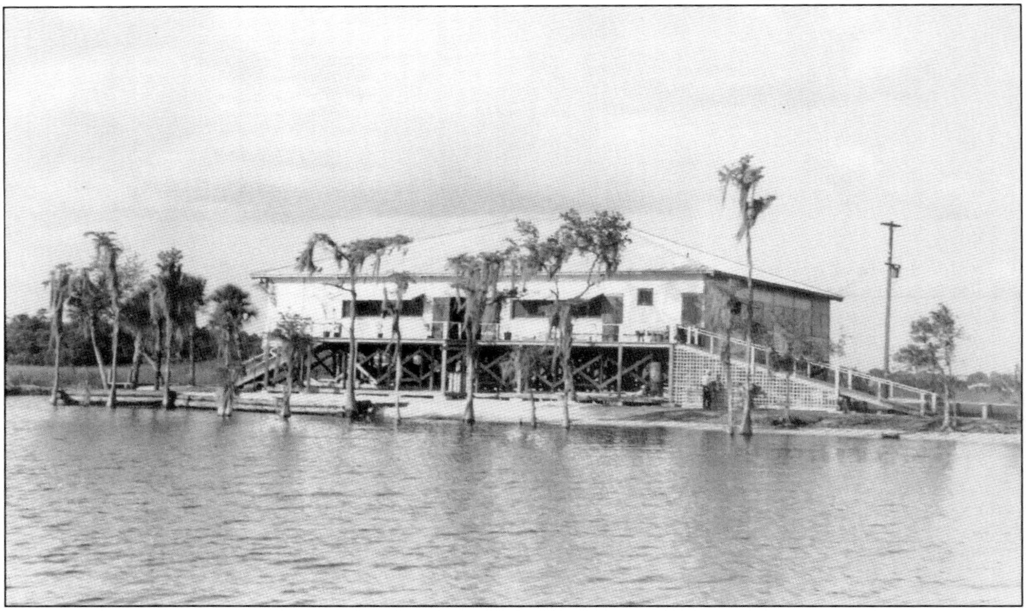

Clermont's land boom went bust, and the Citizens Bank almost failed, but big dreams still existed in the form of projects such as the Yacht Club, built in 1937 between Lake Minnehaha and Lake Winona. The wooden building featured a large dance floor and hosted many social events. The American Legion bought it in 1944, but it was torn down in the 1950s. (Courtesy of Cooper Memorial Library Association.)

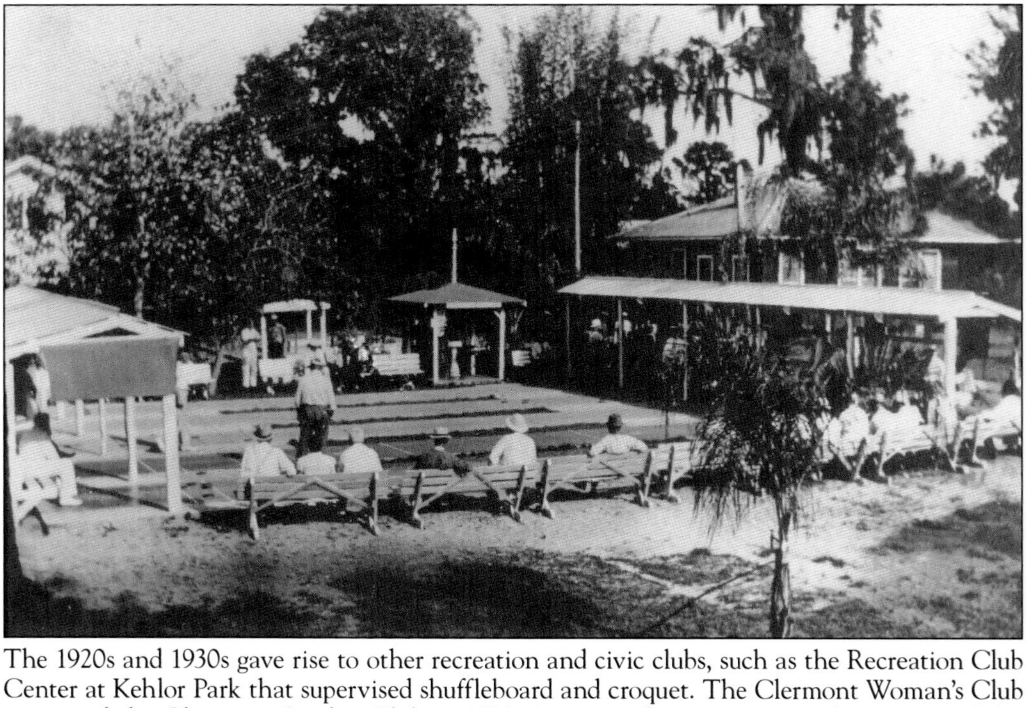

The 1920s and 1930s gave rise to other recreation and civic clubs, such as the Recreation Club Center at Kehlor Park that supervised shuffleboard and croquet. The Clermont Woman's Club organized the Clermont Garden Club in 1931. A group of young women also organized the Clermont Welfare League, which led to the town's first clinic. (Courtesy of Cooper Memorial Library Association.)

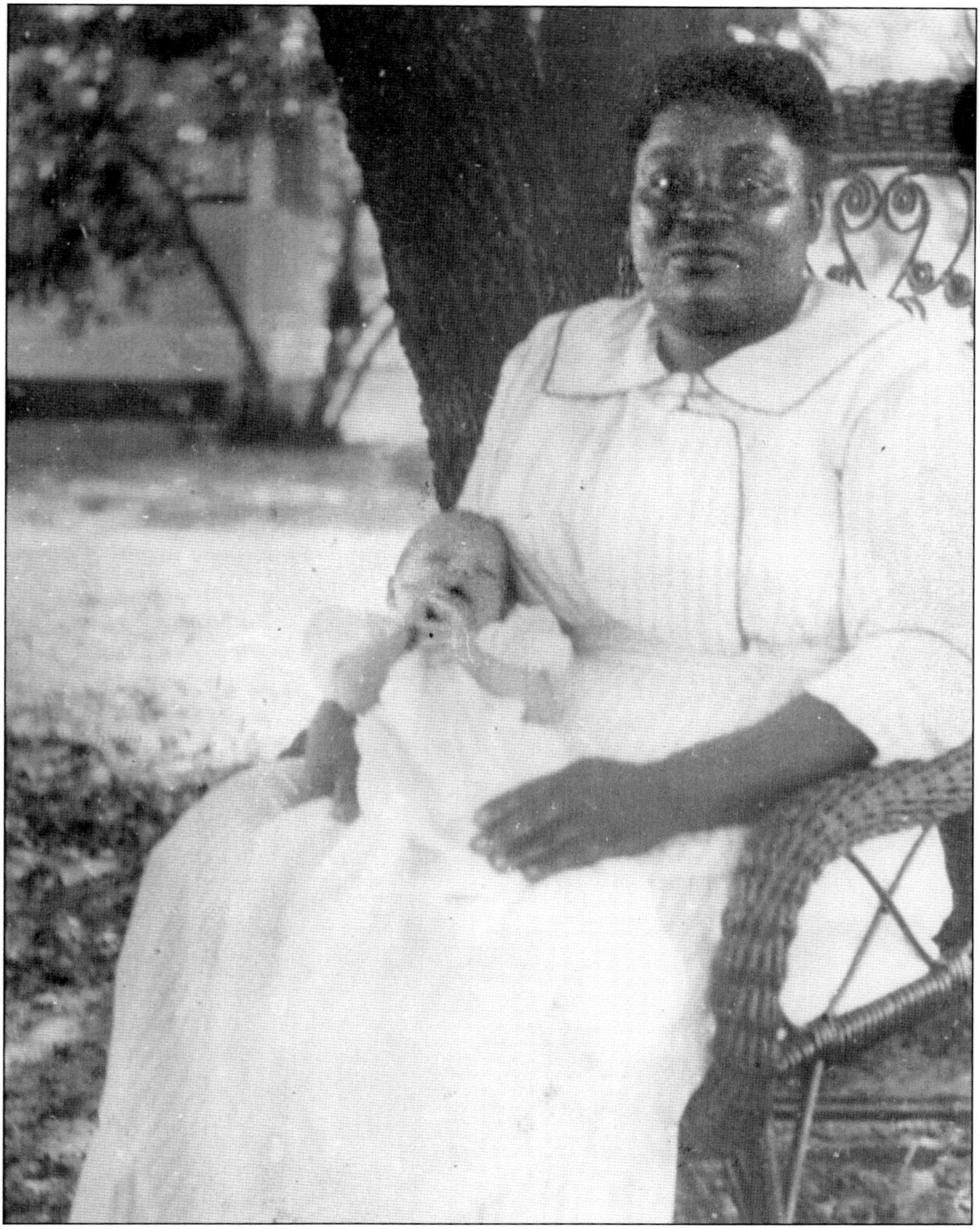

"Aunt" Sallie Townsend was one of Clermont's most beloved citizens. She delivered more than 1,000 infants—almost every baby in the town—over the course of several decades. She is seen here with Charles Roe in 1915. Sallie moved from Tallahassee to Orlando, where she married her Sunday school teacher, James Townsend. They started Clermont's first African American school and the St. Marks African Methodist Episcopal Church. Sallie's brother George DeVaughn was the school's first teacher. She led an effort to build a medical clinic for African Americans in 1947. The Townsends had four children: Bertha, Sadie, Mattie, and James Jr. In 1984, after Sallie died at the age of 81, more than 400 people attended her funeral. (Courtesy of Cooper Memorial Library Association.)

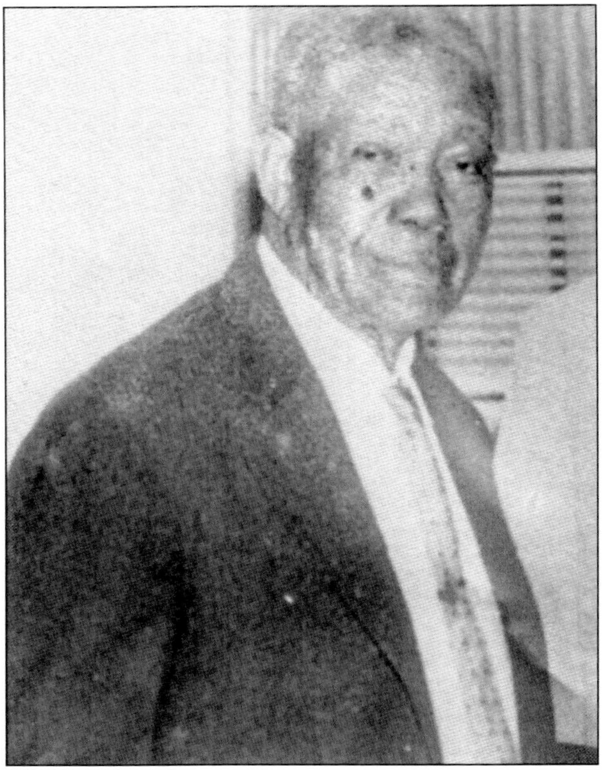

John Dingle came to Clermont in 1908 and delivered water to the Clermont-Minneola School. He worked as an engineer for the electric plant that supplied power to Clermont residents from dark until midnight and on Tuesdays when women did their ironing. He worked for the city from 1922 until he retired in 1963. Other significant families included the Odums, Joneses, and Deans. (Courtesy of Cooper Memorial Library Association.)

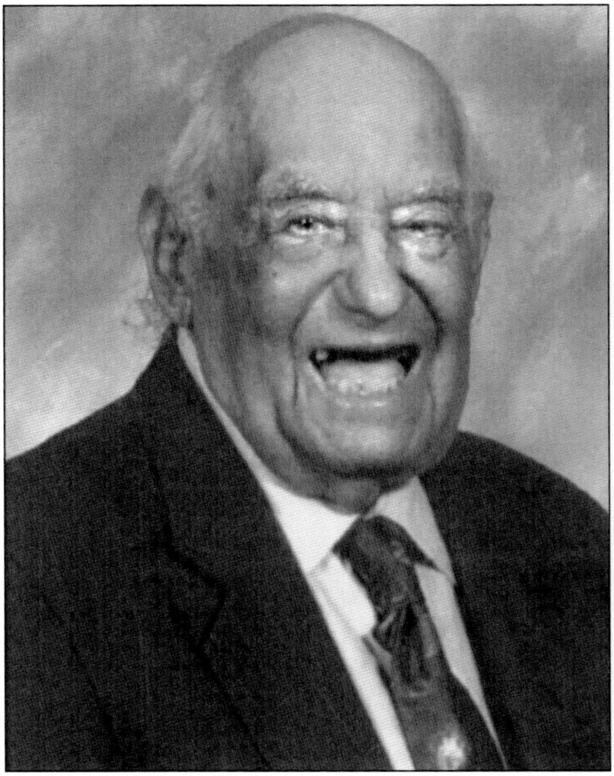

Arthur Dean came to Clermont in 1925. Initially, he filled buckets of water for 15¢, but eventually he helped build roads, including Highway 27. He tended vast citrus acreage, owned a store in the Lincoln Park neighborhood, and drove the first school bus for African American children. “I got a lot of good luck in Clermont,” he said. Dean died in December 2009 at age 98. (Courtesy of Amy Dean Jones.)

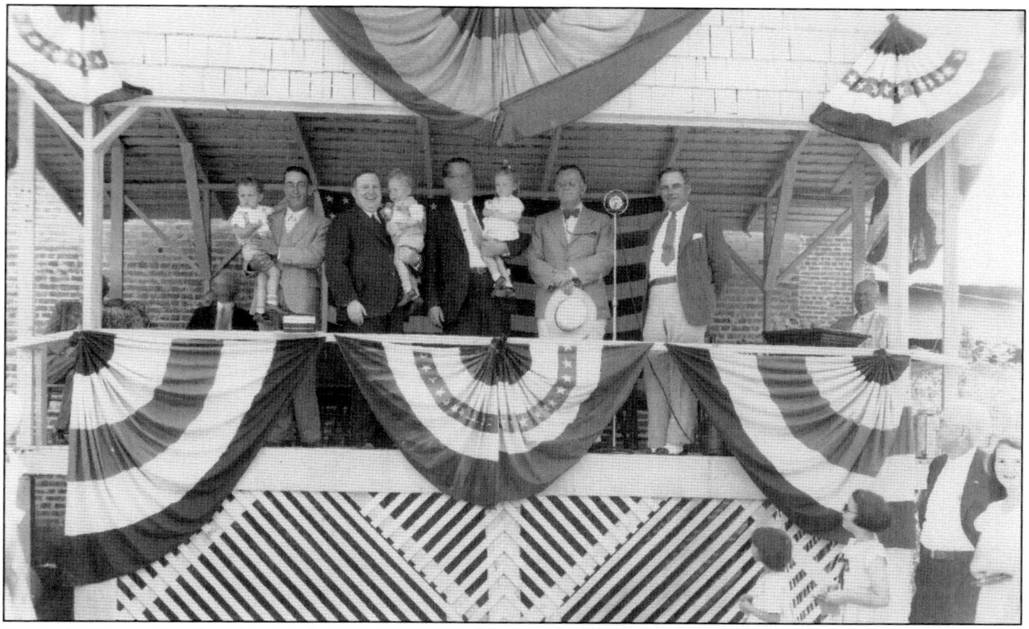

Beulah Hannah, daughter of pioneer Thomas Hooks, gained notoriety when she seconded the nomination of New York governor Franklin Delano Roosevelt for president at the 1932 Democratic Party Convention. The next year, the political rally seen here was held at the old bandstand on Montrose Street. From left to right are I. W. Kennedy, Florida governor David Sholtz, J. G. Futch, H. C. Duncan, and state representative George Westbrook. (Courtesy of Cooper Memorial Library Association.)

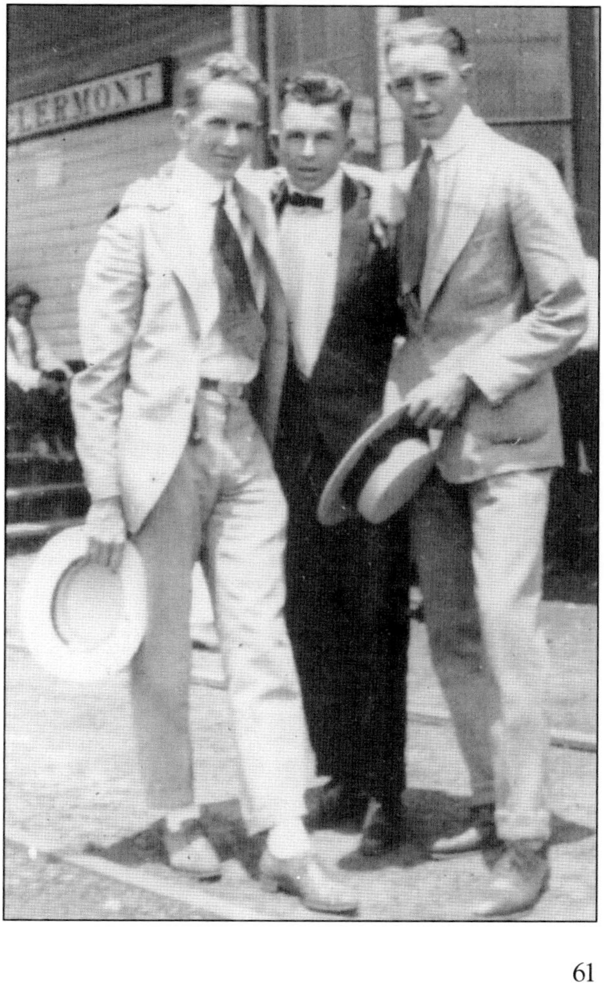


These dapper Clermont men are seen in front of the Clermont train station. From left to right are Clyde Gaines, Holmes Bryson, and Paul Settle. During the 1930s, Gaines was the buyer for Ro-E-Gaines Fruit Company, which represented nine large growers. Settle was a bookkeeper at Citizens Bank and witnessed two robberies over the years, including one reportedly by Fred Barker of Ma Barker infamy. (Courtesy of Cooper Memorial Library Association.)

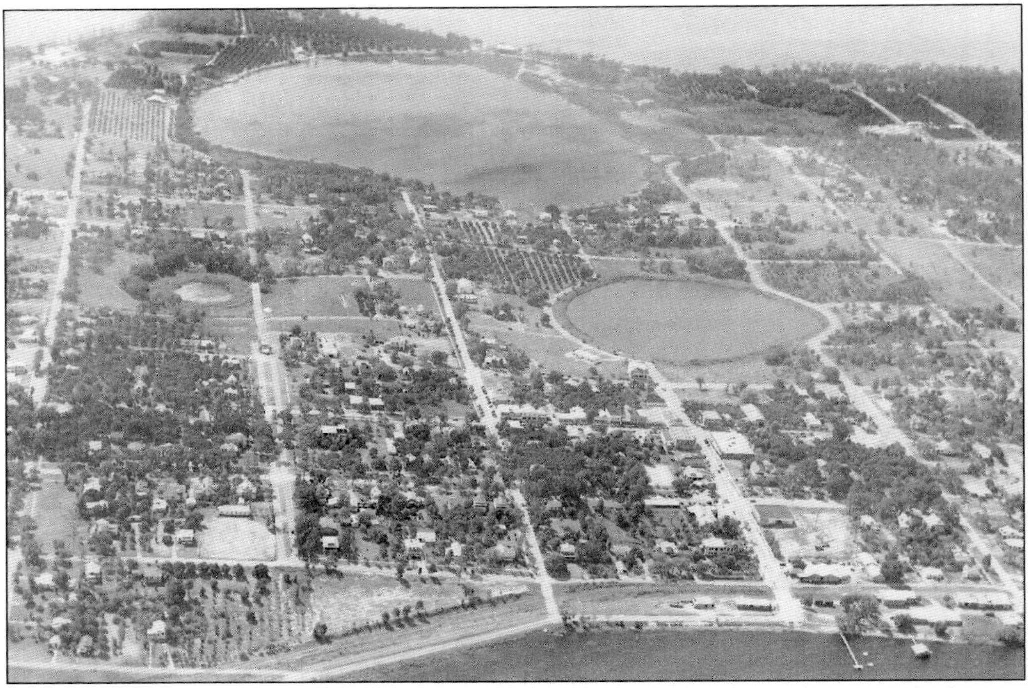

This *c.* 1941 photograph of Clermont shows a thriving downtown between Lake Minneola (bottom of photograph) and Lake Minnehaha (top of photograph). Residents witnessed the heady land boom of the 1920s, followed by bankruptcy in 1939 after bond indebtedness rose to almost $1 million and the millage rate went from 11 to 691 mills. By 1940, however, the town had paid 92 percent of its taxes owed. (Courtesy of the Lake County Historical Society.)

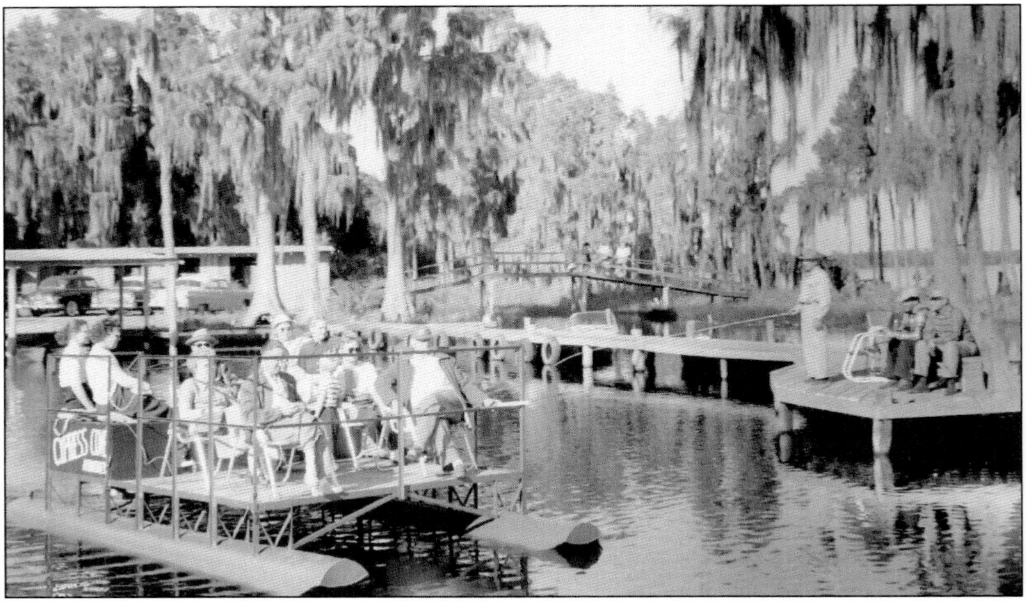

After World War II, tourism picked up as visitors, such as those shown in this late-1950s photograph, came to enjoy the area's many recreational opportunities. Cypress Cove Resort was built on the west side of Lake Minnehaha and included rental units, a marina, and space for mobile homes. (Courtesy of the Lake County Historical Society.)

# *Three*

# CITRUS ERA

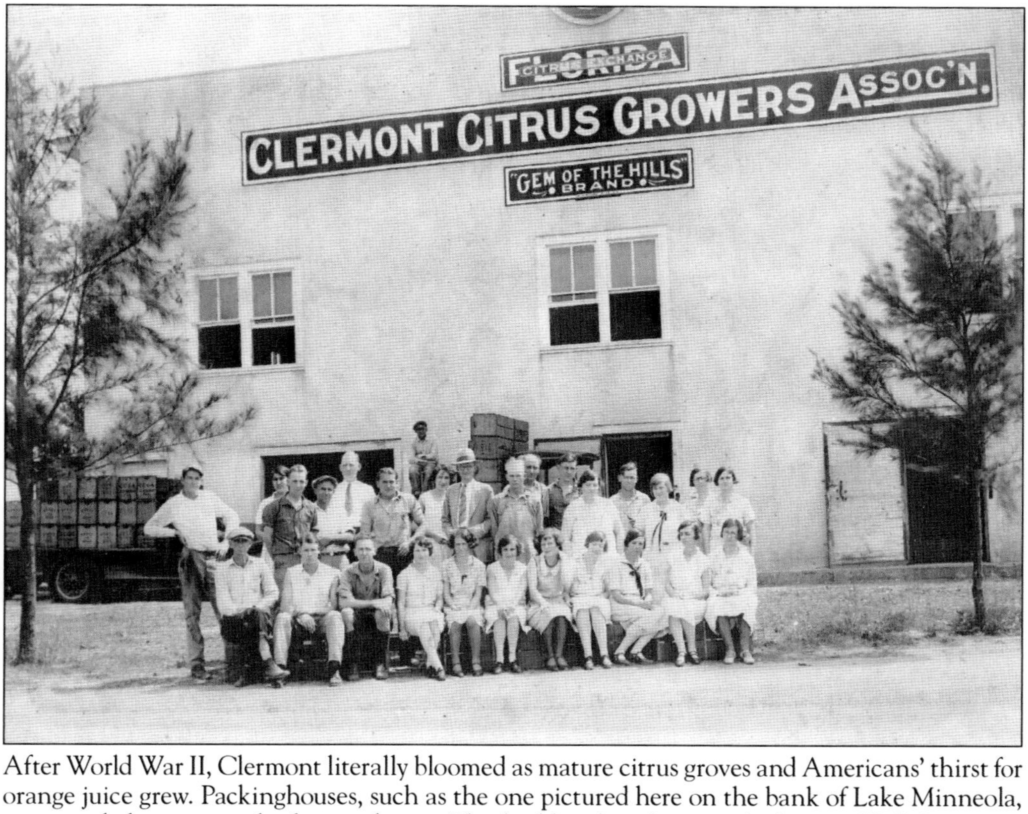


After World War II, Clermont literally bloomed as mature citrus groves and Americans' thirst for orange juice grew. Packinghouses, such as the one pictured here on the bank of Lake Minneola, were needed to process the fruit and juice. This building later became the home of Bell Ceramics. (Courtesy of Cooper Memorial Library Association.)

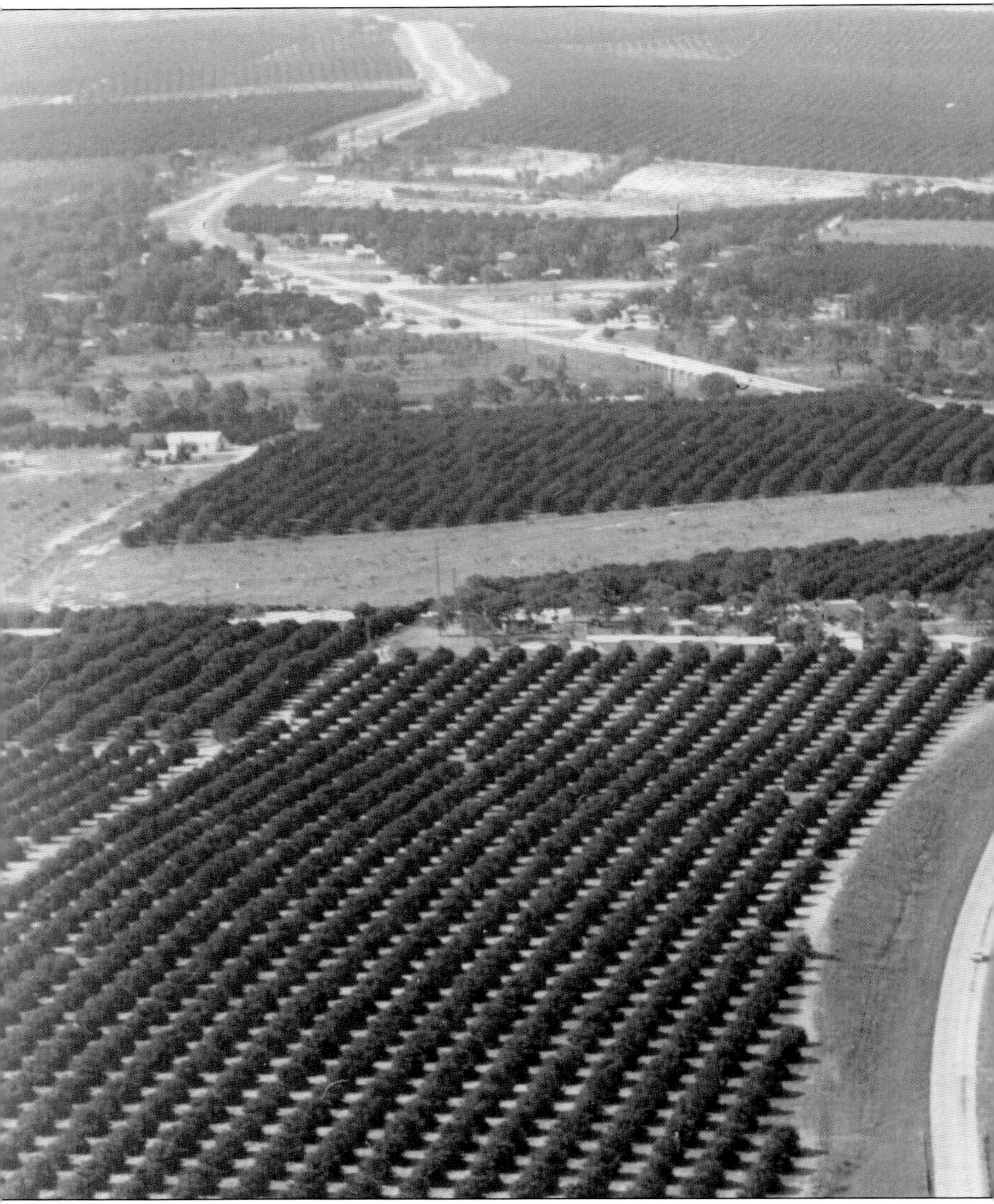

From the end of World War II through 1989, citrus reigned in Clermont. Looking north along Highway 27, tourists and Clermont residents enjoyed a picture-perfect view of the city nestled by miles of lush citrus groves. State tourism officials dubbed the highway "Citrus Boulevard." One commentator quipped that the Citrus Tower, seen at right, was "built by Vitamin C." At the top of Florida's highest observation point, visitors enjoyed a breathtaking 360-degree view that included

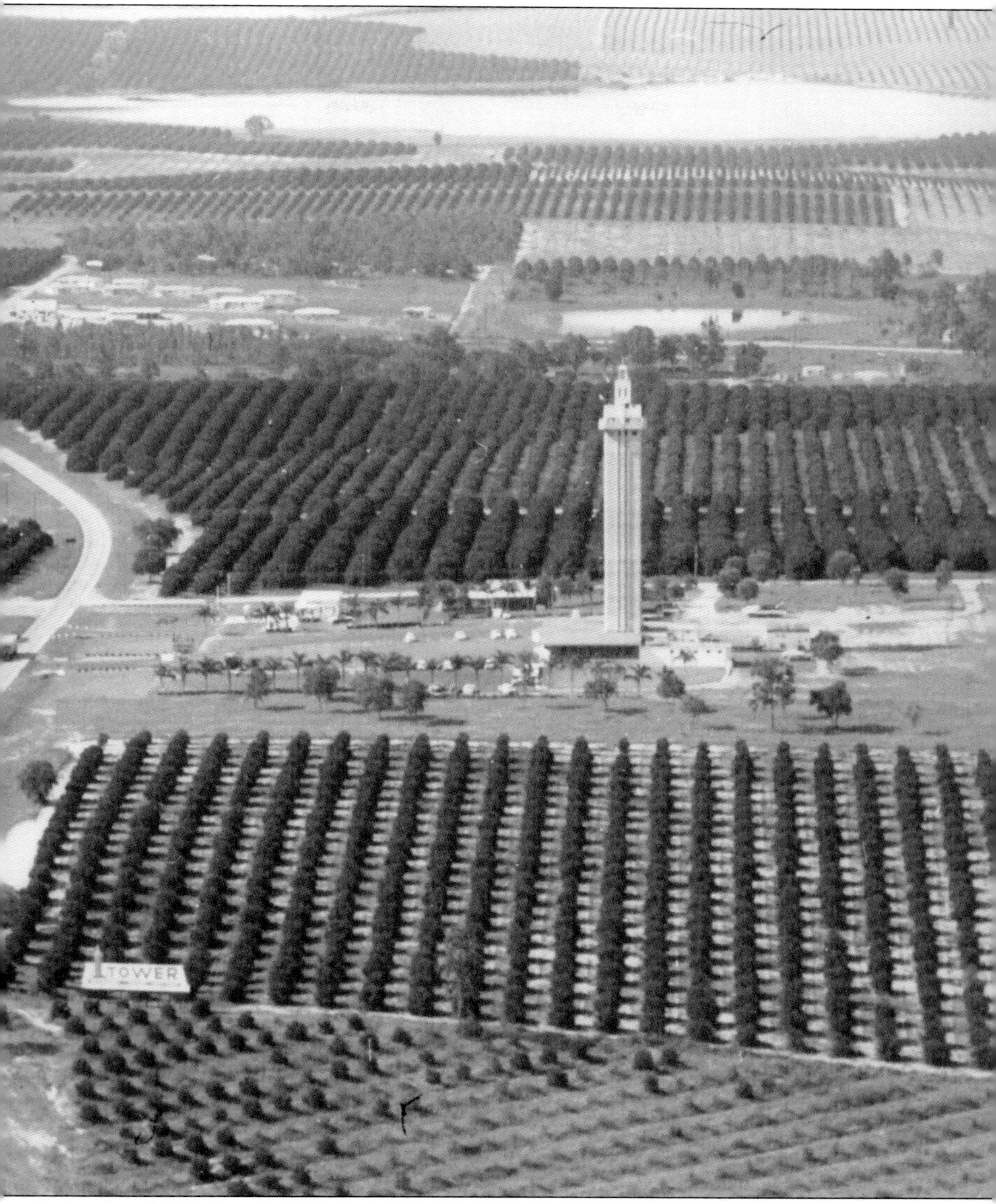


groves extending eastward to the Orange County line. Some of the Clermont citrus names during this era included Charles Bradshaw's Hi-Acres, Blue Goose, Minute Maid, Duke Crittenden, the Langley and Harmon families, Apshawa, and the Postal Colony Company, a cooperative of about 200 postal employees. Roadside fruit stands abounded as families flocked to visit Florida's growing tourist attractions. (Courtesy of the State Archives of Florida.)

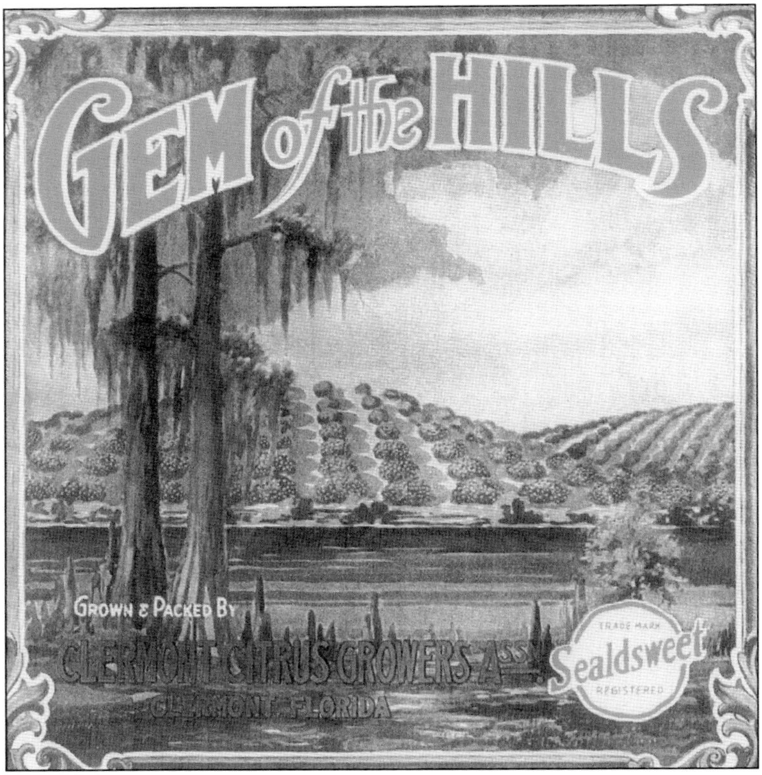


"Gem of the Hills" was a Clermont citrus label under the Seald Sweet trademark. Colorful citrus crate labels are considered collectible art, but they served practical purposes by acting as a small poster to grab buyers' attention. Citrus labels were used from the 1880s until cardboard boxes replaced crates in the 1950s. (Courtesy of A Slice in Time.)

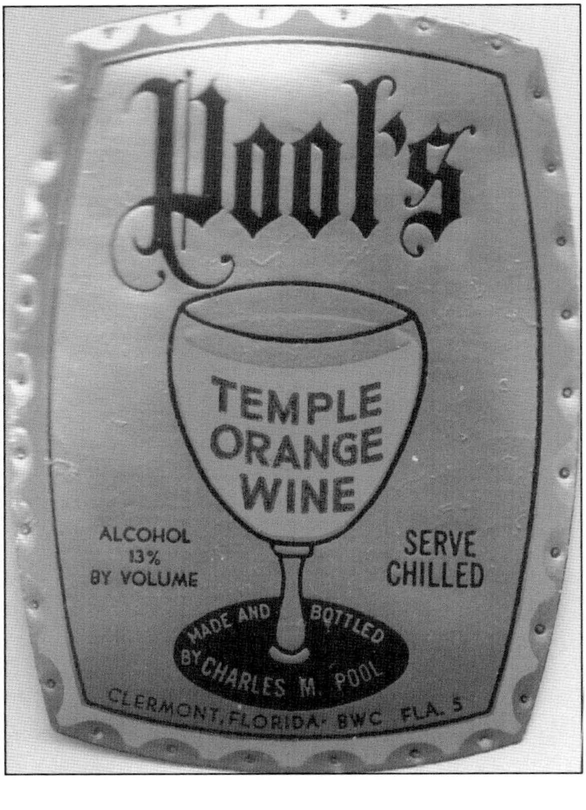


Until the late 1950s, the Pool family developed a thriving citrus wine industry. P. J. and Charles Pool started their enterprise in the 1930s and had a booth at the 1939 New York World's Fair. By the following year, they produced 250,000 gallons of grapefruit wine, alone. They used various citrus, as evidenced by this vintage gold-foil label. (Courtesy of Douglas Hudson.)

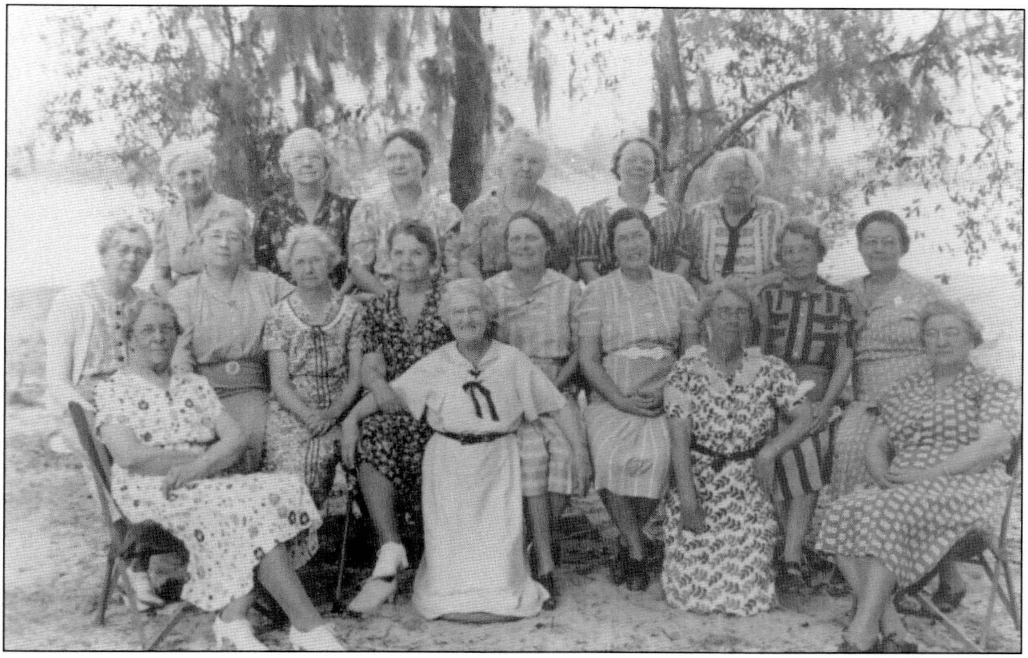

Women's groups remained active in the 1950s. The Clermont Needle Club held its 25th anniversary in 1940. From left to right are (first row) Cole, Roe, Bishop, and Baker; (second row) McNiece, Pollard, Arnett, Sharpe, Thompson, Roe, Lochner, and Richardson; (third row) Roe, Bennett, Bess, Foulke, Middleton, and Workman. (Courtesy of Cooper Memorial Library Association.)

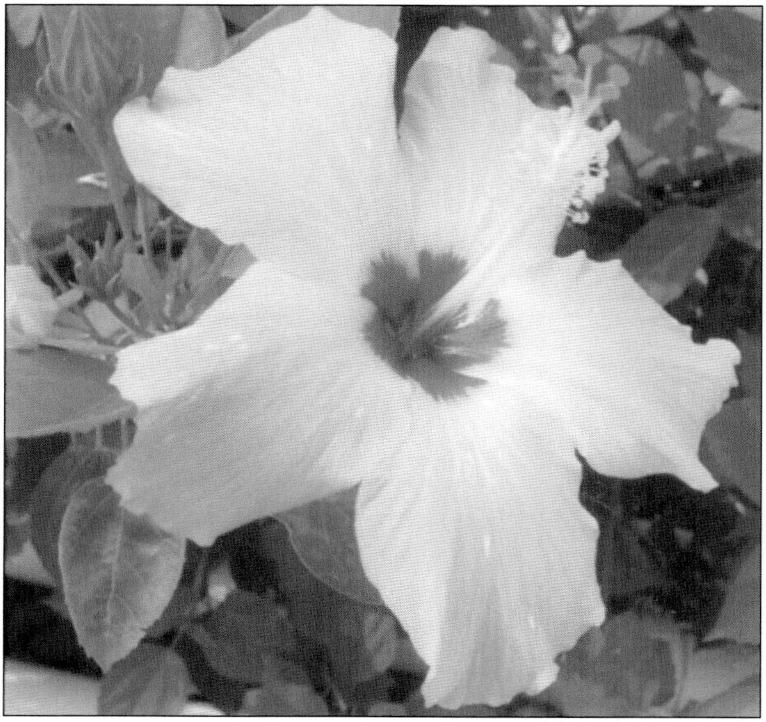

In the early 1950s, the chamber of commerce produced a 30-minute film titled *Discover Clermont—Gem of the Hills*. The film touted the city's many charms with images such as the annual children's fishing tournament and yards laden with hibiscus, the city's official flower, seen in this photograph. More than 25 million people viewed the film, and building permits tripled during the next few years. (Courtesy of Cooper Memorial Library Association.)

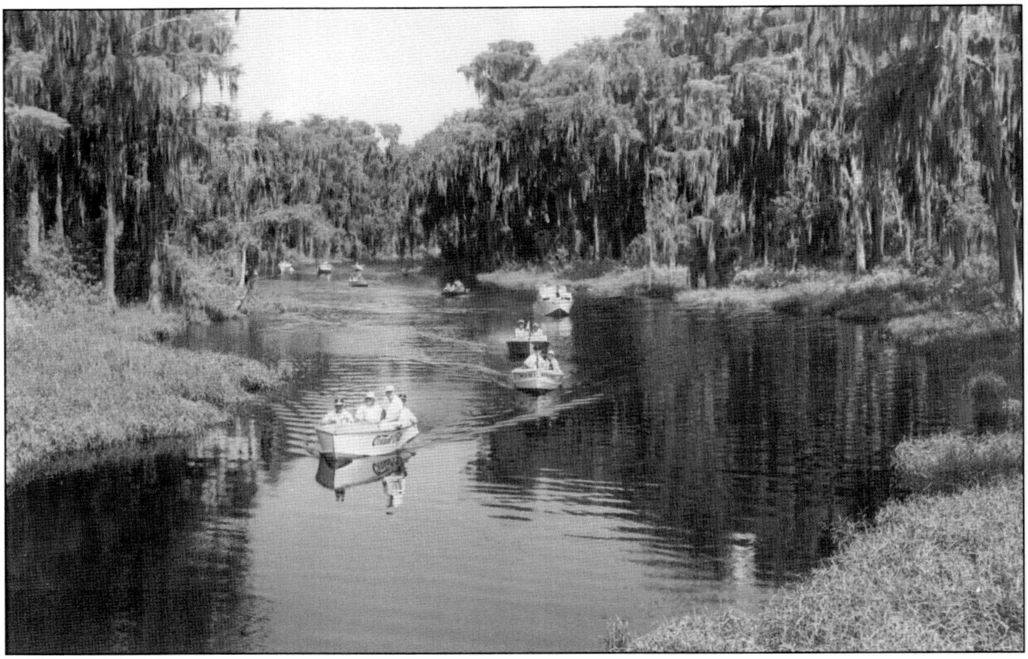

Clermont's many lakes, connected by the Palatlakaha Creek, grew even more in popularity. Boaters could start in Clermont and travel to Silver Springs, a popular Florida tourist attraction. The Tampa Boat Club, seen here idling along the Palatlakaha Creek in 1953, was headed to the Lake Susan Lodge and Cottages. (Courtesy of Elizabeth Geiger Estates.)

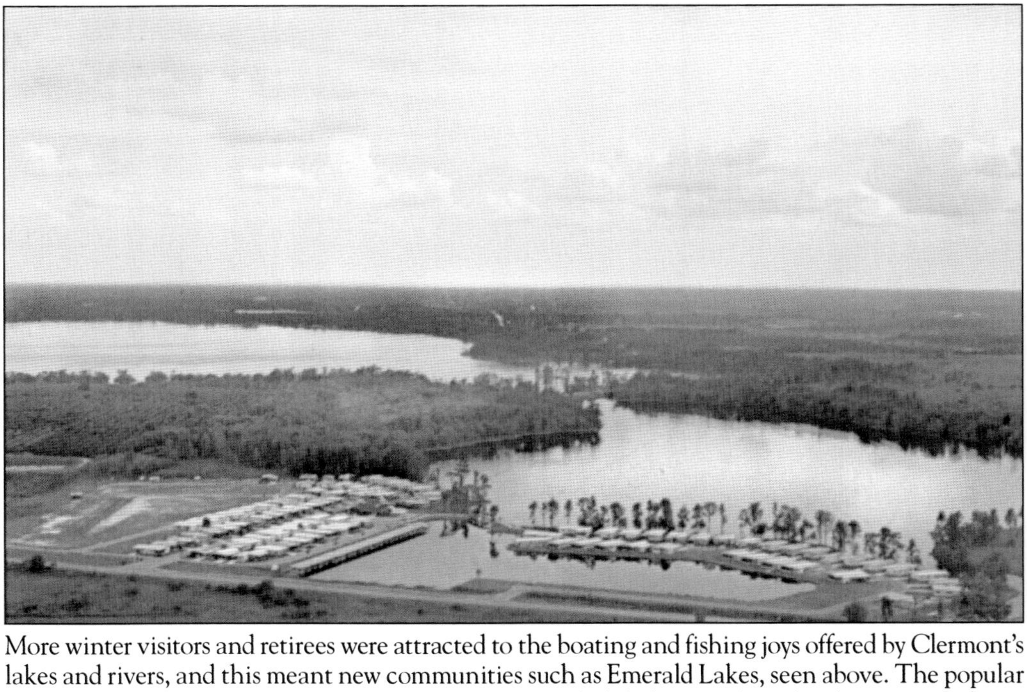

More winter visitors and retirees were attracted to the boating and fishing joys offered by Clermont's lakes and rivers, and this meant new communities such as Emerald Lakes, seen above. The popular mobile home community, developed in 1968, put Palatlakaha Creek and Lake Minnehaha at residents' doorsteps. Since 2000, the park has been owned by residents and administered through their board of directors. (Courtesy of Cooper Memorial Library Association.)

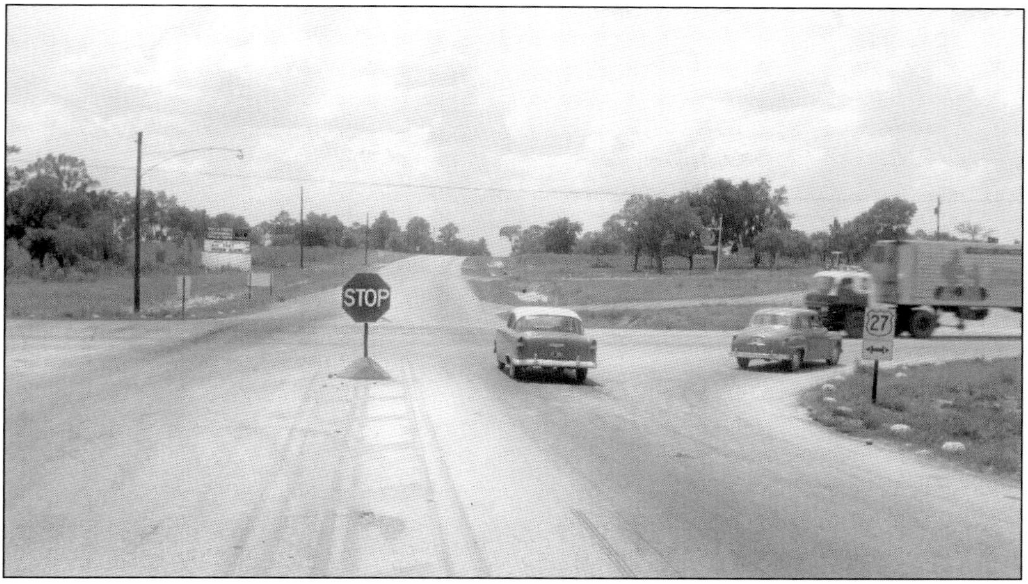


The intersection of U.S. Highway 27 and State Road 50 in Clermont marks the center of Florida, almost equidistant north and south as well as east and west. Highway 27 was a major tourist route when this June 1956 photograph was taken. The road runs from Fort Wayne, Indiana, to Miami, Florida. State Road 50 runs from the Gulf Coast to the Atlantic Ocean. (Courtesy of the State Archives of Florida.)

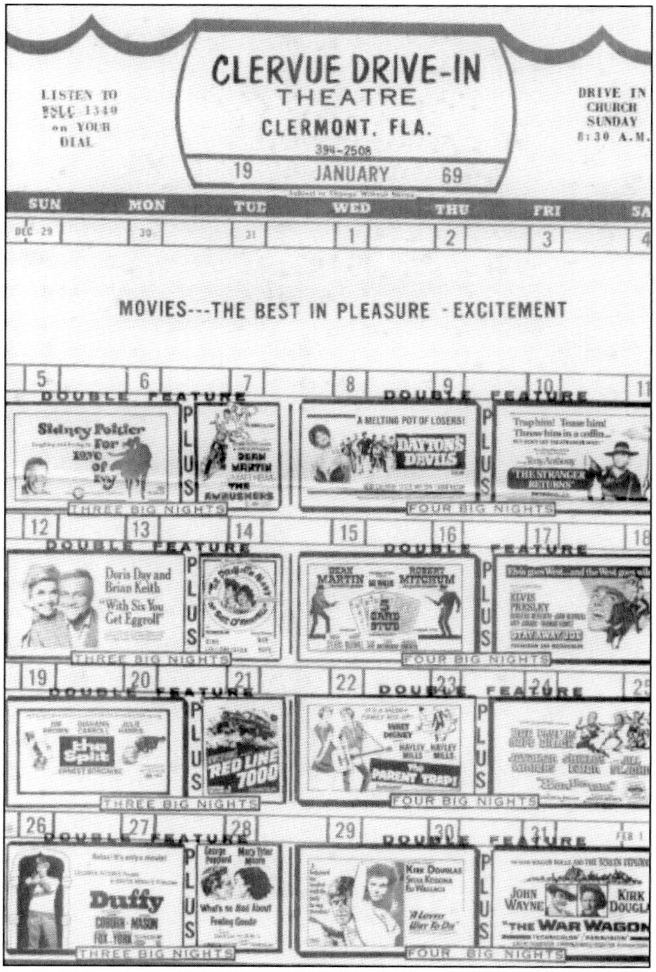


The Clervue Drive-in Theatre, at the intersection of Highways 27 and 50, was a popular destination in the 1950s and 1960s. The first drive-in theater opened in New Jersey in 1933. By 1958, there were more than 4,000 across the United States. Television and air-conditioning doomed most drive-ins. After the Clervue closed in the 1970s, the city council, Peoples State Bank, and Holiday Inn Express saved the marquee, which now advertises the hotel. (Courtesy of Carol Tomlinson.)

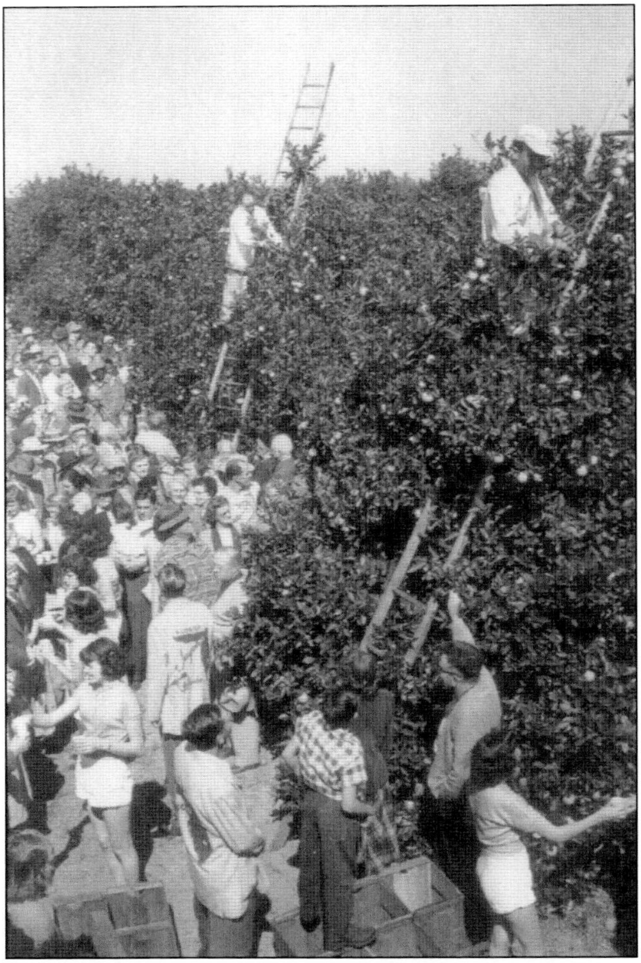

In the early 1950s, central Florida was host to the National Orange-Picking Contest. Clermont's American Fruit Growers, later known as Blue Goose, sent picker Lloyd Harris as their representative. Contestants were judged on how many boxes of oranges they could pick in a two-day contest sponsored by Orlando's Junior Chamber of Commerce. (Courtesy of the State Archives of Florida.)

One of the most enduring citrus operations in the Clermont area was Apshawa Groves. It began in 1934 and lasted more than 50 years. A New Jersey group paid $1,250 an acre for 500 acres north of Minneola and named it Apshawa after a lake back in New Jersey. During World War II, the grove prospered from sales of fruit juice sold to the military. (Courtesy of the Lake County Historical Society.)

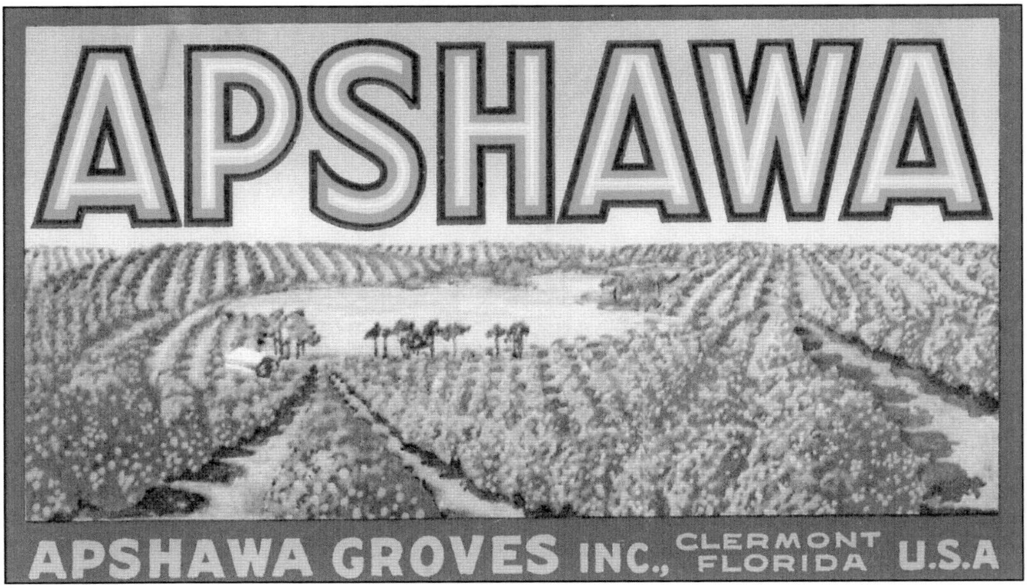

Robert Smythe served as Clermont's fire chief from 1969, when this photograph was taken, to 1990. His charitable work included building a dental clinic in Haiti. His daughter Robin Smythe Weisman, a Clermont native, made history as the news director and vice president of Central Florida's first 24-hour television news station. Robert's other family members include his wife, Mary Adele, four daughters, and twelve grandchildren. (Courtesy of Robin Smythe Weisman.)

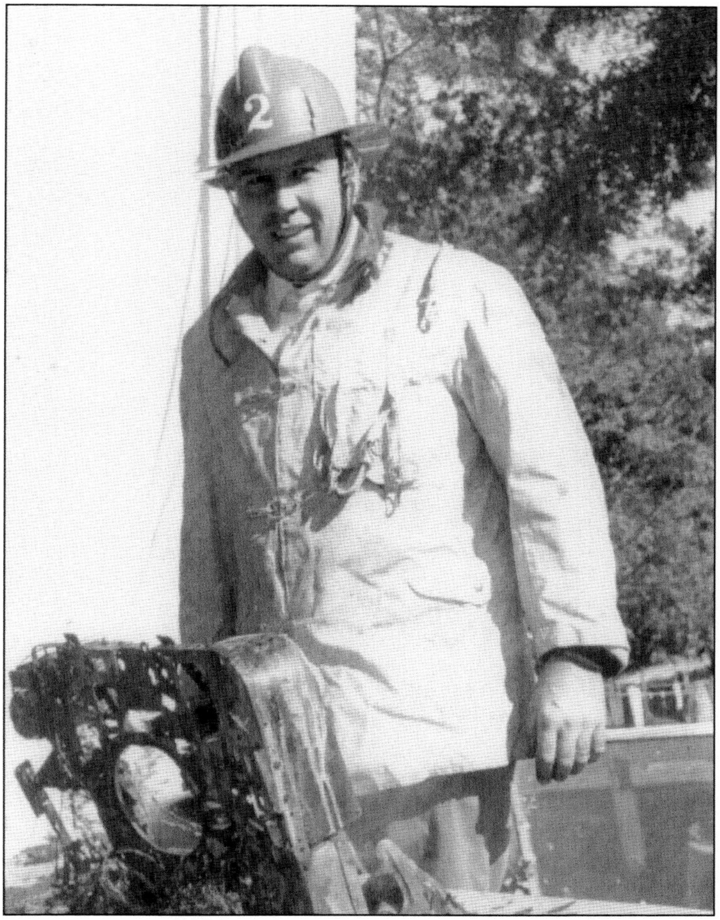

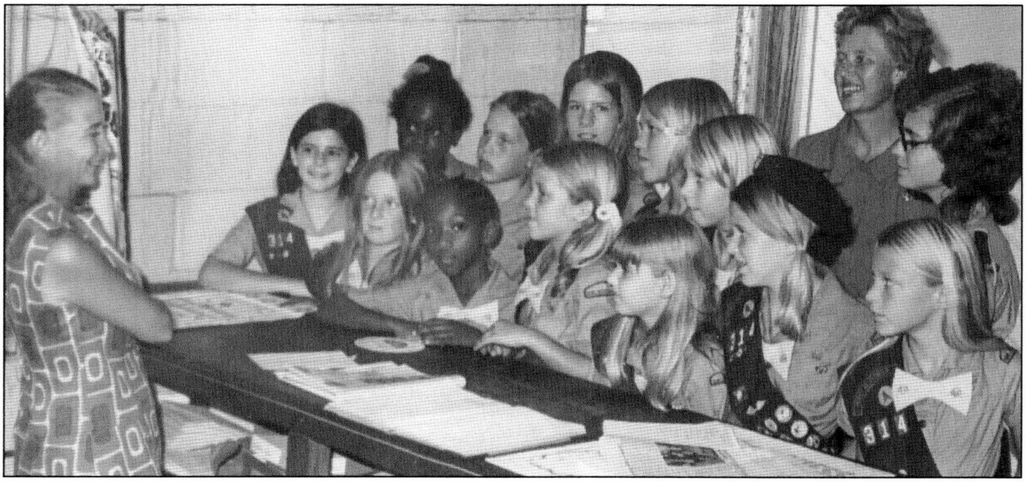

Three enduring Clermont institutions came together in this field trip photograph: Ann Dupee, the *South Lake Press*, and Girl Scout Troop 314. Ann came to Clermont with her husband, former *Wall Street Journal* executive George Dupee, in late 1967. They published their first edition in January 1968, although the newspaper dates back under previous owners to 1913, when it was called the *Clermont Clarion*. (Courtesy of Ann Dupee.)

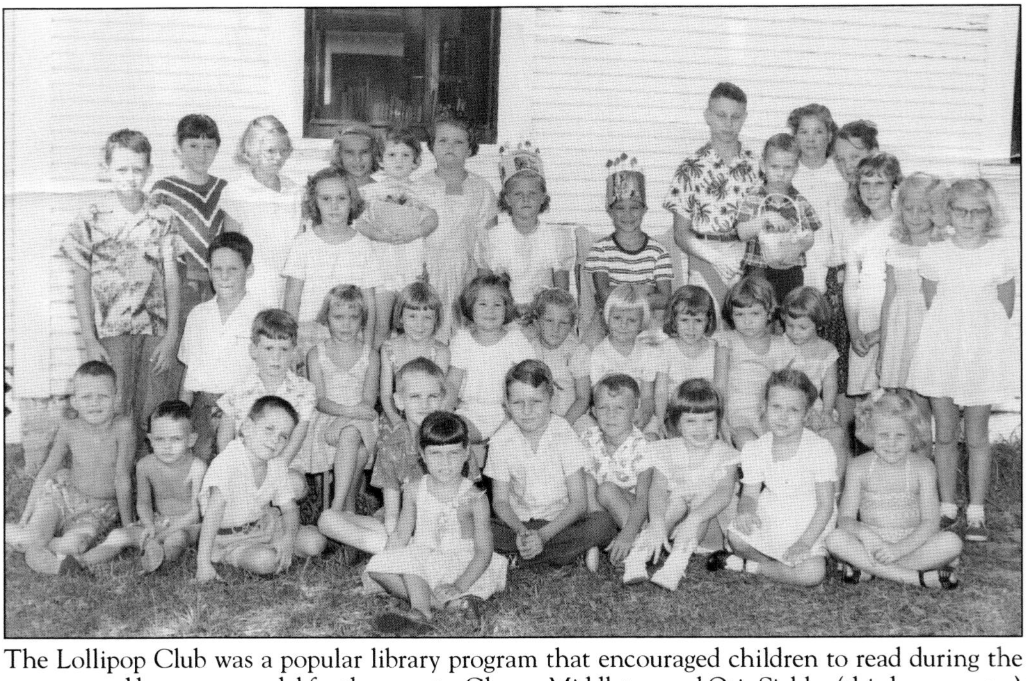

The Lollipop Club was a popular library program that encouraged children to read during the summer and became a model for the county. Glenna Middleton and Otis Sickler (third row, center) were chosen as the club's queen and king in 1953. Glenna also swam across Lake Minneola when she was eight years old to help her father promote the annual All-States Picnic celebrating winter visitors' return home. (Courtesy of Glenna Scaife.)

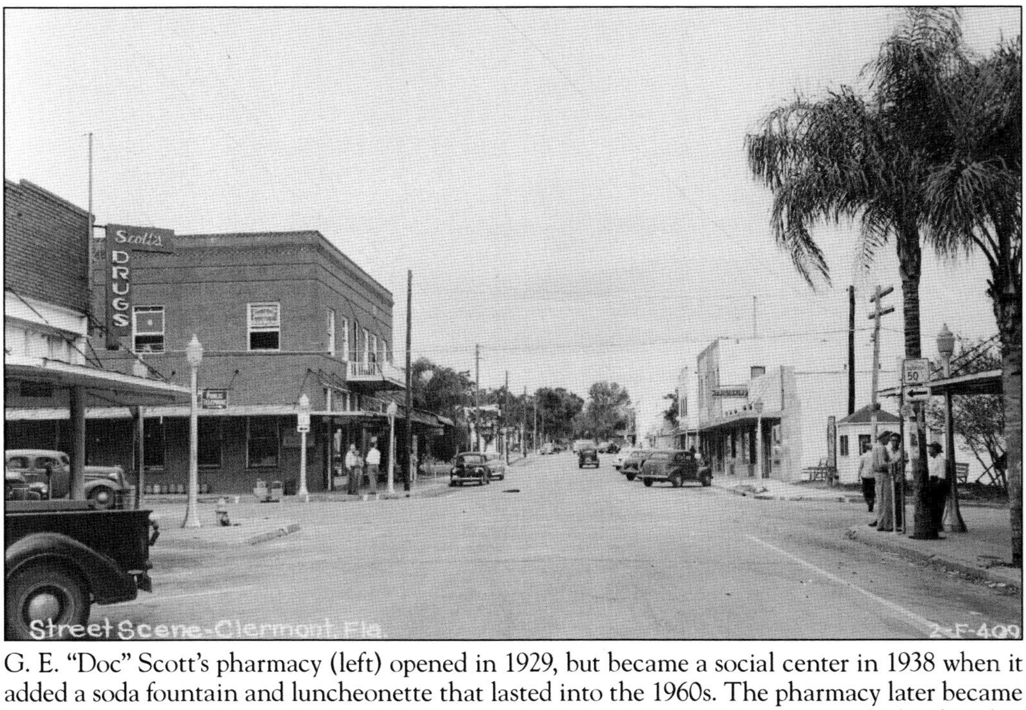


G. E. "Doc" Scott's pharmacy (left) opened in 1929, but became a social center in 1938 when it added a soda fountain and luncheonette that lasted into the 1960s. The pharmacy later became the Grant-Harris Drug Store. Marshall's Pharmacy was also a downtown staple for decades. (Courtesy of Cooper Memorial Library Association.)

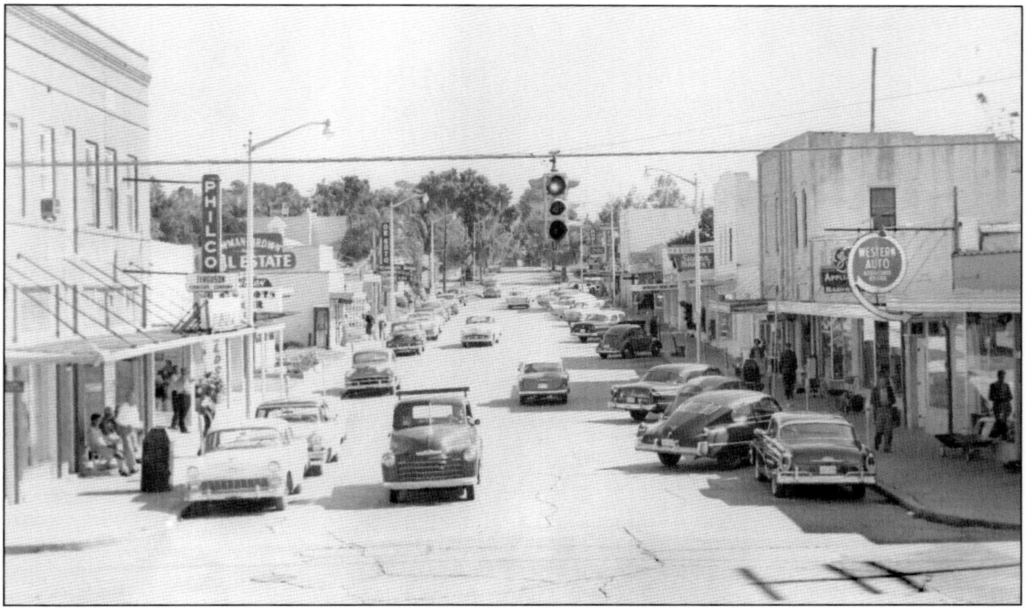


The city's historic downtown bustled with activity in the 1950s and 1960s. This *c.* 1956 eastward-facing view of Montrose Street shows why residents did not need to go far for all their needs. Shoppers had their choice of two grocery stores, a car dealership, a Western Auto, a furniture store, and a real estate office. The business district remains vital today through the Clermont Downtown Partnership. (Courtesy of the Lake County Historical Society.)

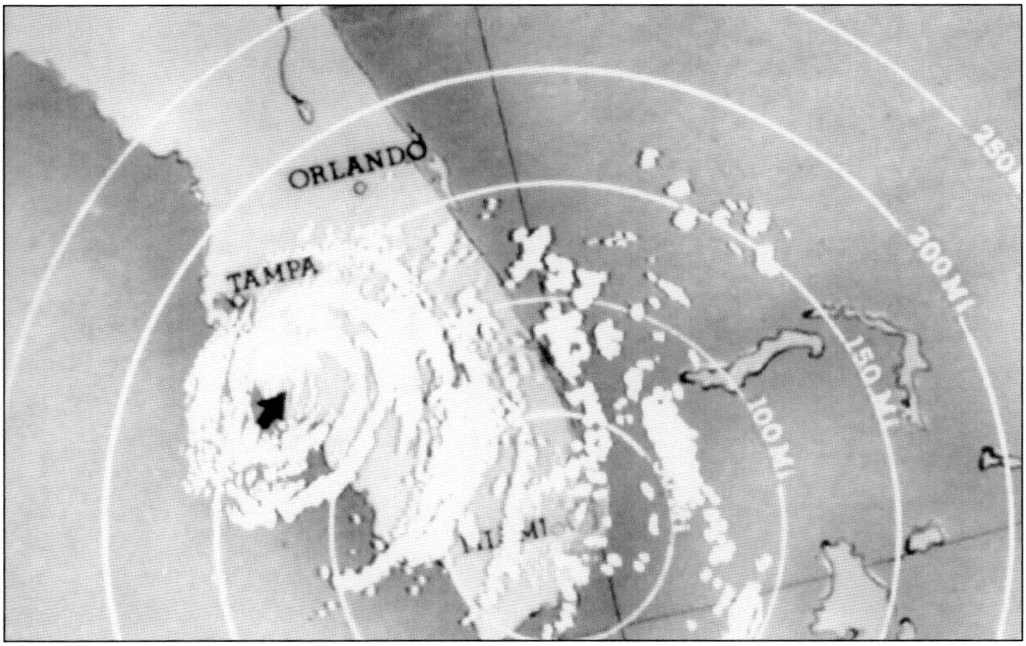


On September 11, 1960, Clermont became the bull's eye for Hurricane Donna. The Category 5 hurricane was the fifth-strongest to hit the United States, with winds peaking at 160 miles per hour and 364 fatalities. After swiping the Florida Keys, the hurricane turned and crawled across Central Florida. Clermont homes, businesses, and citrus groves sustained damages. Mobile homes were lifted off their foundations. (Courtesy of the National Hurricane Center.)

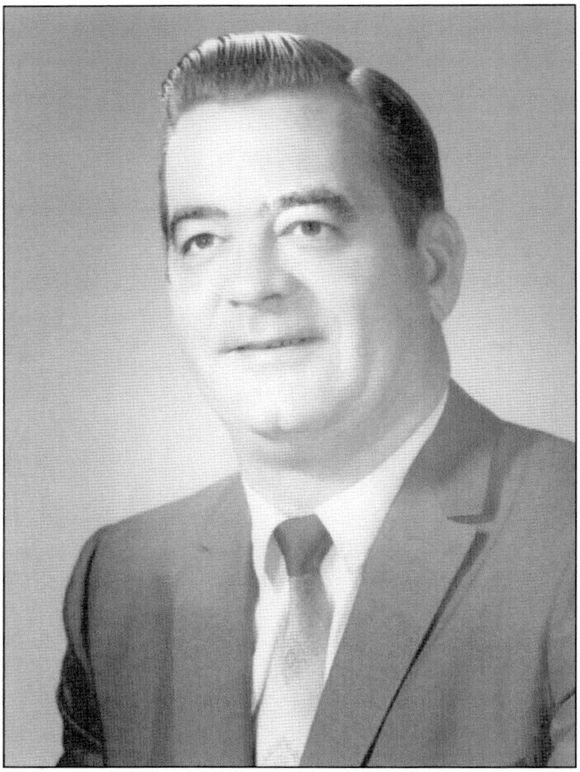

C. Welborn Daniel, a World War II navy veteran, is one of Clermont's most respected and powerful leaders. He served in the Florida legislature from 1956 to 1972, first in the Florida House of Representatives for six years before serving four consecutive terms as state senator for Lake and Sumter Counties. He also served as a circuit judge and on the appeals court before resigning in 1990. (Courtesy of the State Archives of Florida.)

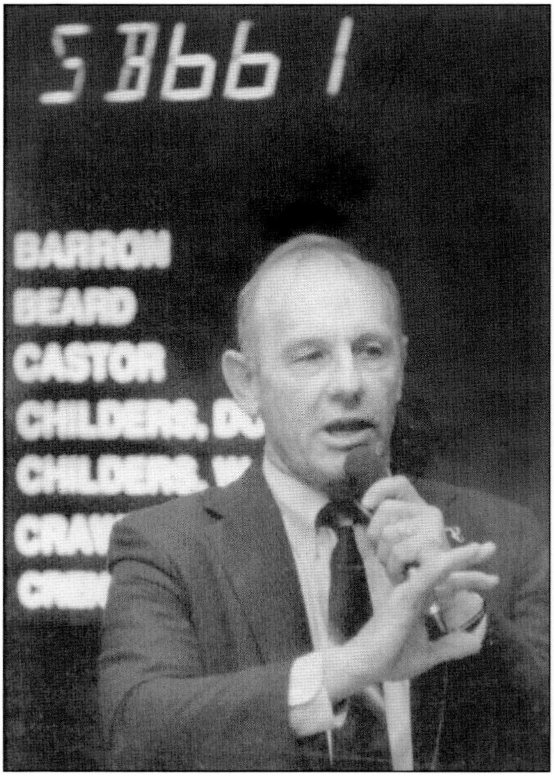


Richard "Dick" Langley is shown arguing in favor of Senate Bill 661 in 1986. The Clermont citrus owner and developer served in the legislature from 1972 to 1978 in the Florida House of Representatives and from 1980 to 1992 as a senator. He was voted the senate's debating champion five times. He later served as Lake County's school board attorney and as chairman of the Lake County Republican Party. (Courtesy of the State Archives of Florida.)

Former senator Dick Langley paid $137 to throw a cream pie in the face of Ann Dupee, former editor and publisher of the *South Lake Press*. The *c.* 1990 event was a charity auction at Clermont Chamber's annual Labor Day festivities. When the following Labor Day rolled around, Dupee had raised $120, enough money to serve Langley a cream pie of his own. The Labor Day festival lasted more than 40 years and drew crowds of 10,000 to Jaycee Beach. Activities included food, live entertainment, and parades. A boat scavenger hunt started the annual event. Attorney Dennis Horton ran in the festival's road race for 20 years. (Both courtesy of Ann Dupee.)

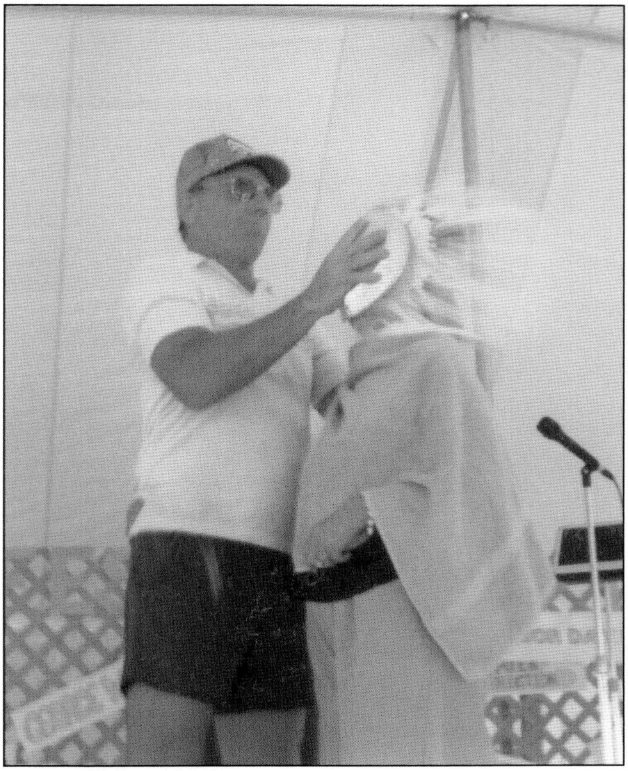

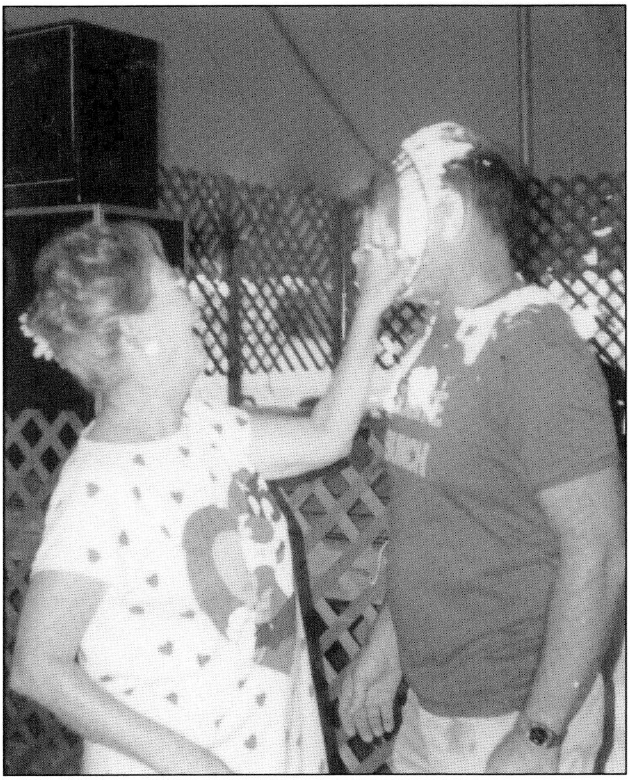

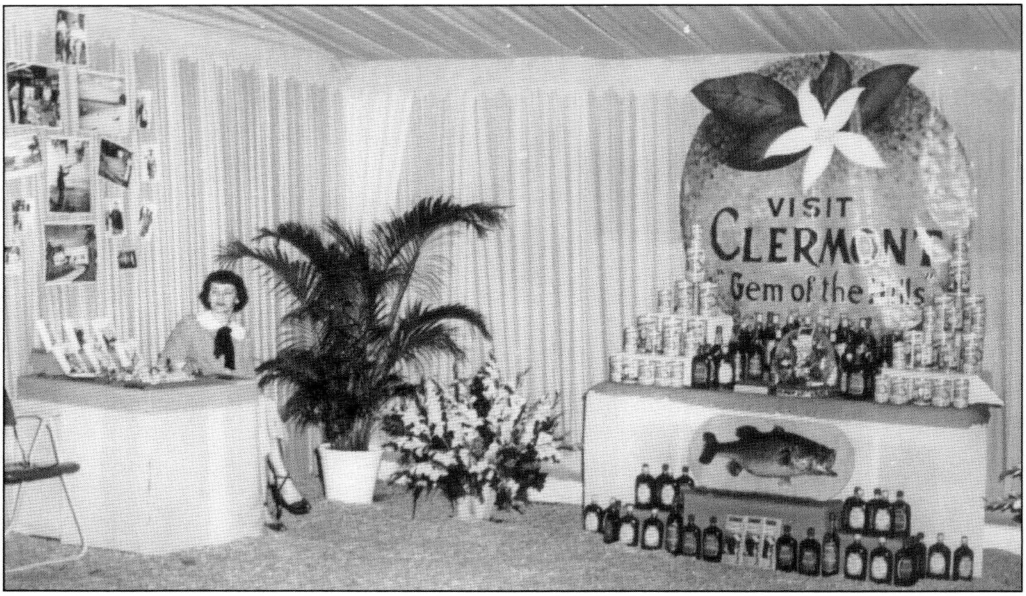

The Lake County Fair was a time when school children looked forward to rides and cotton candy and cities could tout what made their communities special. In this 1950s photograph, Clermont focused on its citrus industry with products made from oranges and a large display with the city's famous slogan, "Gem of the Hills." The fair has promoted youth and agriculture for 89 years. (Courtesy of the Lake County Historical Society.)

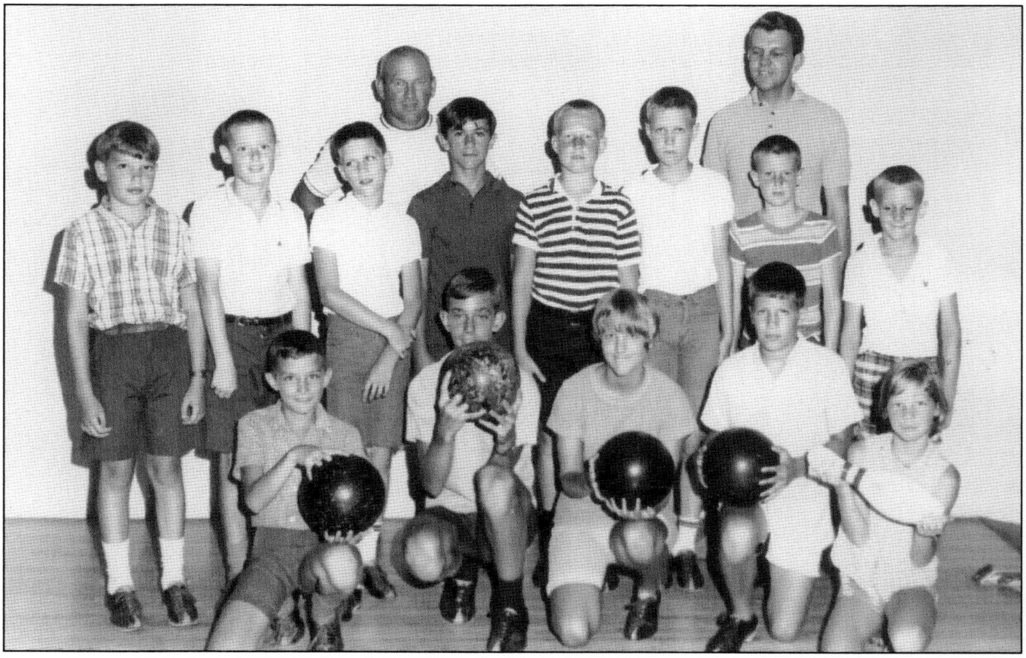
This summer recreational bowling league was held at the Clermont Bowling Lanes built by Martin Winther in 1960. Winther was also president of the First Federal Savings and Loan Association. Clermont is home to several professional bowlers, including Professional Bowlers Association Tournament of Champions winner Jason Couch, Hall of Famer Norm Duke, and TV commentator Randy Pedersen. (Courtesy of Ann Dupee.)

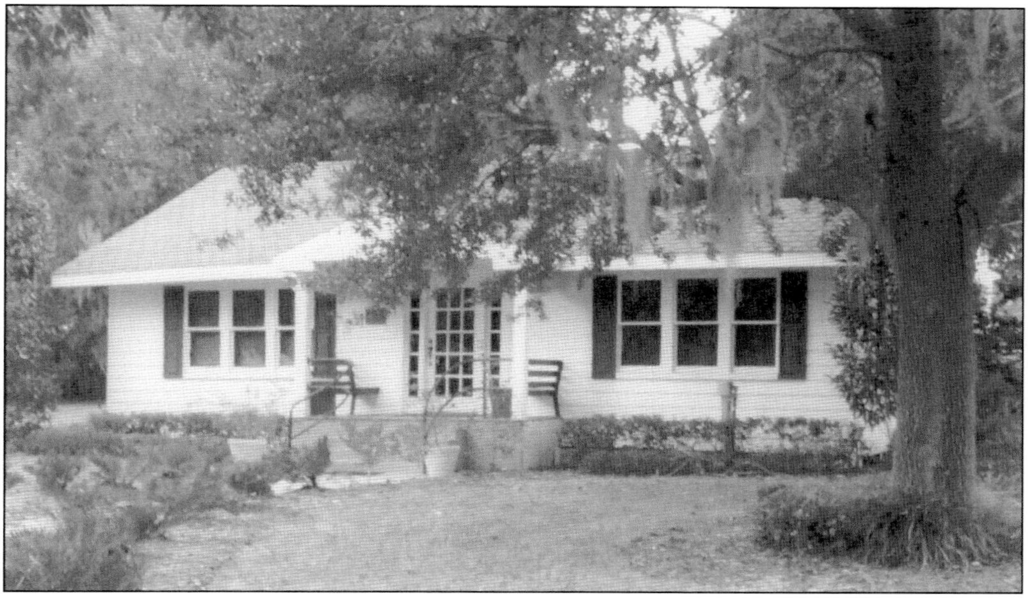

Clermont Woman's Club became the city's only building to be listed on the National Register of Historic Places in 1993. The 655 Broome Street location is the site of a one-room schoolhouse built in the 1880s. The Clermont Woman's Club was first organized as the Clermont Civic Club in 1921. For many years, they raised money for the library and served as volunteer librarians. (Photograph by Doris Bloodsworth.)

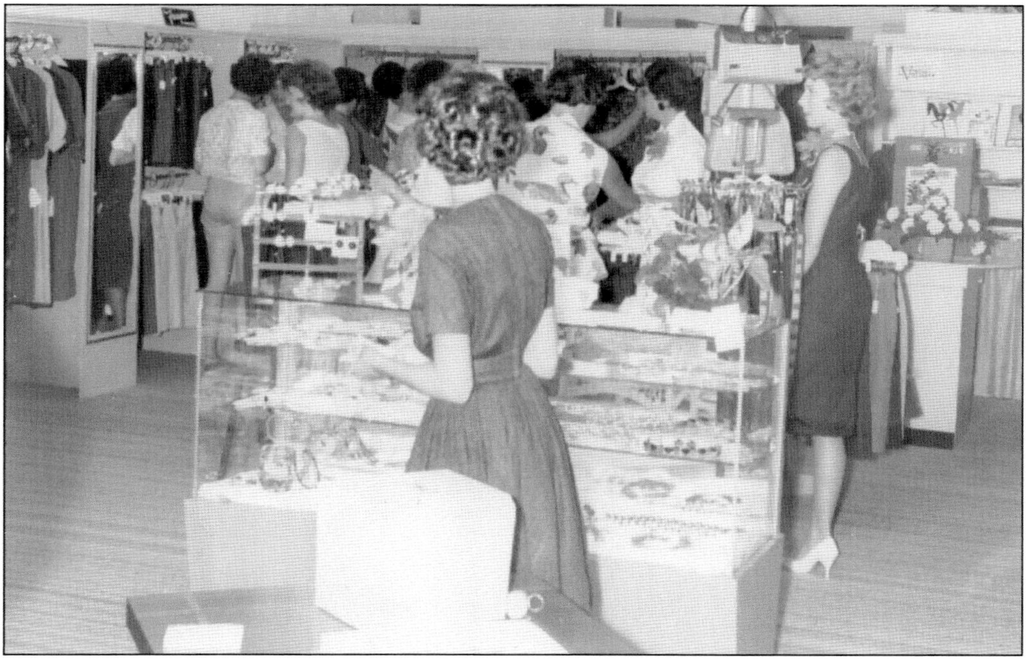

Enthusiastic shoppers welcomed Patti-Lu Casuals' grand opening in 1963. The ladies' apparel shop, located at 626 Eighth Street, was named after co-owners Pat Grant and Lucy Johnson. In 1965, a new shopping center called South Lake Plaza opened on Highway 50 with a Publix supermarket as its main tenant. In 1969, Patti-Lu Casuals moved from the downtown business district to the shopping center. (Courtesy of Cooper Memorial Library Association.)

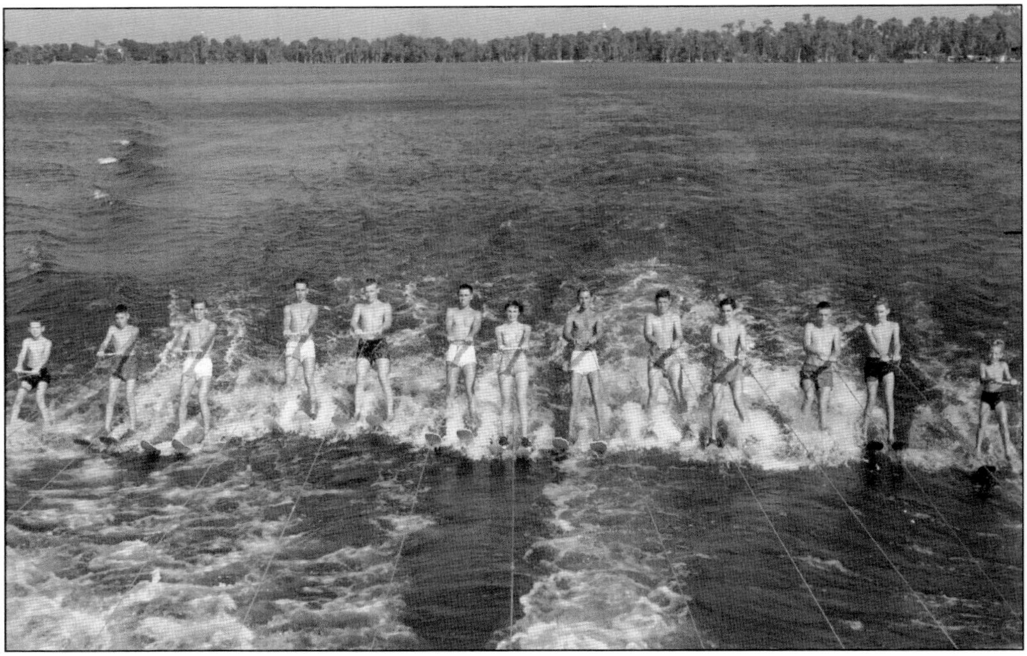

These 13 members of the Clermont Ski Club are shown during a 1950s visit to Cypress Gardens, a theme park in Winter Haven, Florida, that operated from 1936 to 2009. Some of the waterskiing club members, such as Tiffany and Glenna Middleton, were descendants of the city's pioneer families. Cypress Gardens was known as the Water Ski Capital of the World. (Courtesy of Cooper Memorial Library Association.)

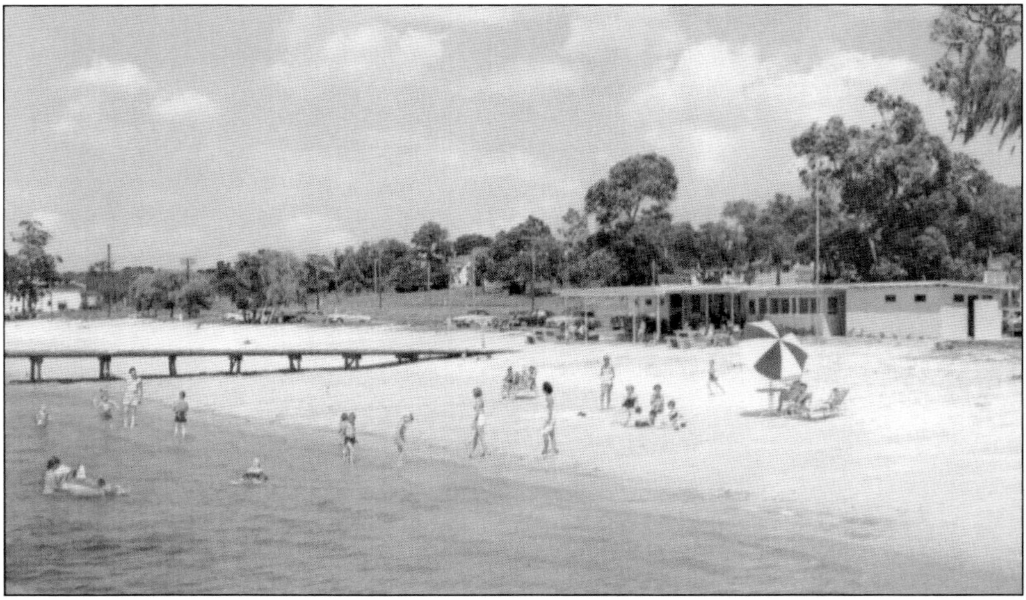

During the 1950s, Clermont's Junior Chamber of Commerce (Jaycees) created what became Florida's largest inland freshwater sand beach, more than 1,000 feet long. The Jaycees worked for almost a year on the project, which included a dock, boat ramp, beach house, restaurant, and parking. Across the street was the Highlander Hut, where teen dances were held during the 1960s. (Courtesy of Cooper Memorial Library Association.)

# *Four*

# New Vistas, New Neighbors

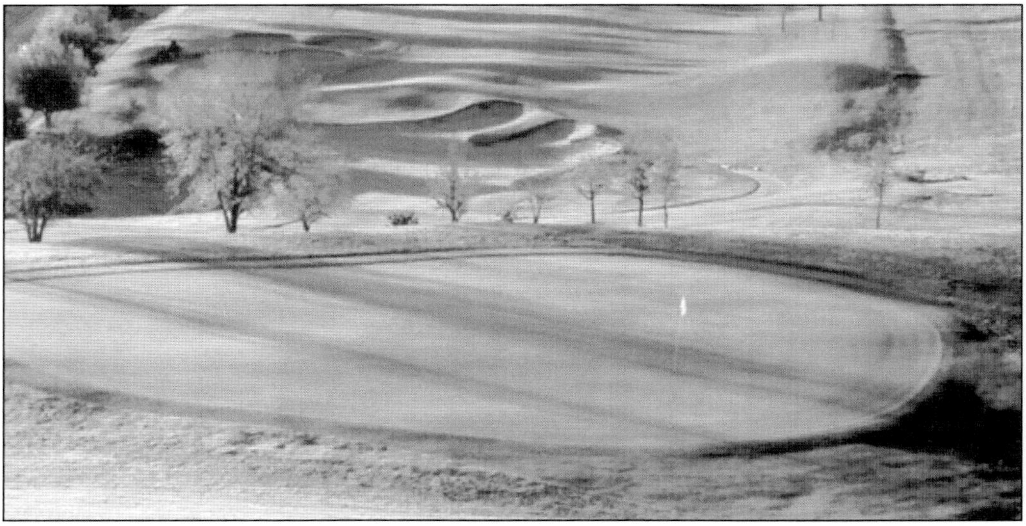

Clermont's citrus era ended in the 1980s when Central Florida was hit by three hard freezes in 1983, 1985, and 1989. Within months after the Christmas 1989 freeze, the rolling green hills became brown and barren. Although fortunes were lost, it opened the doorway for new developments, such as the Diamond Players Club, now called Sanctuary Ridge Golf Club. The landscape changed, bringing new vistas and new neighbors. (Courtesy of Sanctuary Ridge Golf Club.)

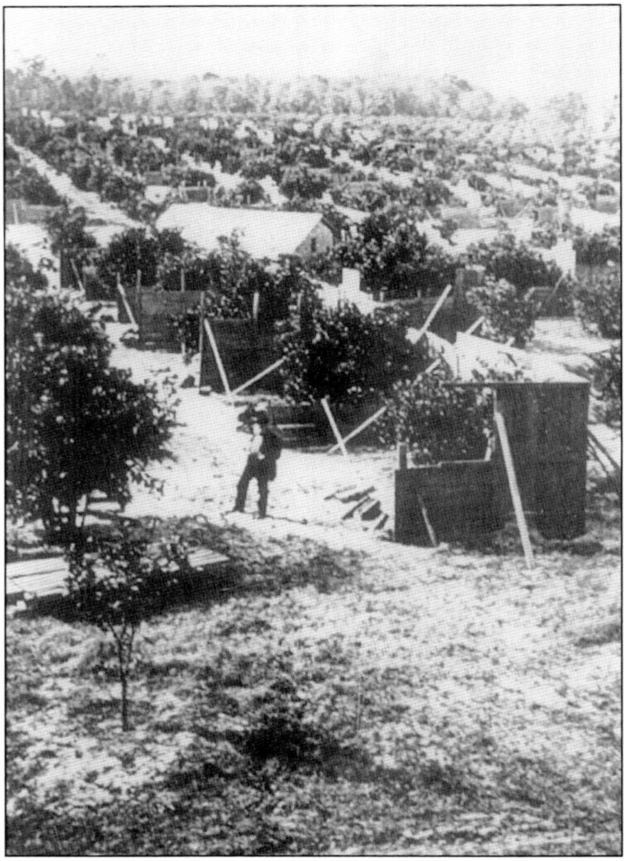

On Christmas Eve 1989, snow fell and the Lake Louisa weather station registered a low of 19 degrees. The third hard freeze in a decade wiped out Central Florida's citrus industry. A century earlier, grove owners, seen in this photograph trying to protect their orange trees a few miles north of Clermont, had faced a similar fate during the Great Freeze of 1894–1895. (Courtesy of the Lake County Board of County Commissioners.)

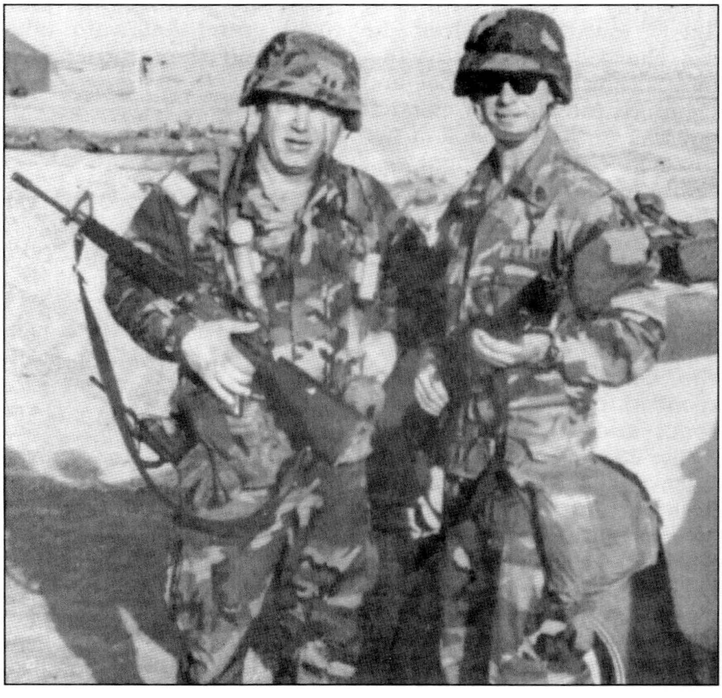

Clermont felt the impact of the Persian Gulf War in 1991 when Clermont High School's longtime booster club member Chuck Kindig (left) and teacher/coach Bruce Kregloe (right) served, in addition to local resident George Miller, in Operation Desert Storm. The school welcomed Kindig and Kregloe home with a big pep rally while the band played "Proud to be an American." (Courtesy of the *South Lake Press.*)

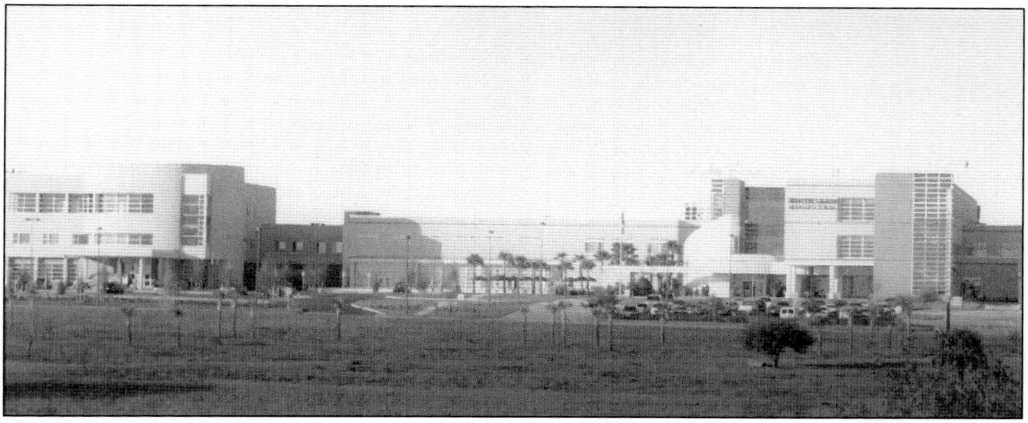

The expansion of South Lake Hospital was one of the silver linings in the aftermath of the 1980s freezes that crippled the area's economy. The community hospital started as a nine-bed clinic in 1941 and grew modestly in the decades that followed at its location overlooking Center Lake. In 1995, the hospital joined with the Orlando Regional Healthcare System, which led to an expansive 180-acre campus. (Courtesy of South Lake Hospital.)

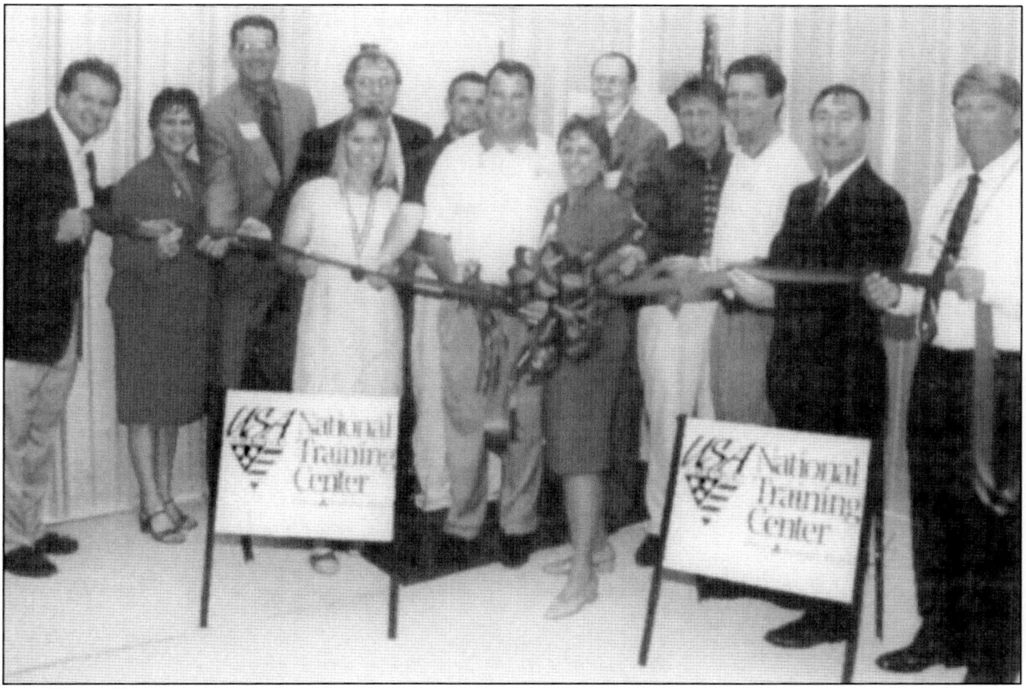


Clermont gained a new identity in the early 1990s: "The World's Triathlon Destination." The town hosts more triathlons than any other city. Athletes found the pristine area lakes and scenic countryside perfect for the events that include a swim, bicycle ride, and run. In 1999, the USA Triathlon organization moved the educational arm of its organization to Clermont. Pictured here is the grand opening. (Courtesy of the National Training Center.)

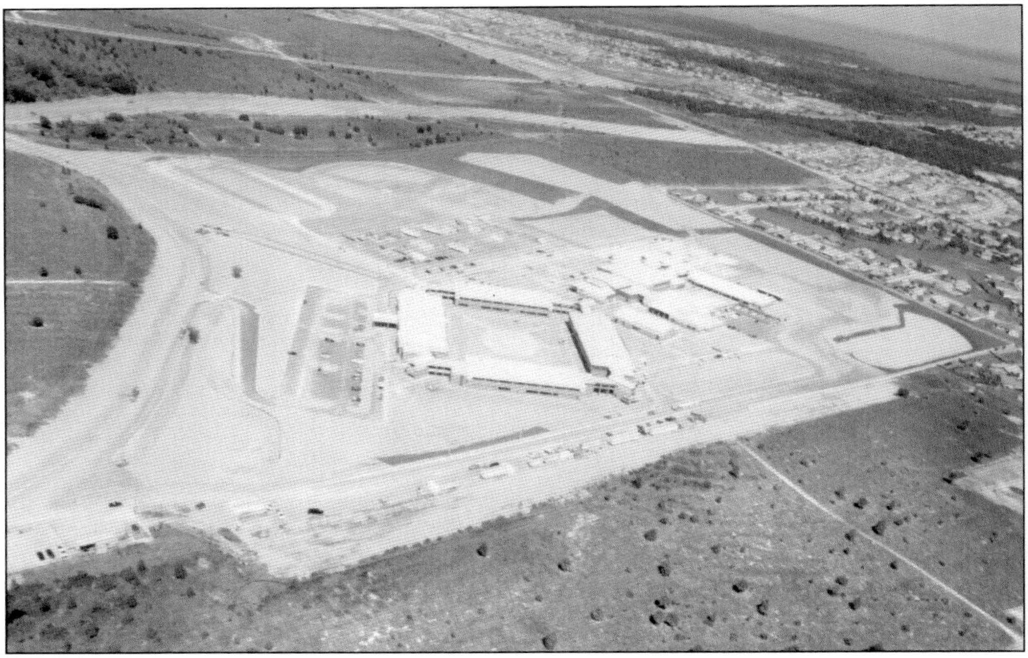

This aerial view shows Clermont's East Ridge High School under construction. It is the largest school in Lake County and has more than 3,000 students. It was built in 2002 to accommodate the population explosion the city experienced as residential construction took off in the 1990s. (Courtesy of Ann Dupee.)

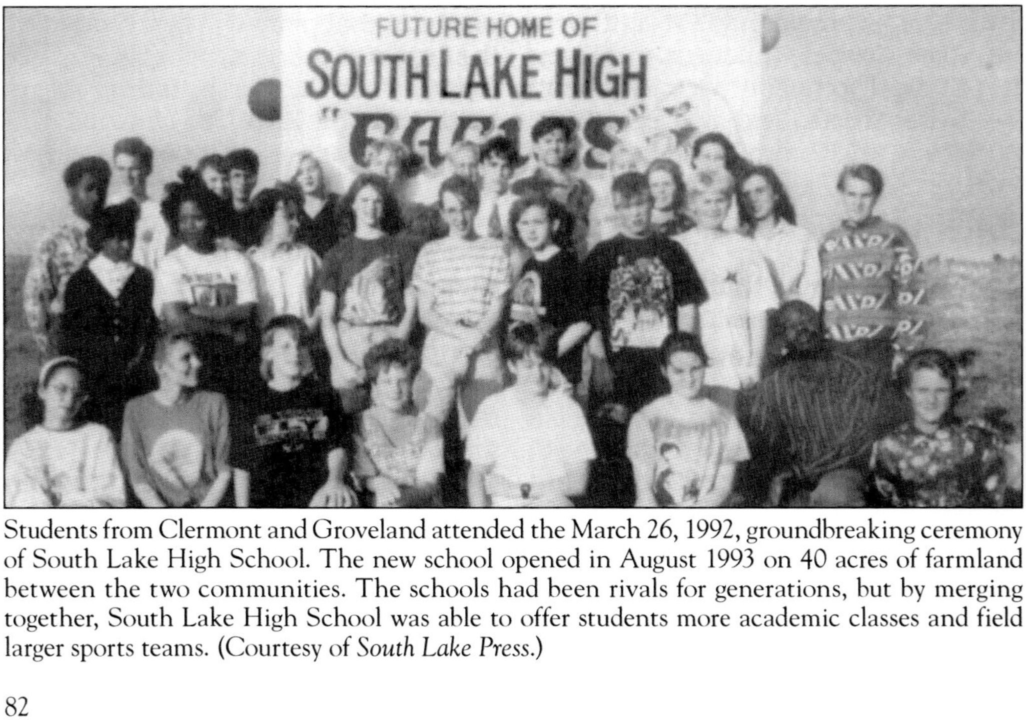


Students from Clermont and Groveland attended the March 26, 1992, groundbreaking ceremony of South Lake High School. The new school opened in August 1993 on 40 acres of farmland between the two communities. The schools had been rivals for generations, but by merging together, South Lake High School was able to offer students more academic classes and field larger sports teams. (Courtesy of *South Lake Press.*)

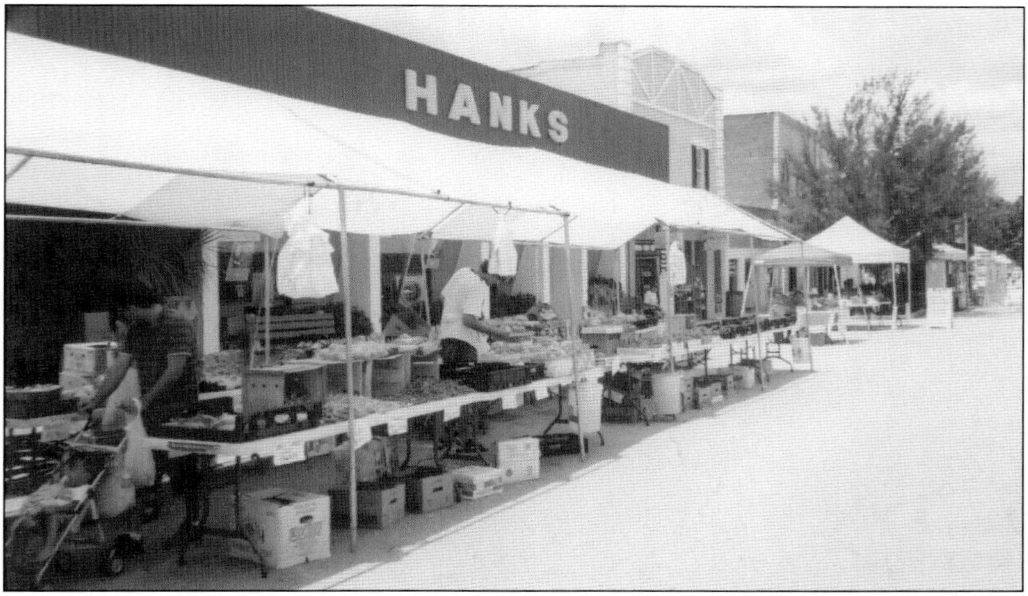


Early pioneers would be happy to see that historic downtown Montrose Street is still home to many of Clermont's oldest businesses and city hall. The Clermont Downtown Partnership sponsors its popular farmers' market every Sunday where shoppers can choose from local delicacies, such as Yalaha bread and barbecue. (Photograph by Doris Bloodsworth.)

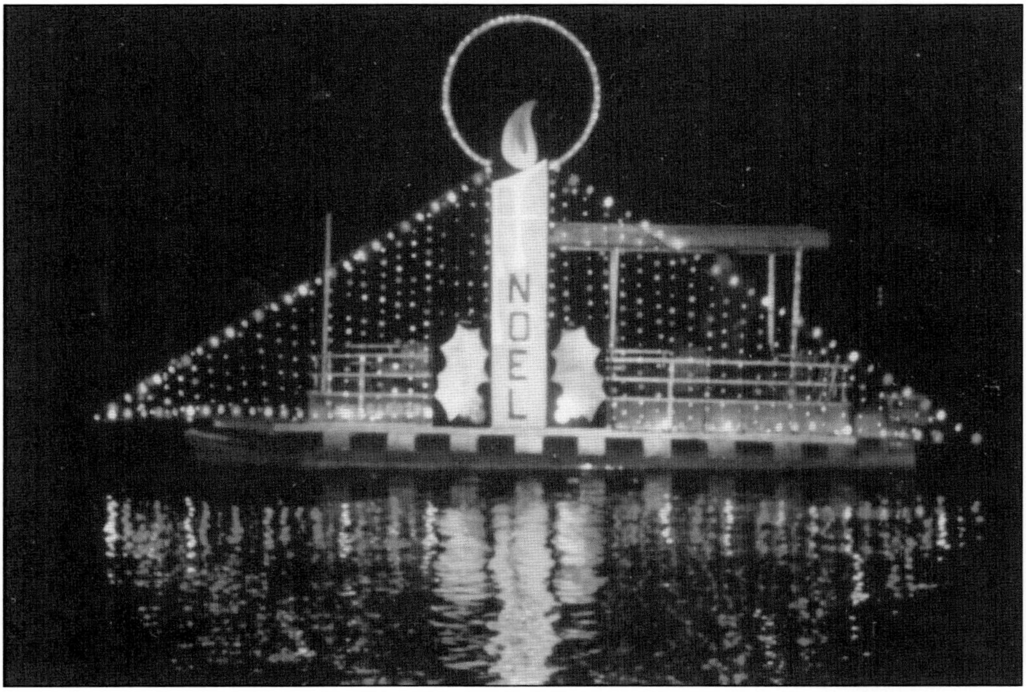


One of the city's holiday traditions during the 1990s was the lighted boat parade initiated by the Clermont Kiwanis Club and later cosponsored by the South Lake Kiwanis Club. Jack and Jackie Ulch won first place one year with their decorated pontoon boat. The floating parades were held on Lake Minneola while thousands of spectators watched from lakeside. (Courtesy of Jack and Jackie Ulch.)

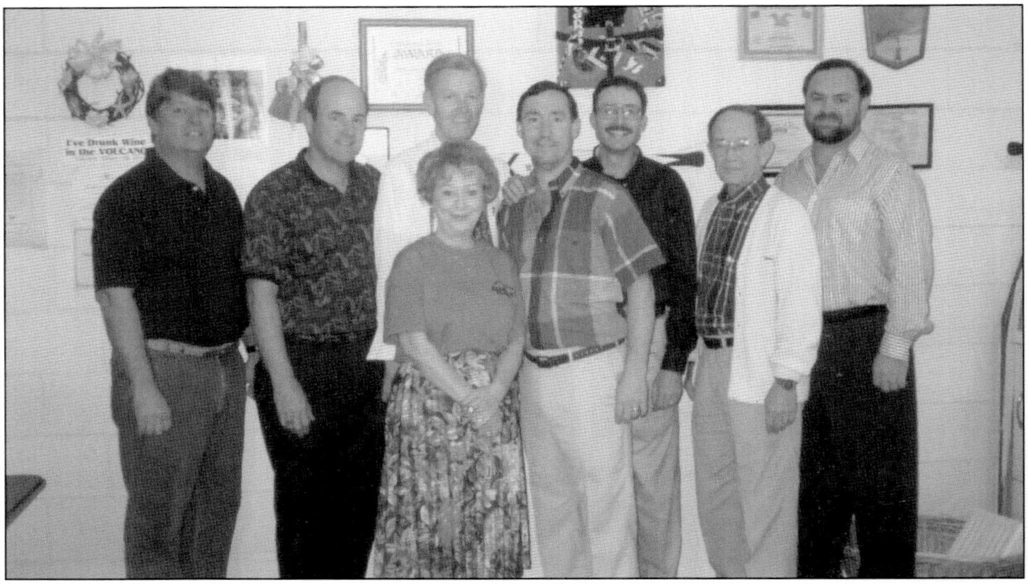

This gathering includes decades of Clermont leadership. From left to right are Hal Turville, Clermont's current mayor; Mike Conley, former city council member; Charley Beals, the city's youngest-ever city council member; Ann Dupee, city council member and former owner of the *South Lake Press*; Bob Pool, former mayor; George Forbes, former city manager; Jim Hoskinson, former mayor and county commissioner; and Wayne Saunders, finance director and city manager since 1985. (Courtesy of Ann Dupee.)

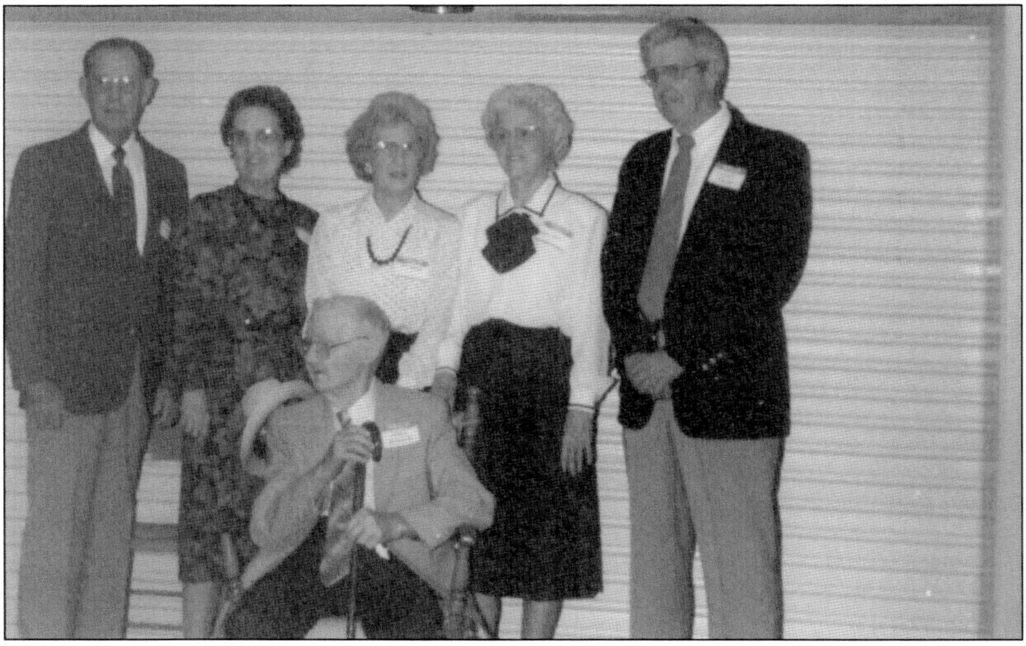

Max Hooks (seated), a pioneer, celebrated his 100th birthday with family and friends in 1993. Hooks lived three more years. He was the grandson of Herring Hooks, who moved to the Clermont area in 1868. Max was the city tax collector in 1916. He also owned a dairy farm and later citrus groves on what is now Max Hooks Road. From left to right are Oakley Seaver, Elizabeth Seaver Magruder, Dorothy Seaver Lassiter, Nelle Seaver, and Max Leonard Seaver. (Courtesy of Leonard Seaver.)

In 1998, Clermont got a new signature event called Pig on the Pond. Like the Labor Day celebrations of the 1950s through the 1990s, the festivities are held on Jaycee Beach. The barbecue competition and festival averages 20,000 people and raises significant funds for scholarships and education throughout South Lake County. One of the most popular events is the pig race, shown at right. (Courtesy of Pig on the Pond.)

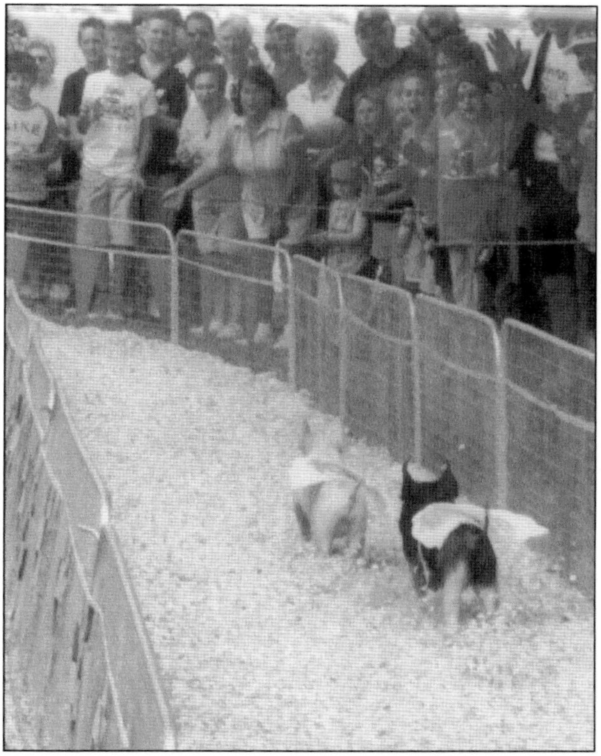

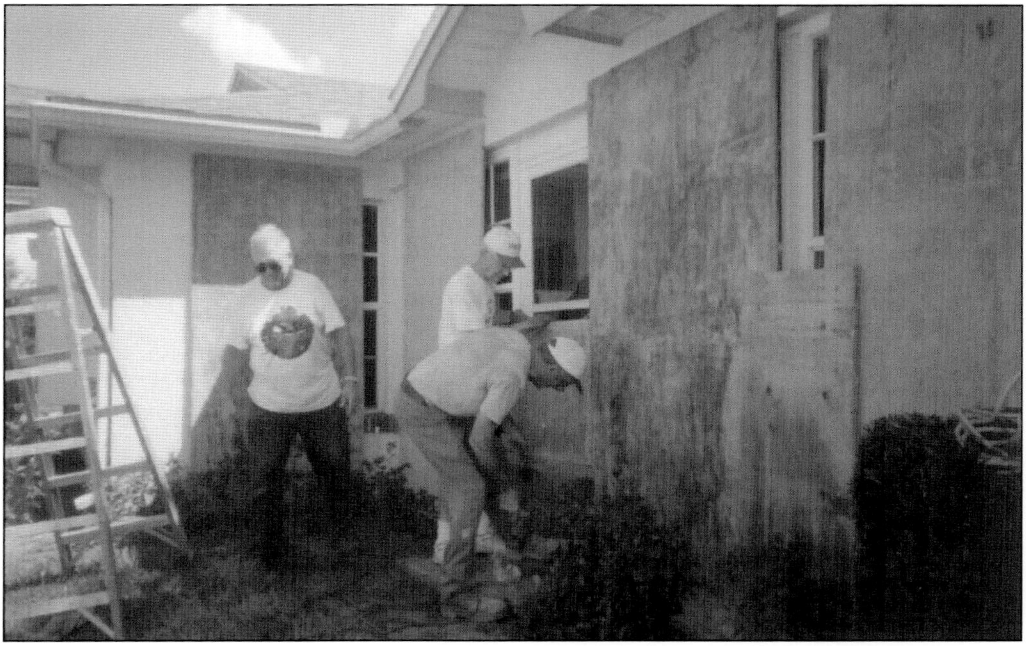

Clermont residents boarded up their homes in 2004. Hurricanes Charley, Frances, Ivan, and Jeanne stormed through the area, and other hurricanes sent heavy rainfall. It was the first time in history that two hurricanes hit Florida within 24 hours of each other. It was also the first time that four hurricanes struck one state in one season. Damages were in the billions, and the death toll exceeded 3,000. (Courtesy of Ann Dupee.)

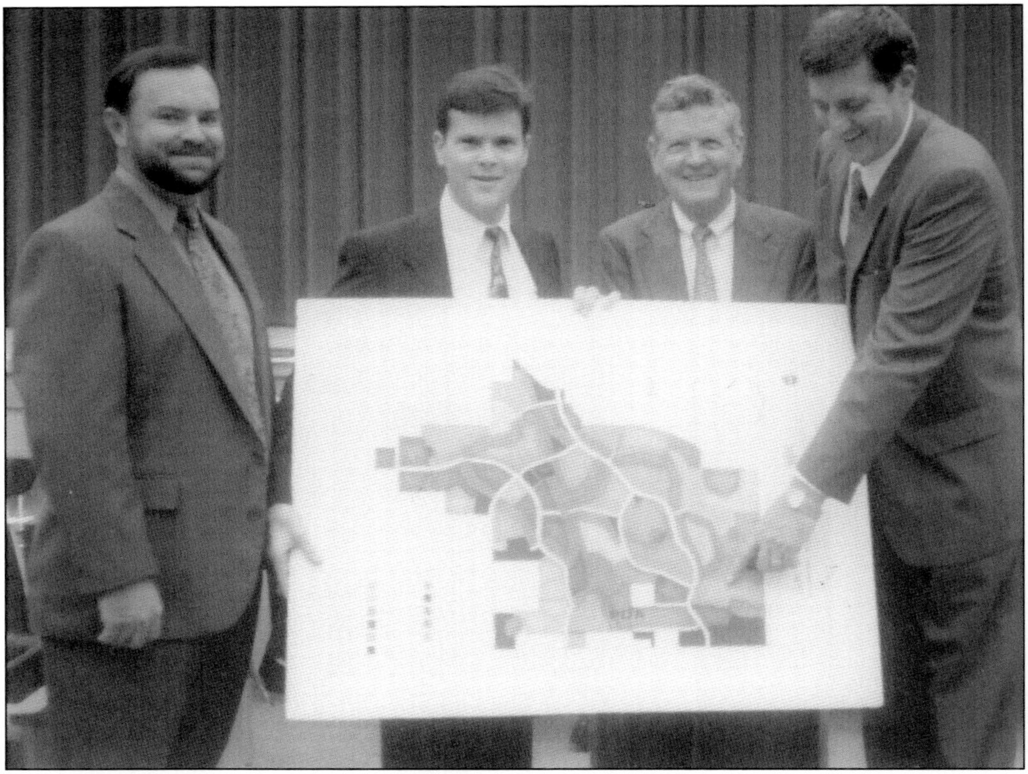

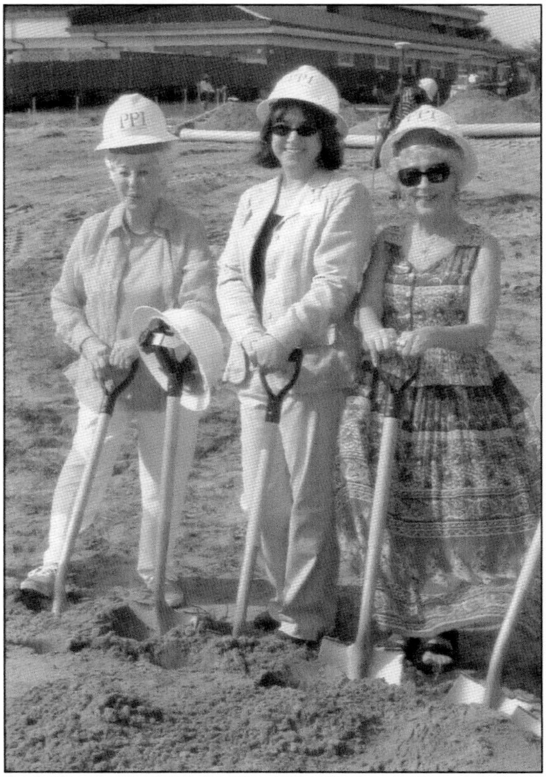

In 1993, Orlando-based Maury Carter and Associates donated 40 acres on a hilltop off Hancock Road for a South Lake branch of Lake-Sumter Community College. Subsequently, the University of Central Florida joined with the college to offer a variety of undergraduate programs. From left to right are Wayne Saunders, Clermont city manager; Daryl and Maury Carter; and Bob Westrick, president of Lake-Sumter Community College. (Courtesy of Ann Dupee.)

From the 1894 Cooperville Literary Club to the largest library in Lake County, Clermont's growth and heritage came together at the June 2008 groundbreaking ceremony for the new 50,000-square-foot Cooper Memorial Library. From left to right are Ann Reaves, major donor to the children's room; Tracy Swank, regional branch manager; and Ann Dupee, a longtime supporter for whom the library's Café Dupee was named. (Courtesy of Ann Dupee.)

# *Five*

# Tourism and Historic Businesses

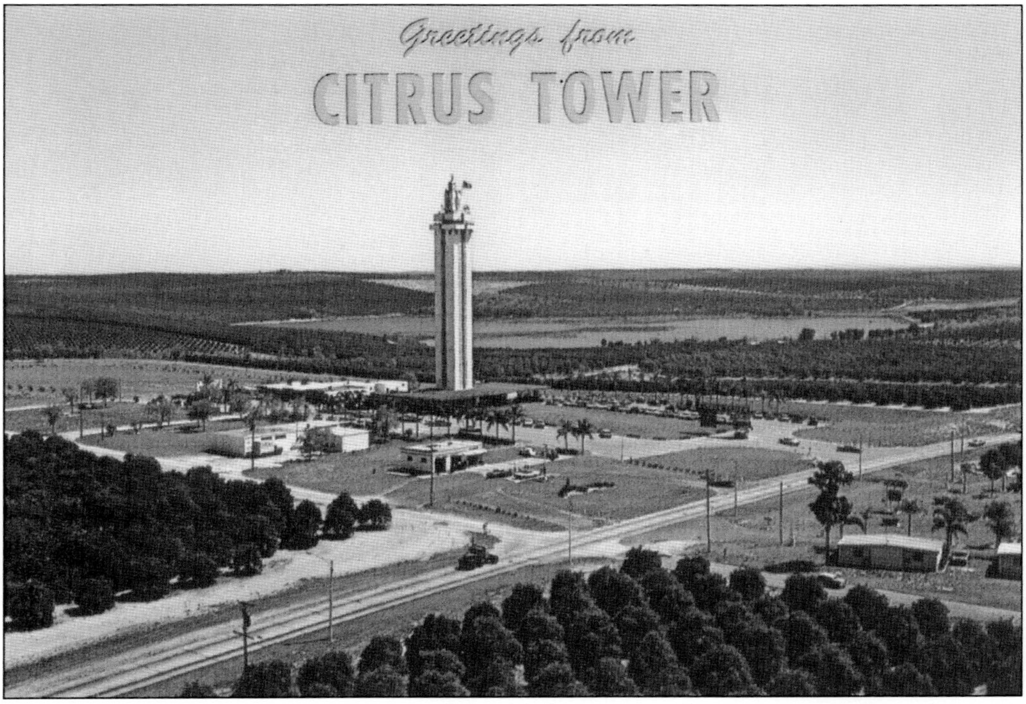


Built in 1956, the Citrus Tower was one of Florida's first man-made attractions and was the state's highest observation point. The observation decks offer an unrivaled view of 2,000 square miles. The tower cost about $250,000 and eventually included a post office and glassblowing studio. Citrus Tower was the brainchild of former Pittsburgh residents Jack Toole and A. W. Thacker, owner of Skyline Motel on Highway 27. Toole also founded the Presidents Hall of Fame next to Citrus Tower. (Courtesy of Clayton Bishop.)

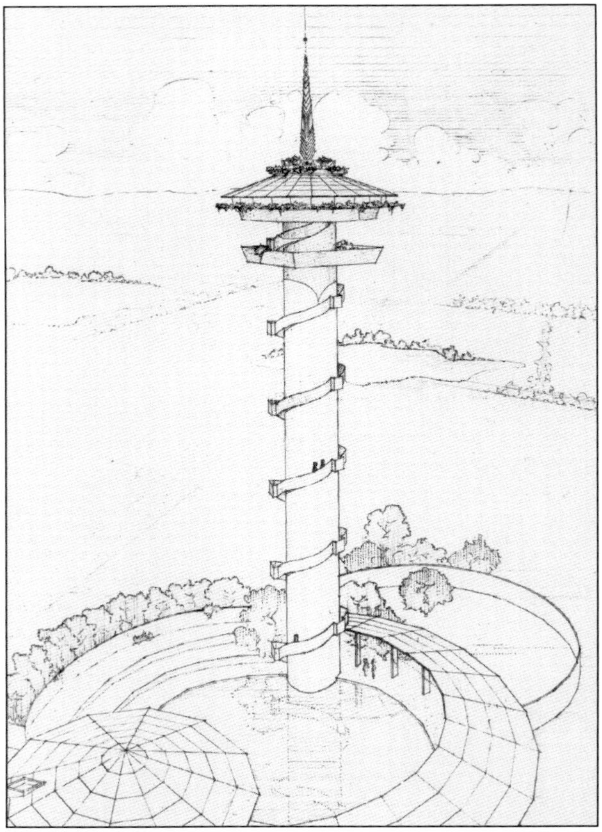

Don McCaffrey, who owned a moisture-proof saltshaker company called Airko, proposed a Clermont tower as early as 1953. A. Wynne Howell of Lakeland, an understudy of Frank Lloyd Wright, designed the proposal pictured at left. Howell's design, which showed people climbing on the outside of the tower, was rejected. (Courtesy of the Lake County Historical Society.)

The winning design came in 1954 from Thomas Russell of Pennsylvania. When completed in July 1956, the tower consisted of 5 million pounds of concrete and rose more than 500 feet above sea level. Shown third from left in the first row, Florida governor Farris Bryant attended the grand opening with representatives from Silver Springs and Cypress Gardens who brought water from their attractions to christen the tower. (Courtesy of Greg Homan.)

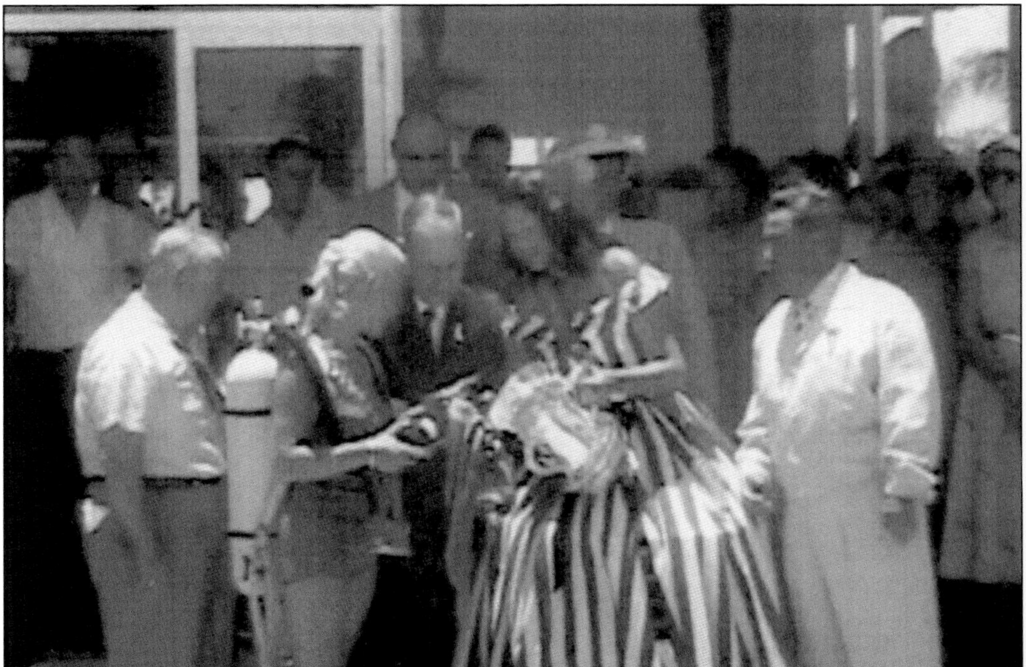

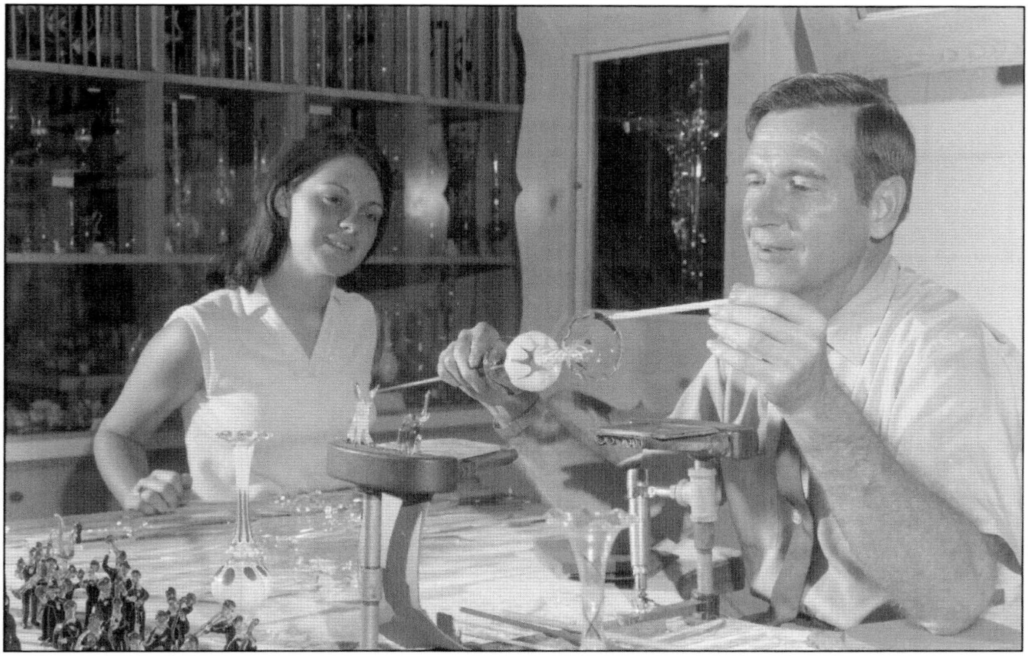

In 1958, the Citrus Tower added a glassblowing studio where visitors could watch Don Boutz and his family create vases and figurines. Boutz had been in the circus and came from a family of Bohemian glassblowers. (Courtesy of the State Archives of Florida.)

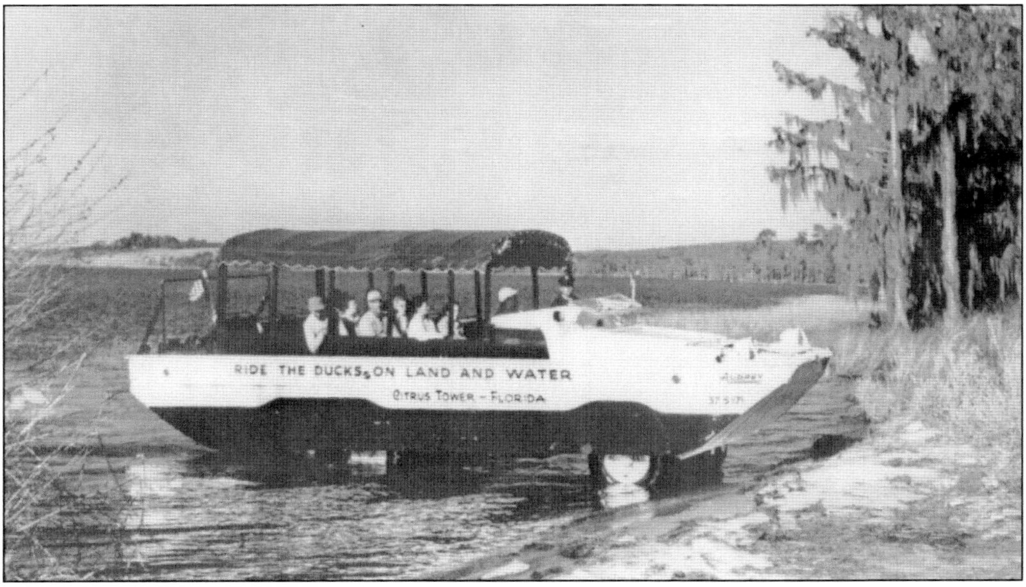


Tourists wanting to see Clermont by land and water could do so on the Citrus Tower's Duck Boat Tours, as pictured in this 1958 photograph taken at Lake Minnehaha. The amphibious vehicles called DUCKS were developed in 1942 during World War II and manufactured by GMC. They are still considered one of the most successful amphibious vehicles ever invented. (Courtesy of the State Archives of Florida.)

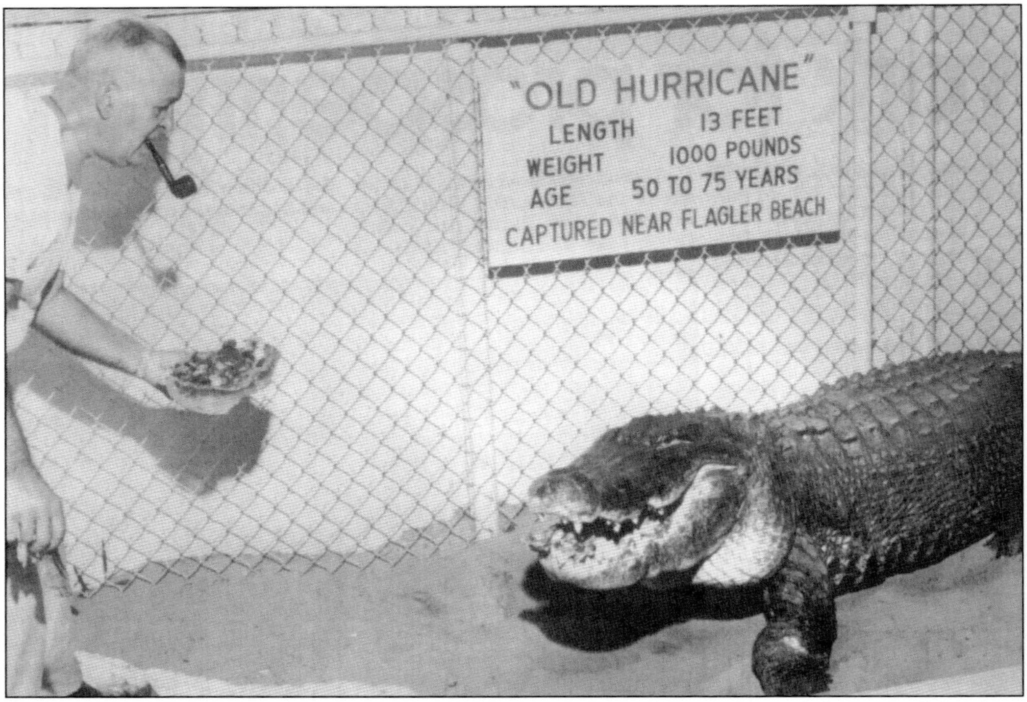


In 1959, Jack Raymon opened his Wildlife Arena at the Citrus Tower. One of the stars of the show was "Old Hurricane," believed to be the largest alligator in captivity in 1961, when this photograph was taken. Raymon is feeding the alligator its first meal after winter hibernation. Wildlife expert Hal Granberry later leased the exhibit. (Courtesy of Cooper Memorial Library Association.)

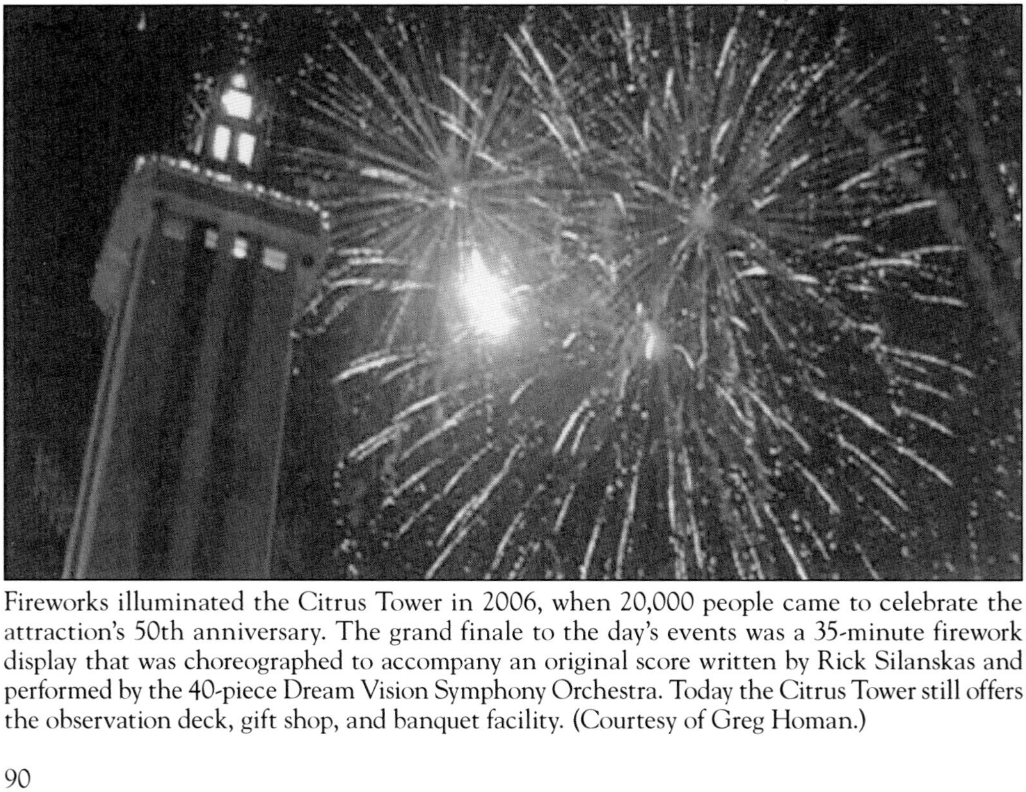

Fireworks illuminated the Citrus Tower in 2006, when 20,000 people came to celebrate the attraction's 50th anniversary. The grand finale to the day's events was a 35-minute firework display that was choreographed to accompany an original score written by Rick Silanskas and performed by the 40-piece Dream Vision Symphony Orchestra. Today the Citrus Tower still offers the observation deck, gift shop, and banquet facility. (Courtesy of Greg Homan.)

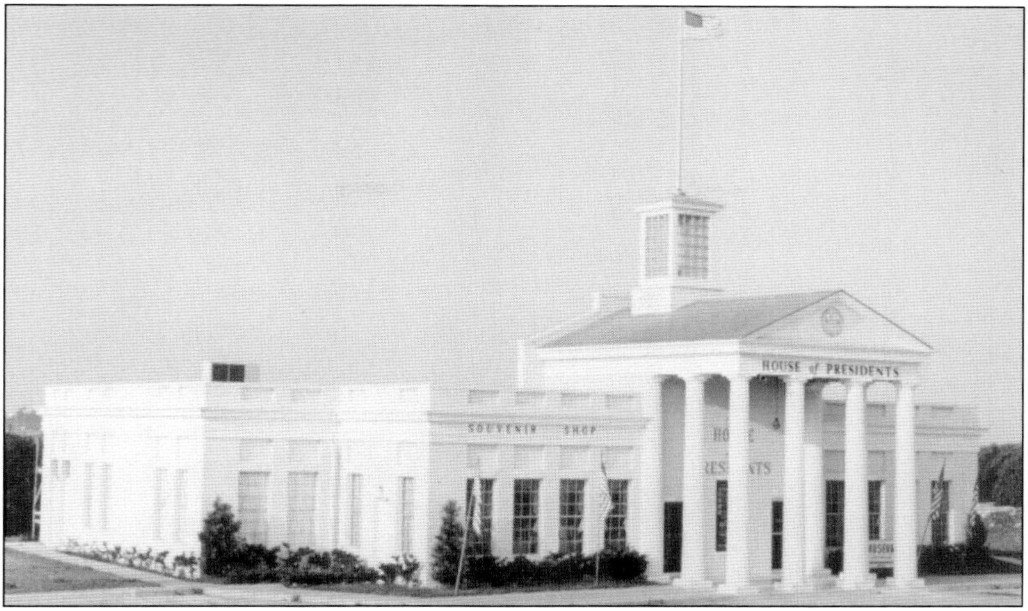


Pres. Ronald Reagan proclaimed the Presidents Hall of Fame "a true national treasure." The attraction opened beside the Citrus Tower in 1960 as a wax museum of U.S. presidents. It expanded in 1990 to include a miniature replica of the White House created by John and Jan Zweifel. The *Guinness Book of World Records* calls the replica the world's largest dollhouse. (Courtesy of Cooper Memorial Library Association.)

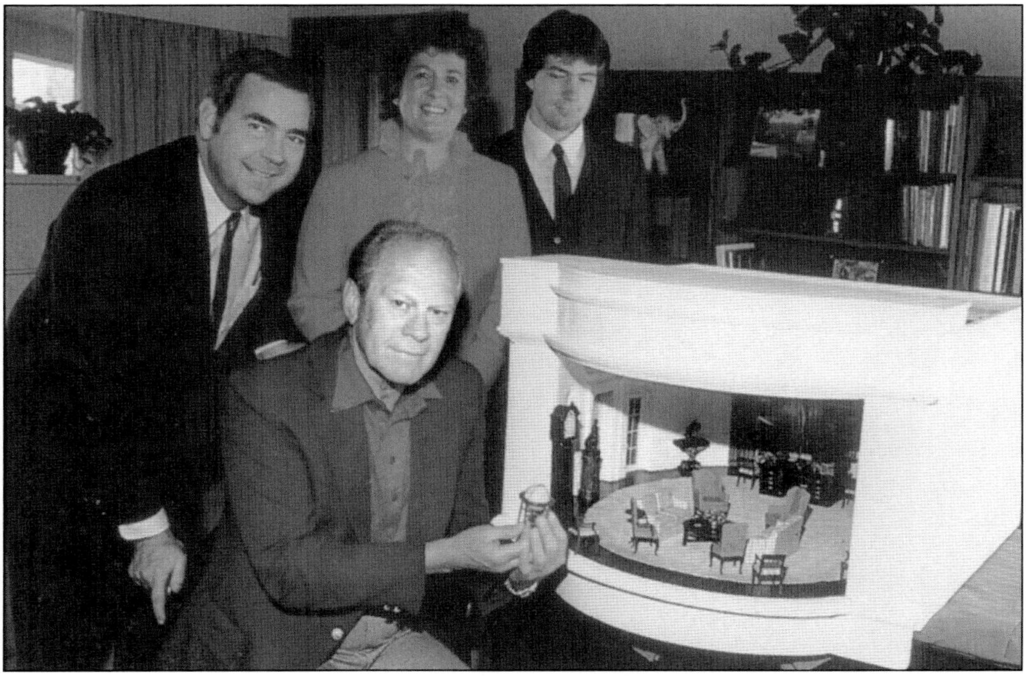

John, Jan, and Jack Zweifel (standing) show their replica of the Oval Office to Pres. Gerald Ford at his California home in 1982. John Zweifel dreamed of building a miniature White House since he visited the real one in 1956. After repeated attempts to photograph and measure the White House were denied, President Ford and his wife, Betty, gave their blessing. (Courtesy of John Zweifel.)

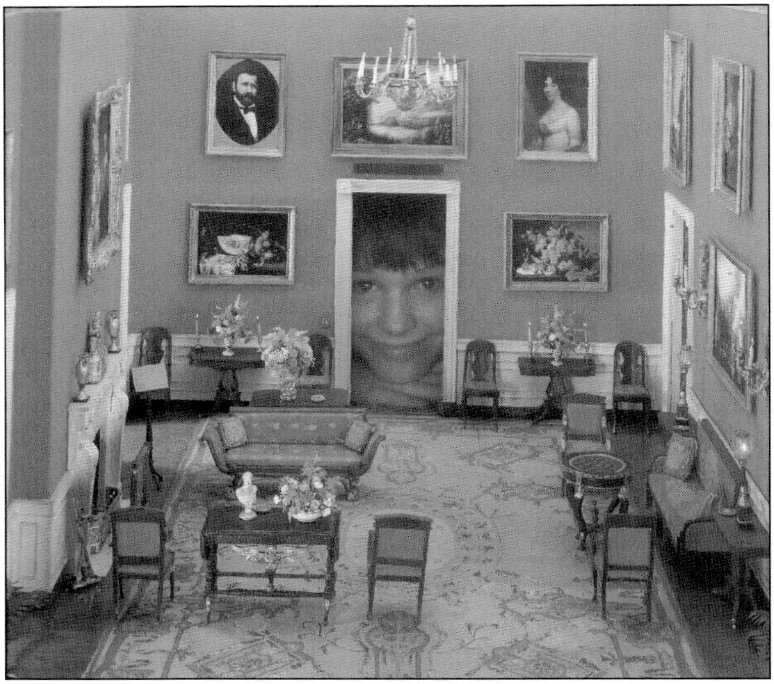

Kevin Buckland peeks through the doorway of the Red Room, giving perspective to the 1:12 scale. Replica builder John Zweifel's desire was to make the White House available to people who couldn't travel to Washington, D.C. During a 1982 tour in the Netherlands, terrorists attacked the display. It took Zweifel six weeks to make repairs. Each room cost an estimated $20,000. (Courtesy of John Zweifel.)

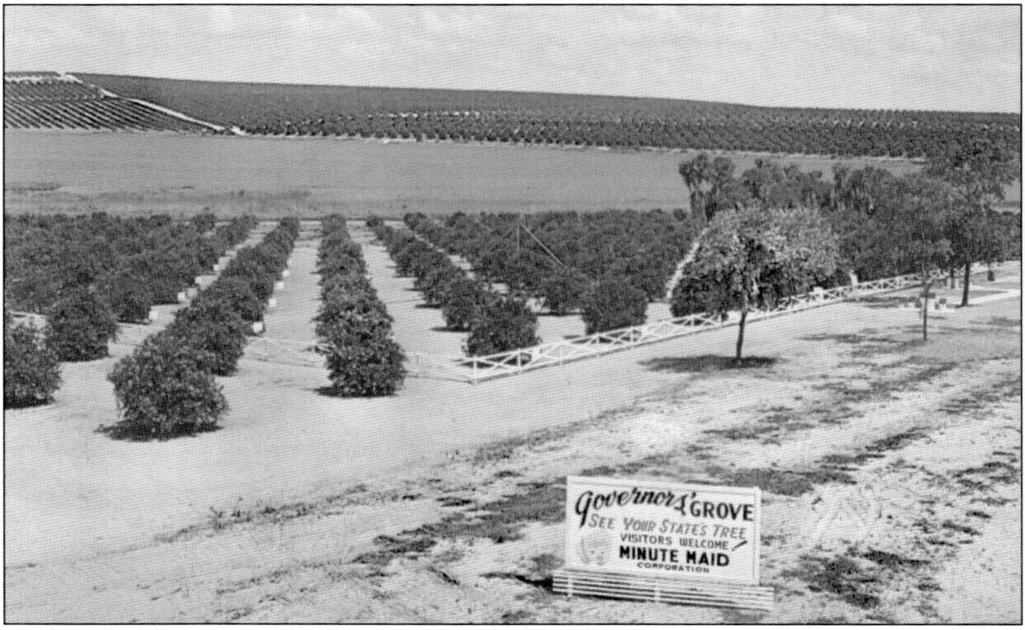


Tourists could picnic beside Governors' Grove, planted by Minute Maid in 1958 near Lake Felter and present-day Kings Ridge. The company planted the grove as a sign of friendship between Florida and the other states. Each governor had a Valencia orange tree and received the fruit after it was picked. The attraction was the site for an episode of Jack Linkletter's *On the Go* television show around 1958. (Courtesy of Elizabeth Duncan.)

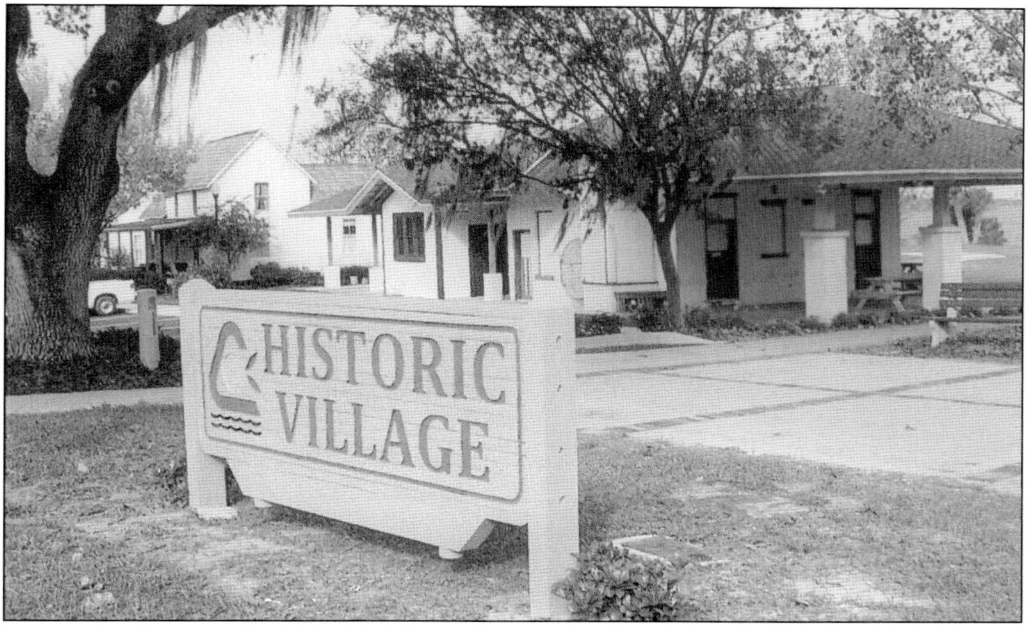


The South Lake County Historical Society led by Micki Blackburn started the Clermont Historic Village by Lake Minneola in 2002. The historic site includes the original homes of James and Sallie Townsend, the first African American settlers in Clermont, and Alexander and Eleanor Kern, owners of the city's first public water system. The village also includes the old train depot and the original town library. (Photograph by Doris Bloodsworth.)

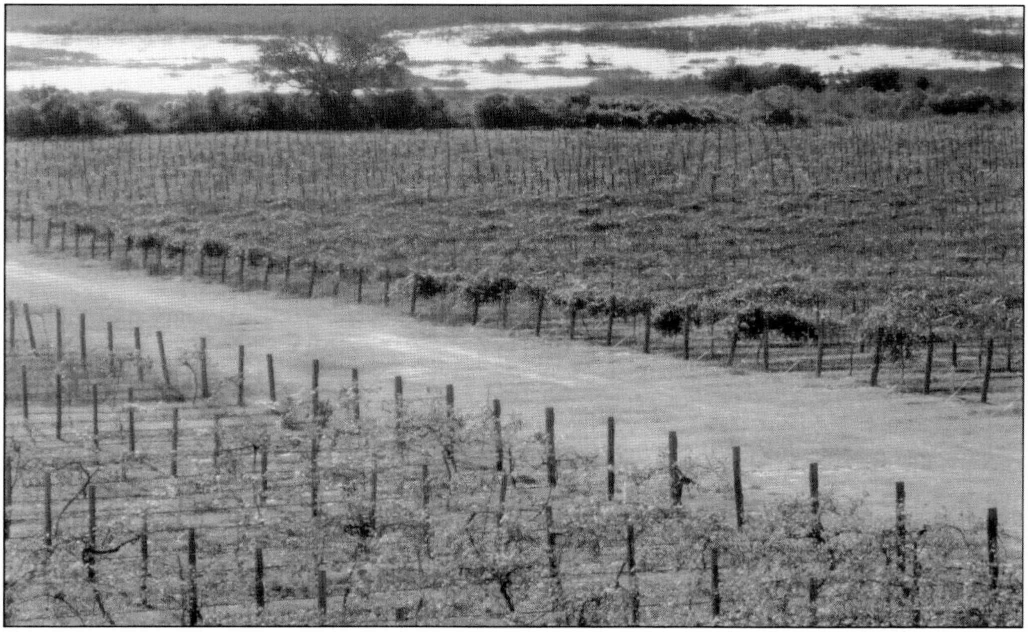

While citrus took a hit in 1989, the grape industry made a revival with the start of Lakeridge Winery and Vineyards, now the state's largest premium winery. The vineyard sits among 127 acres of rolling countryside. More than 110,000 people annually visit the winery, which includes a tasting room and complimentary tours. The Lakeridge wines have won more than 700 awards for excellence. (Courtesy of Lakeridge Winery and Vineyards.)

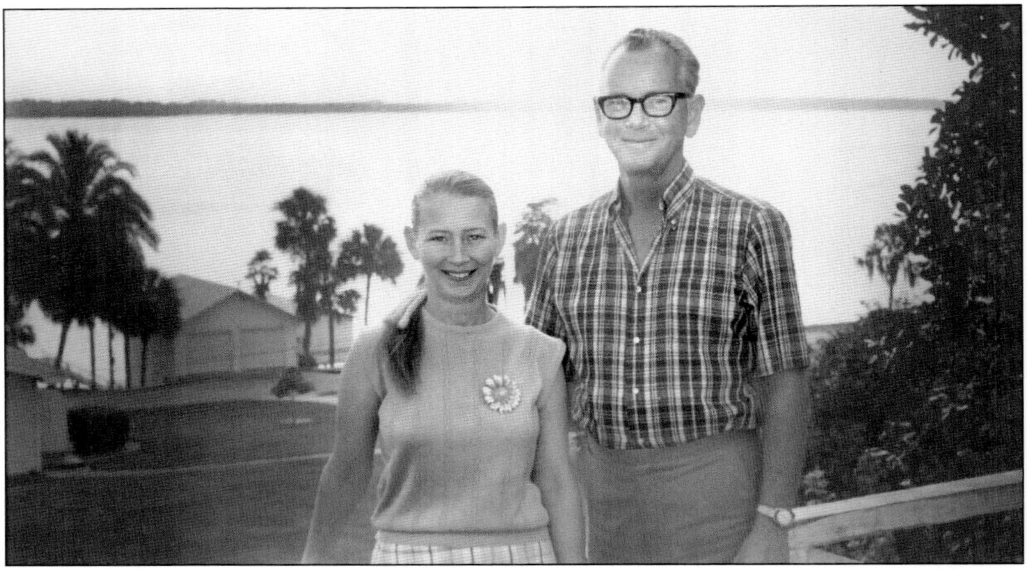

The *South Lake Press* is one of Clermont's oldest businesses, tracing its roots to 1913. Ann and George Dupee purchased the paper in 1968. They came from New York where George was head of the *Wall Street Journal*'s East Coast advertising. The *South Lake Press* still publishes weekly from the Montrose Street address it had in 1935. (Courtesy of Ann Dupee.)

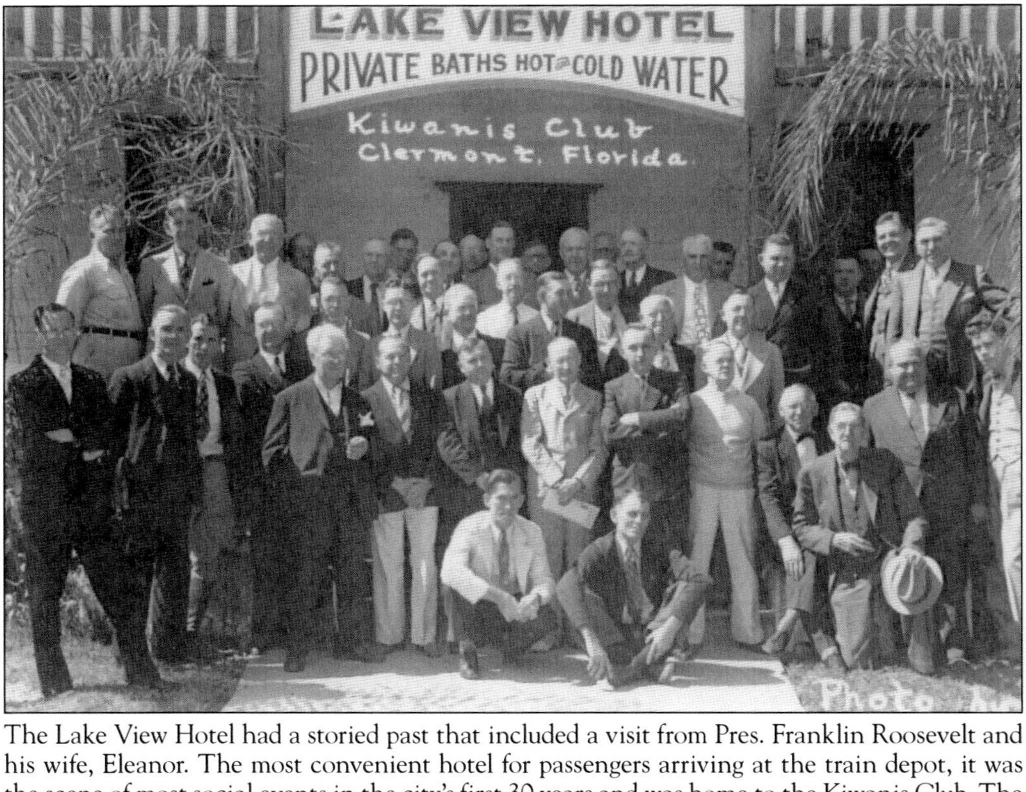


The Lake View Hotel had a storied past that included a visit from Pres. Franklin Roosevelt and his wife, Eleanor. The most convenient hotel for passengers arriving at the train depot, it was the scene of most social events in the city's first 30 years and was home to the Kiwanis Club. The landmark was torn down in 1959 to make way for a grocery store. (Courtesy of Cooper Memorial Library Association.)

Hull Well and Pump Service has been helping Clermont residents since 1912, when Clayton Hull bought his first steam-powered drill. Great-grandson Eddie Hull now runs the company. The company was honored as one of the city's oldest businesses in 2009 during the 125th anniversary of the official founding of Clermont. The Hull family also helped found Minneola. (Courtesy of Eddie Hull.)

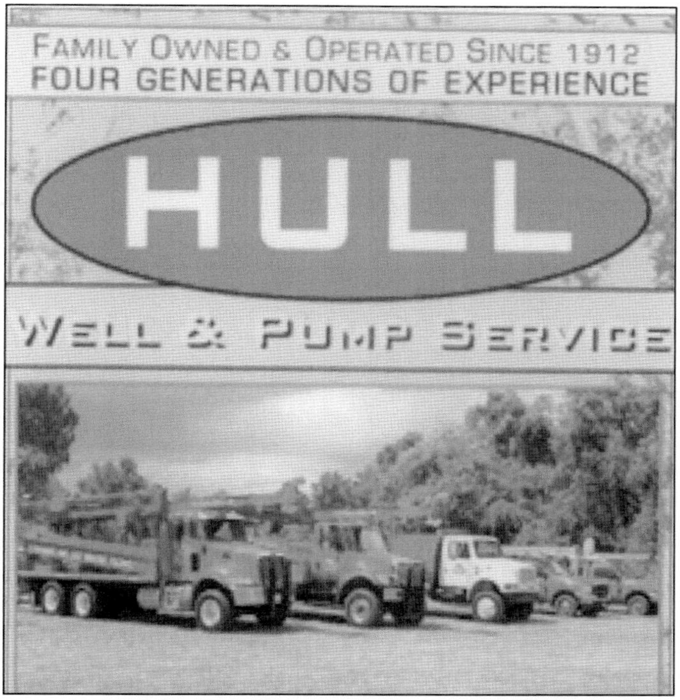


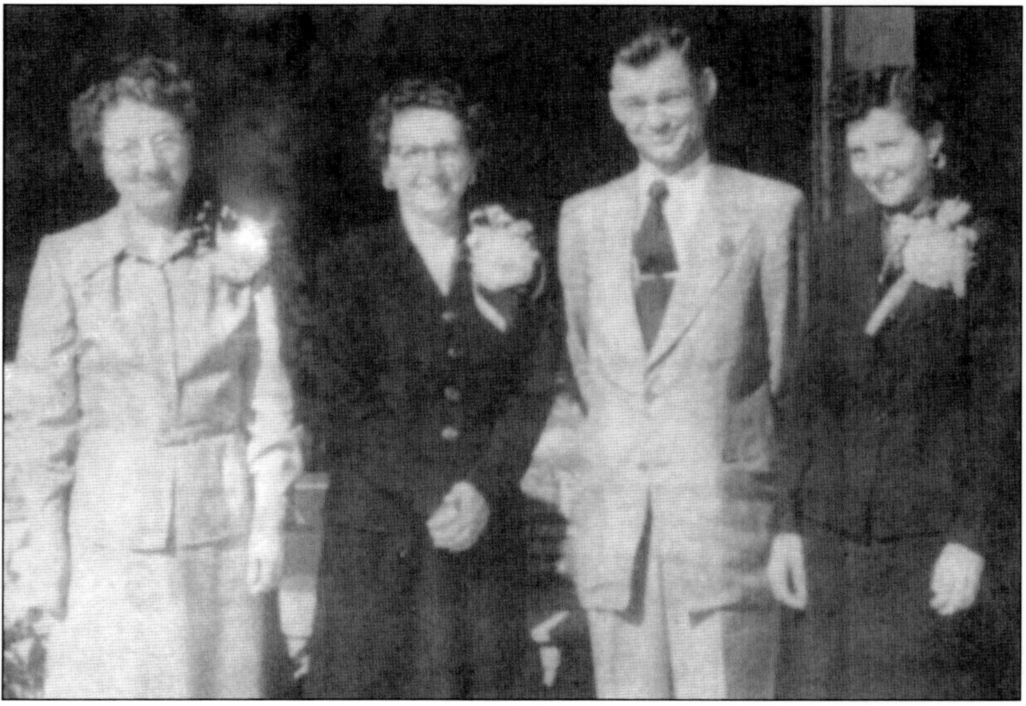

Olivenbaum Insurance has been part of Clermont's historic downtown since 1929. Axel Olivenbaum was an agent at Stokes and Fields Insurance Agency started in 1929. He bought the company around 1949. From left to right are Anna Olivenbaum Braddock, Severina Olivenbaum, Axel Olivenbaum, and Ruth Harrison. In the early days, owners kept insurance policies in a notebook with them at all times so they could help people away from the office. (Courtesy of Olivenbaum Insurance.)

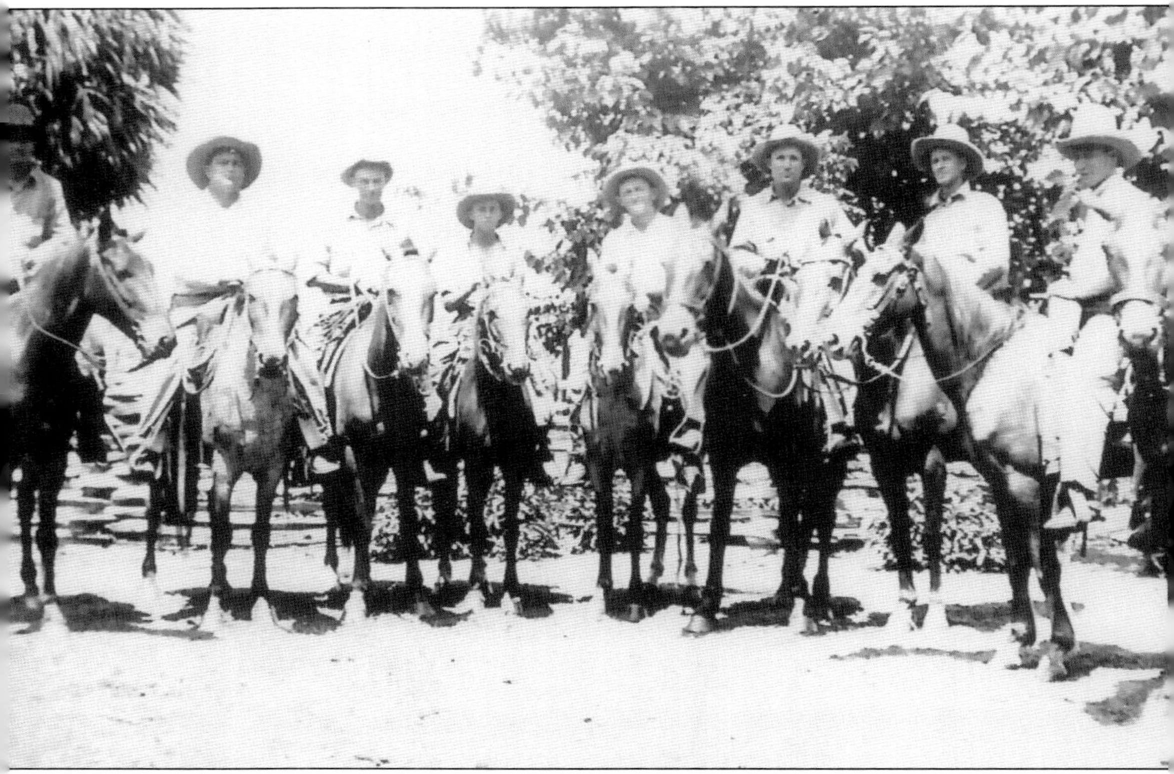

The Bronson family is one of the most famous in Florida. They have been in agriculture continuously since 1635. The Range Riders seen in this 1935 photograph show the cowboys who helped the Bronsons on the South Lake County open range. Many had cattle ranches across South Lake County. From left to right are L. R. Bronson, Allison Story, Alfred Story, Buster Story, Walter Bridges, Oliver Knowles, Lewis ?, Charles Knowles, and Jim Tomlinson. The Bronson name is one of the most famous in Florida. Irlo Bronson is the namesake of the highway leading to Walt Disney World. He served in the Florida House and Senate. Since 2001, Charles Bronson has been Florida's commissioner of agriculture. The family once owned almost 1,800 acres that was purchased by the state, which turned the property into Lake Louisa State Park. (Courtesy of Dennis Bronson.)

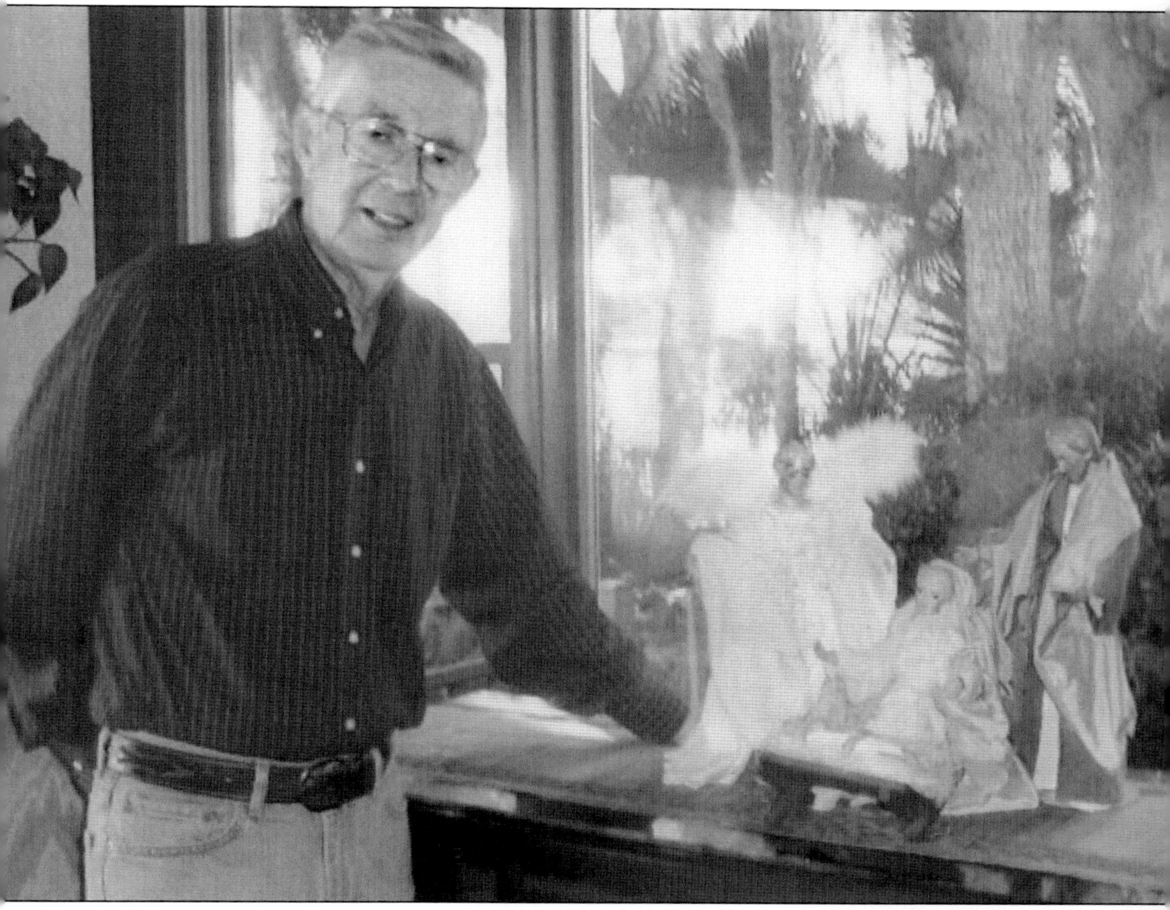

The Bell Ceramics, Inc. factory got its start in 1946 when New Jersey mother Mildred Bell took up painting. This hobby led her and husband Harry Bell to start an art school. She wrote a book titled *Practical Ceramics* and sold the art school to create Bell Ceramics, Inc. The company manufactured and sold an array of products related to ceramics and doll making. The Bells moved to Clermont in 1965 and opened their business in a former citrus-packing plant. Their son Richard Bell, pictured here, became president, and the company expanded worldwide, racking up sales of up to $5 million. In 1986, the company founded the International Foundation of Doll Makers to preserve and promote the art of creating porcelain dolls. In 2005, the company's prime assets were sold to a Texas manufacturer, ending a true Cinderella business story in Clermont. (Courtesy of Toni Bell.)

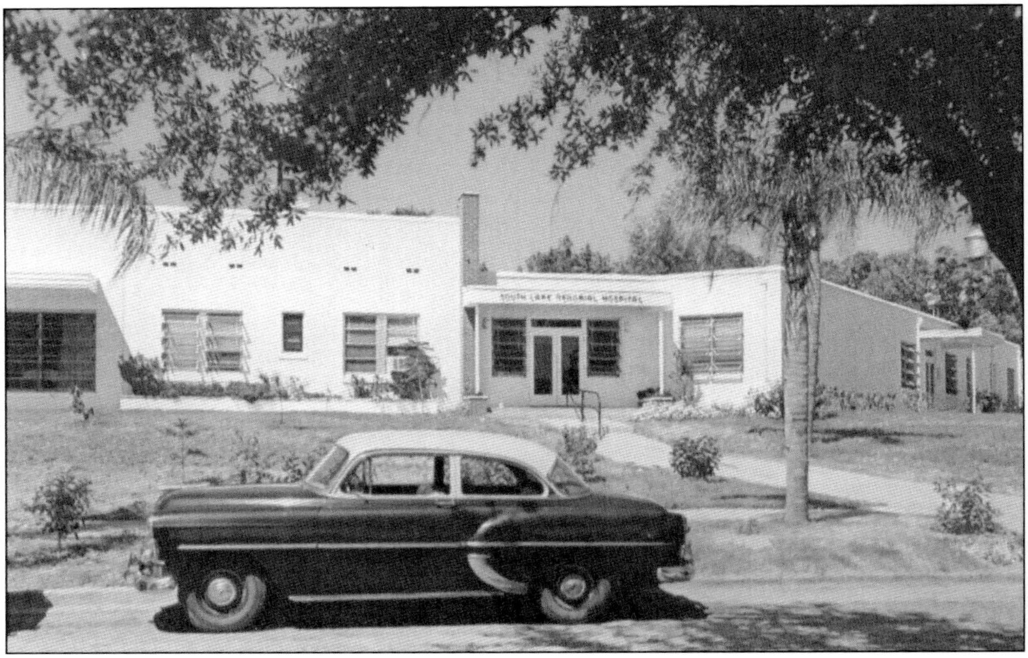

In 1939, a group of 15 women organized the Clermont Welfare League. They raised money to establish a first-aid station. But their dream grew, and in 1941, they built a nine-room clinic overlooking Center Lake. The building expanded again in 1955 (above) to include 15 beds, an emergency room, and an ambulance entrance. That same year, 25 women organized the first Red Cross Gray Ladies volunteer chapter in Lake County (below). The Pink Ladies and candy stripers later joined the volunteer ranks. The Gray Ladies helped with nonmedical needs, such as reading to patients or writing letters for them. A wing dedicated to pioneer Harry Stokes and a three-story addition brought the total beds to 68 by 1972. (Both courtesy of South Lake Hospital.)

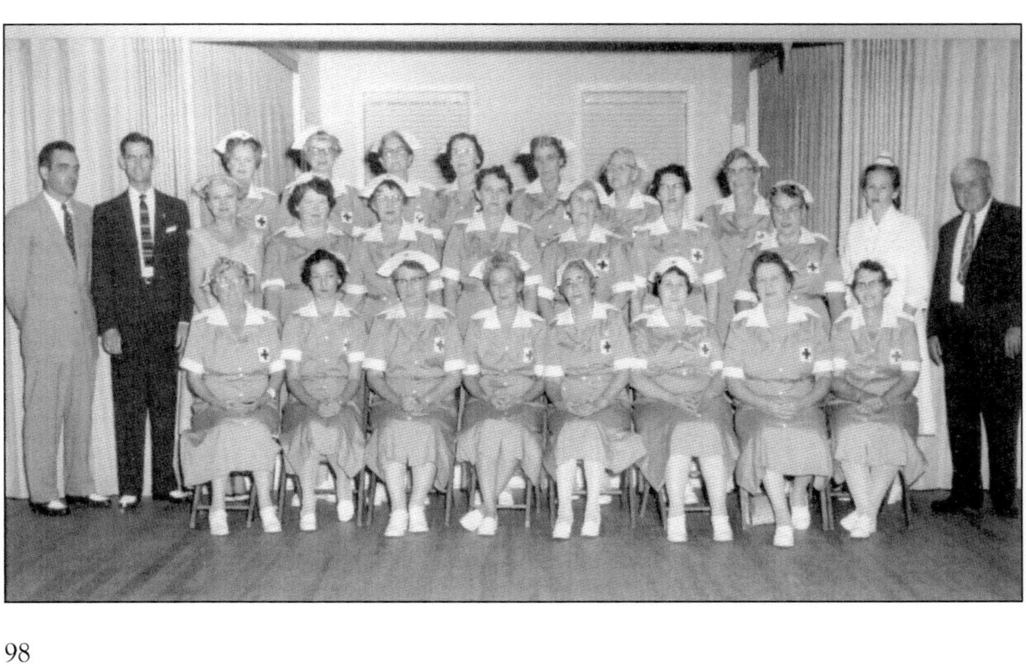

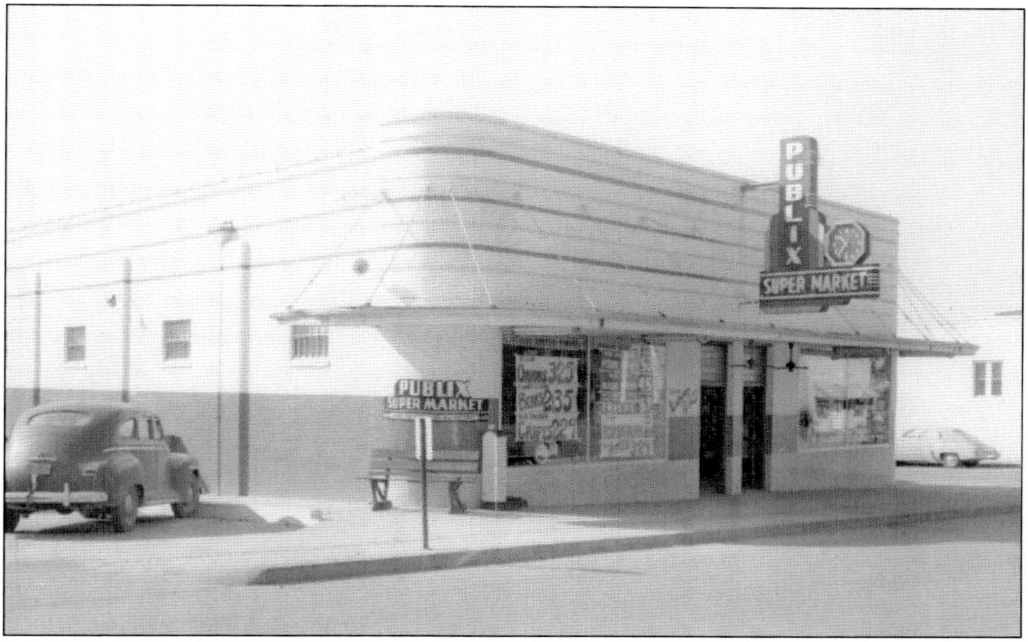


Publix Super Markets in Lakeland opened a new 51-foot-by-111-foot grocery store at Montrose and Seventh Streets in June 1948. Eighteen years later, George Jenkins, president of Publix, donated the building to the City of Clermont. The building is now Jenkins Auditorium. (Courtesy of the South Lake Chamber of Commerce.)

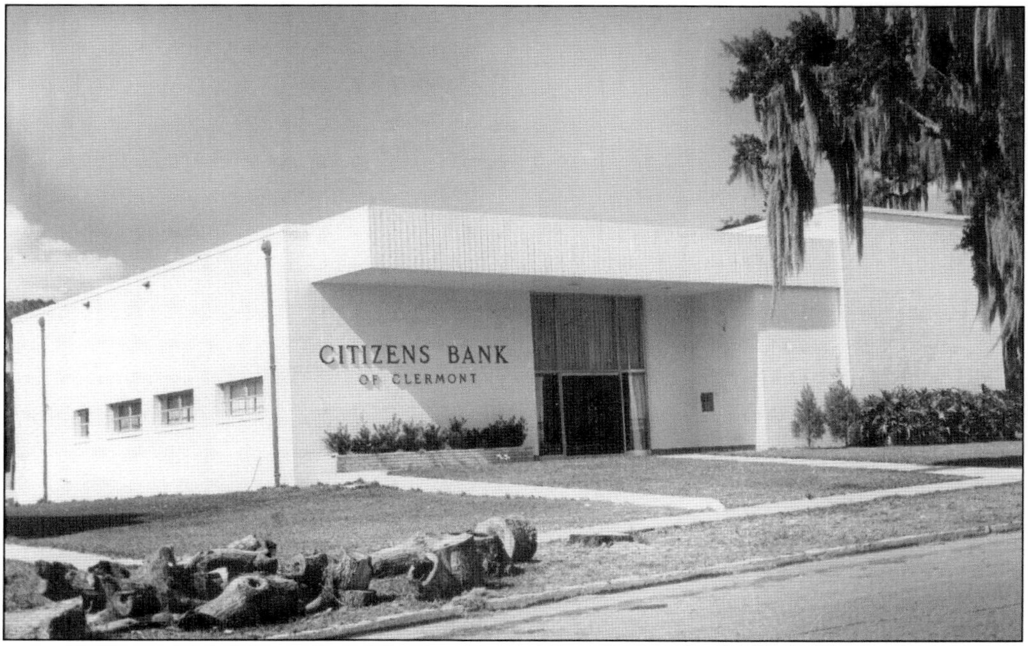


Citizens Bank of Clermont, pictured here in 1961, formed in 1930 when two local banks merged. It was the Great Depression, and many banks failed. At one point, the bank was down to about $1,000 in deposits, but the bank received a loan, and by World War II, deposits grew to $2 million. The bank remained Citizens Bank until it was sold in the 1970s. (Courtesy of Cooper Memorial Library Association.)

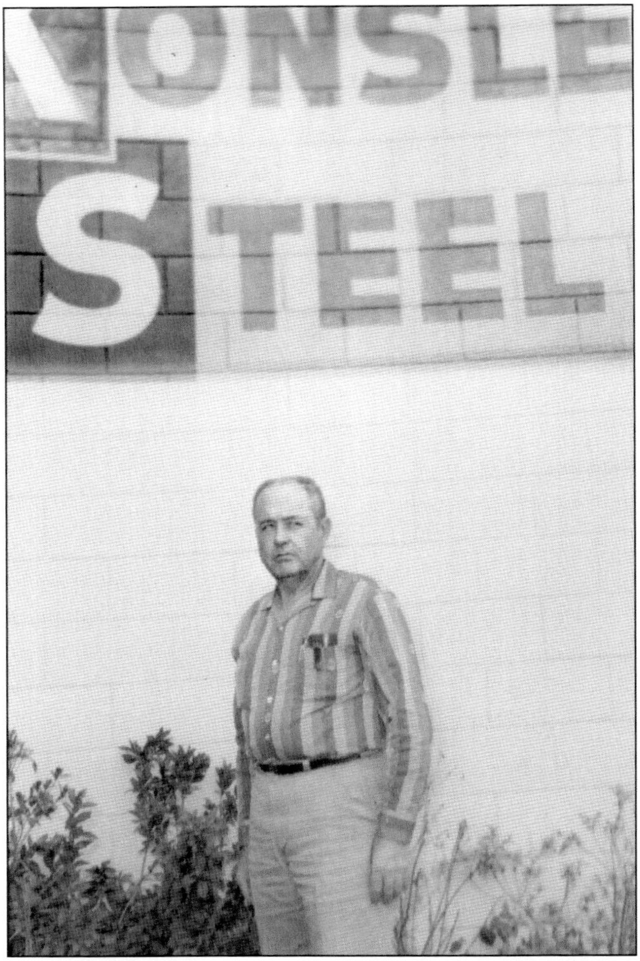


In 1945, Ellis Konsler (left) and his brother Charles started a steel fabricating and welding business. They initially worked out of a gas station at the corner of Montrose Street and West Avenue before they moved beside Clermont Builders Supply. In 1960, Konsler Steel built a 20,000-square-foot building at Highway 50 and Twelfth Street (below). S. W. Williams and Homer Allen bought Konsler Steel in 1971. The plant more than doubled its square footage and employed 175 workers. Their patented spiral fruit-holding bin sold worldwide. Williams sold the company in 1988, and the name changed to Exceletech of Clermont. Williams got the company back in 1992. The company specialized in bridges, power plant stacks, and military projects. After the first Gulf War, the company earned national recognition for hiring veterans. Today the company operates as Exceletech Coating and Applications. (Courtesy of the Konsler family.)

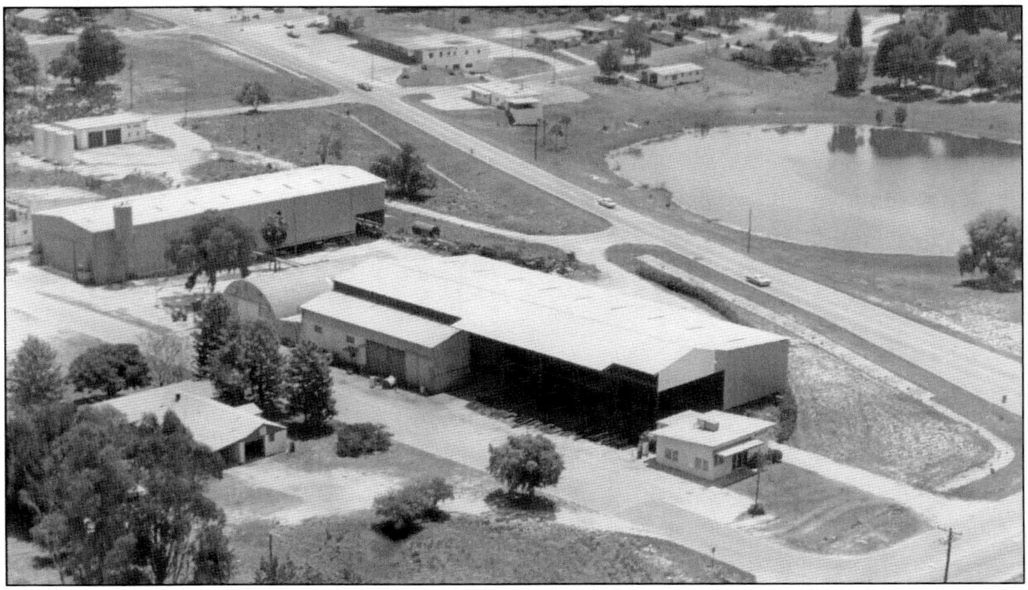

# *Six*
# Schools and Churches

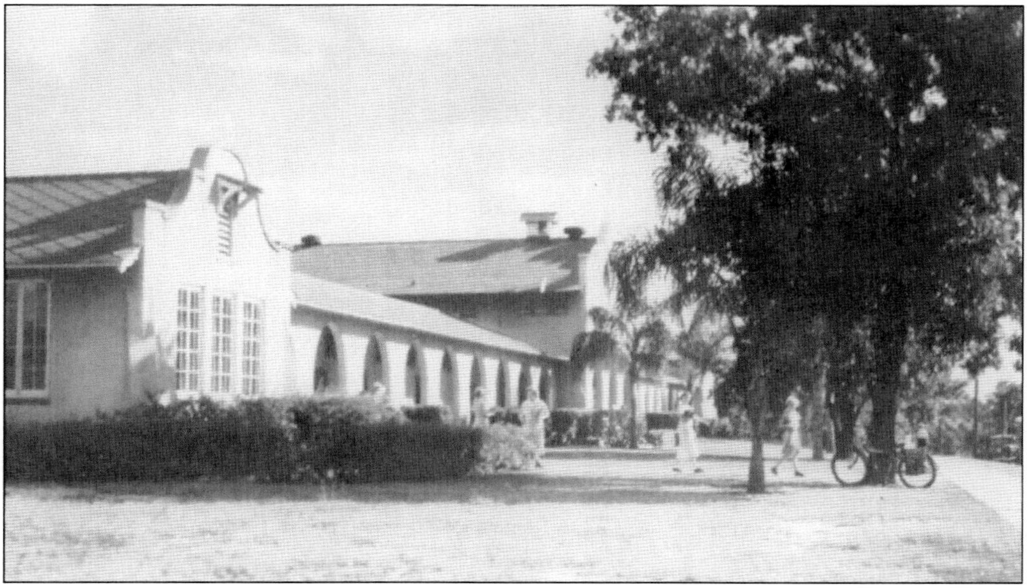

Schools and churches are the heart of the Clermont community. This photograph of the Clermont-Minneola School, built in 1924 on Second Street at a cost of $50,000, shows the popularity of the Spanish Mission architecture in that era. The school was only used for secondary grades. The new building had six classrooms, an industrial shop, a home economics room, and a large auditorium used by the school and community. (Courtesy of the Lake County Historical Society.)

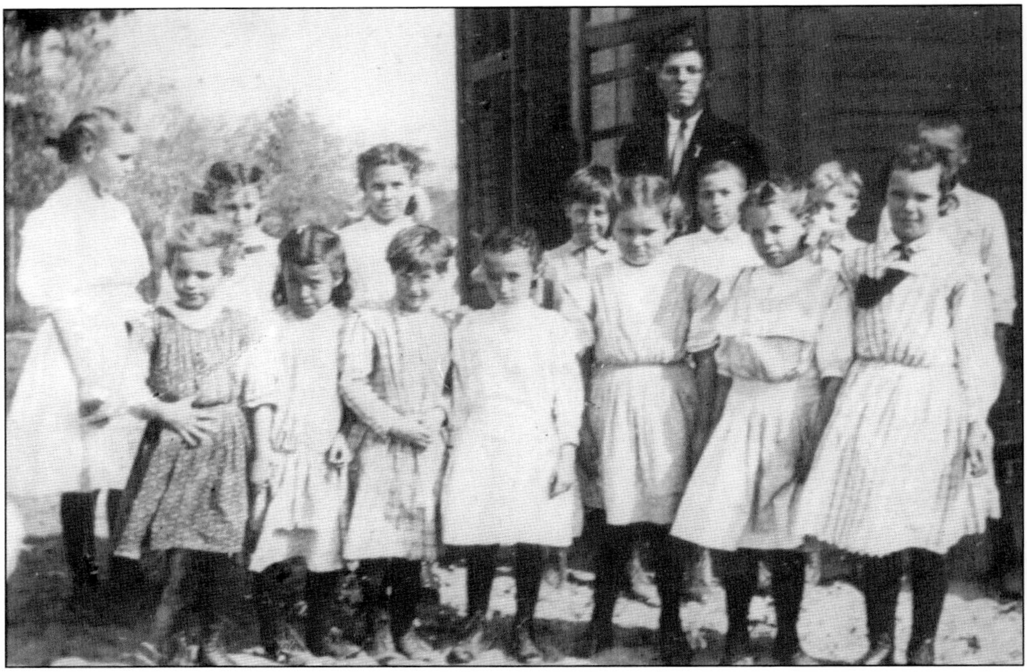

Around 1910, Clermont's one-room schoolhouse was located on Broome Street at the present site of the Clermont Woman's Club. Pictured here from left to right are (first row) Nellie Bailey, Grace Husband, Lorene Smith, Dorothy Hooks, Edith Bailey, Susie Johnson, and Isla Mims; (second row) Beth Hooks, Florence Johnson, "Bim" Smith, Donald Husband, Lamar Mims, and two unidentified. Teacher Wesley Knightis standing in the back right. (Courtesy of Cooper Memorial Library Association.)

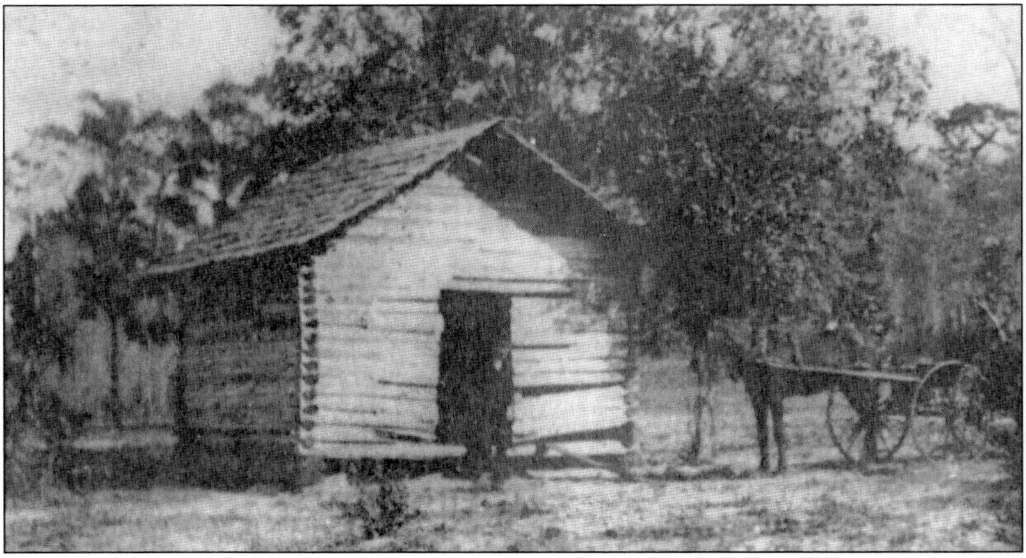

This 1882 photograph shows Clermont's schoolhouse before Lake County was formed. The school was near the present-day intersection of Highways 50 and 27. The first teacher was the wife of Thomas Hooks, the man who brokered the 1884 sale of land to Clermont's original four investors. She had 12 students, and the school term was about five months long. (Courtesy of Harold Cummings.)

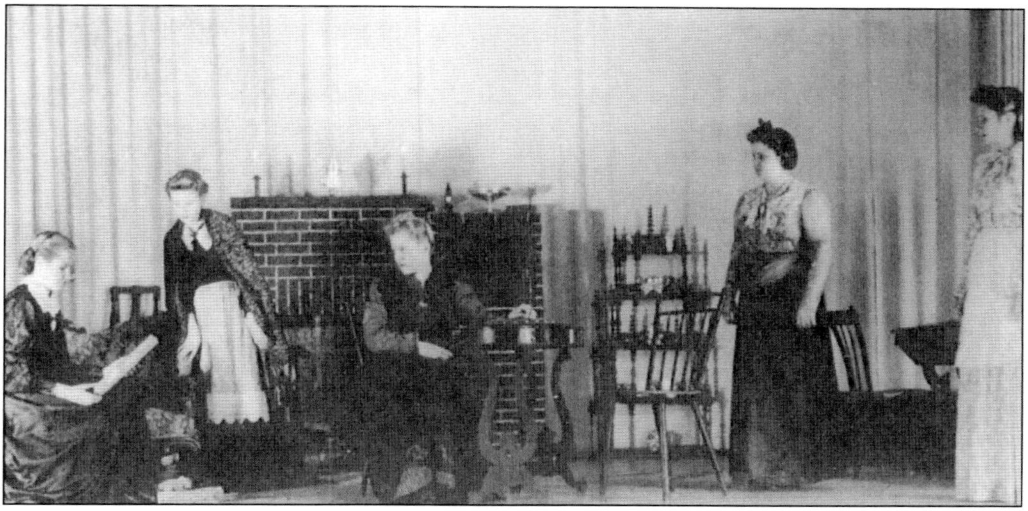

During World War II, some older male students and teachers, such as coach A. J. "Happy" Hayes, were away in the military. This 1945 photograph shows the cast of the senior play, *Ladies in Retirement*. (Courtesy of the *Clerola*.)

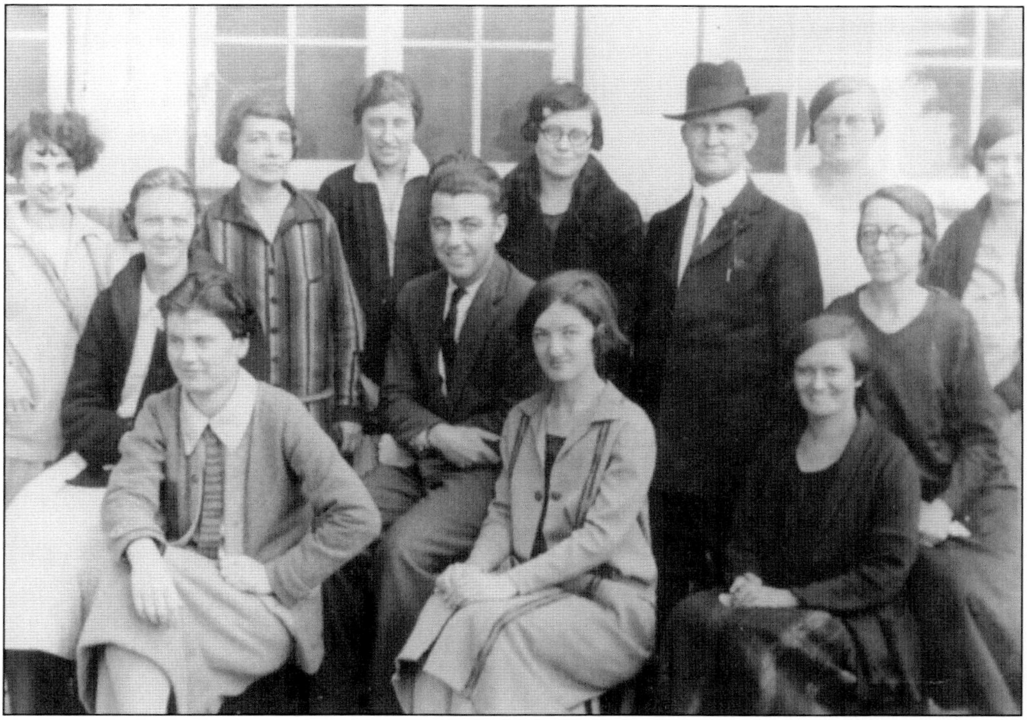

Professor D. M. Halsey (third row, fifth from left) was Clermont School's sixth principal, serving from 1924 to 1926. The other 1925–1926 faculty members from left to right are (first row) Bernice Johnson, Anna Olivenbaum Braddock, and Lelia Lassiter; (second row) Wilma Kay, ? Vincent, and Edna LaVeigne; (third row) two unidentified, Lila Johnson, unidentified, Halsey, Lottie Baker, and Mary Sammons. (Courtesy of Cooper Memorial Library Association.)

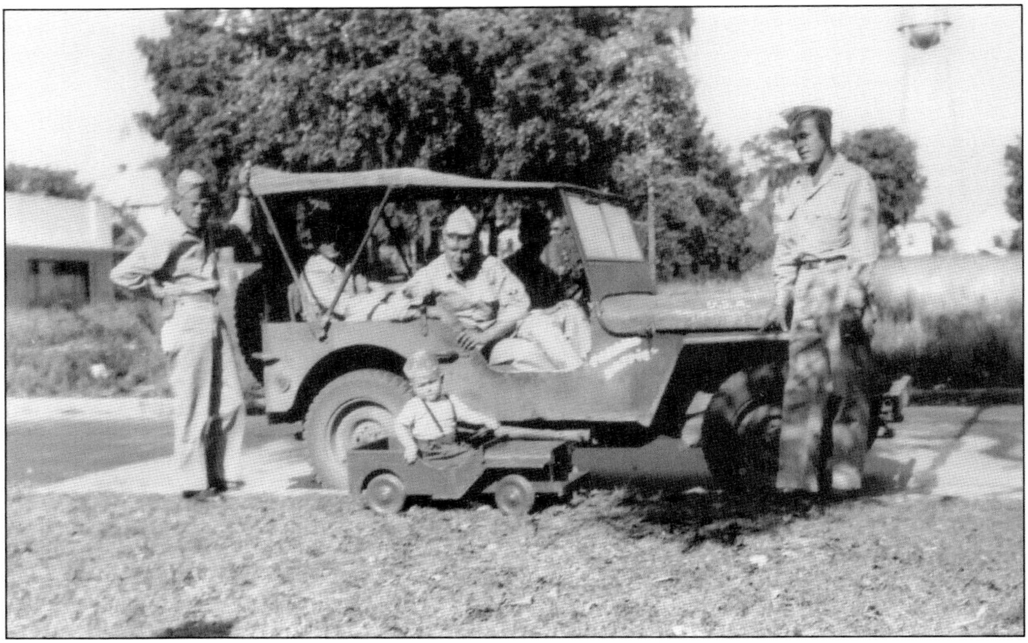

During World War II, a soldier stationed in Clermont coached the high school football team, and residents experienced blackouts to protect the city from potential enemy aerial raids. Clermont five-and-dime store owner Earle Winston made a small Jeep for Bob Hadley, the boy seen in this photograph. Some Signal Corps soldiers saw the child riding along Seventh Street and asked that the boy's aunt take a picture. (Courtesy of Jo Ann House Seaver.)

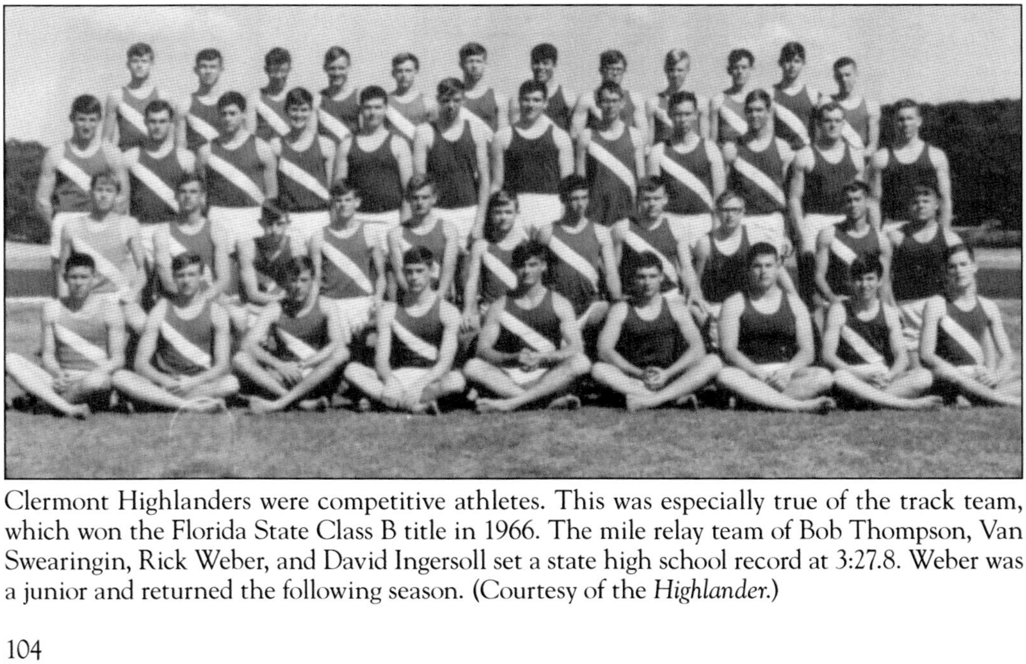

Clermont Highlanders were competitive athletes. This was especially true of the track team, which won the Florida State Class B title in 1966. The mile relay team of Bob Thompson, Van Swearingin, Rick Weber, and David Ingersoll set a state high school record at 3:27.8. Weber was a junior and returned the following season. (Courtesy of the *Highlander*.)

Rev. William McKinney was the principal of Lincoln Park High School, which served the African American community from 1961 to 1967. Before that he was principal of Clermont Junior High School from 1950 to 1961. McKinney was known as a fair but firm disciplinarian. He also served as pastor of New Jacob's Baptist Church. Aurelia Cole, his daughter, served as principal of Clermont's East Ridge High School. (Courtesy of Aurelia McKinney Cole.)

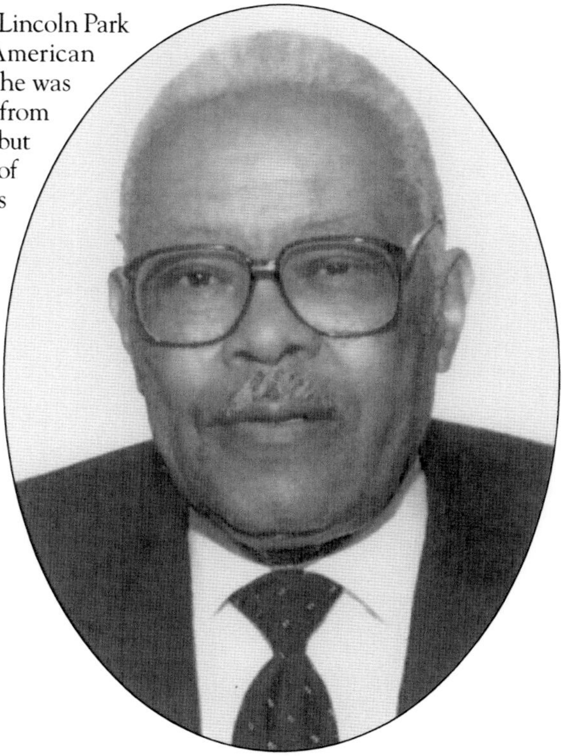

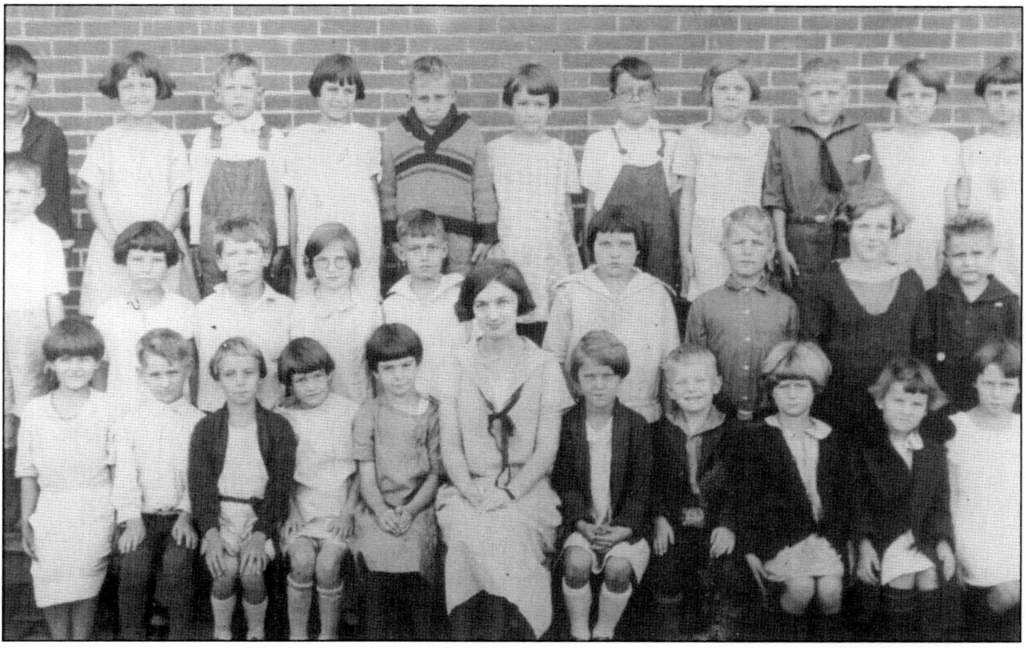

From 1915 to 1924, Clermont-Minneola's redbrick school housed all 12 grades. This 1926 photograph shows that there were still plenty of students that remained after the new high school was built. Seated at center of the first row is teacher Anna Olivenbaum Braddock. Longtime Clermont family names among the students include the Seavers, Johnsons, McClanahans, and Baileys, among others. (Courtesy of Cooper Memorial Library Association.)

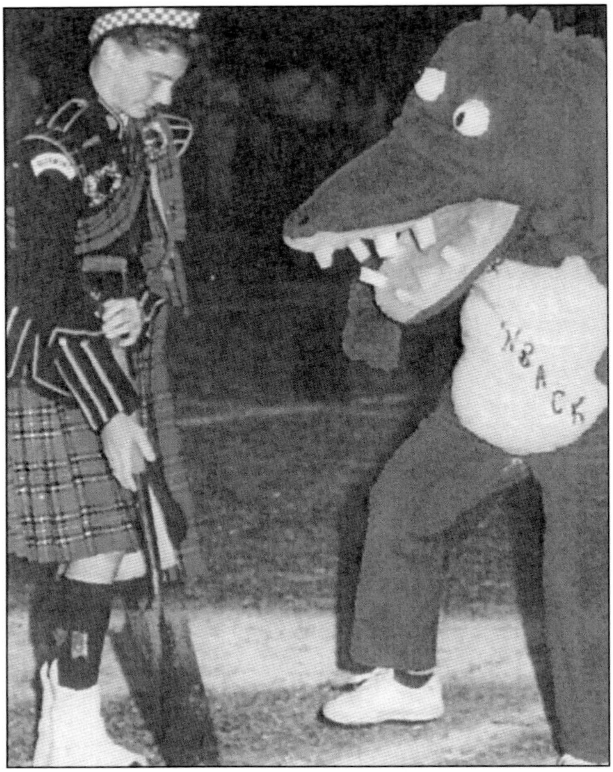

The 1992–1993 school year brought an end to Clermont High School with the merger of Clermont and Groveland High Schools the following year. The two schools had enjoyed a 57-year rivalry. After the teams' last football game in November 1992, attended by 2,500 people, both schools' mascots buried a symbolic hatchet at midfield. This was followed by the arrival of the new South Lake High School eagle mascot riding onto the field in a limousine. (Courtesy of *A Final Glance at CHS.*)

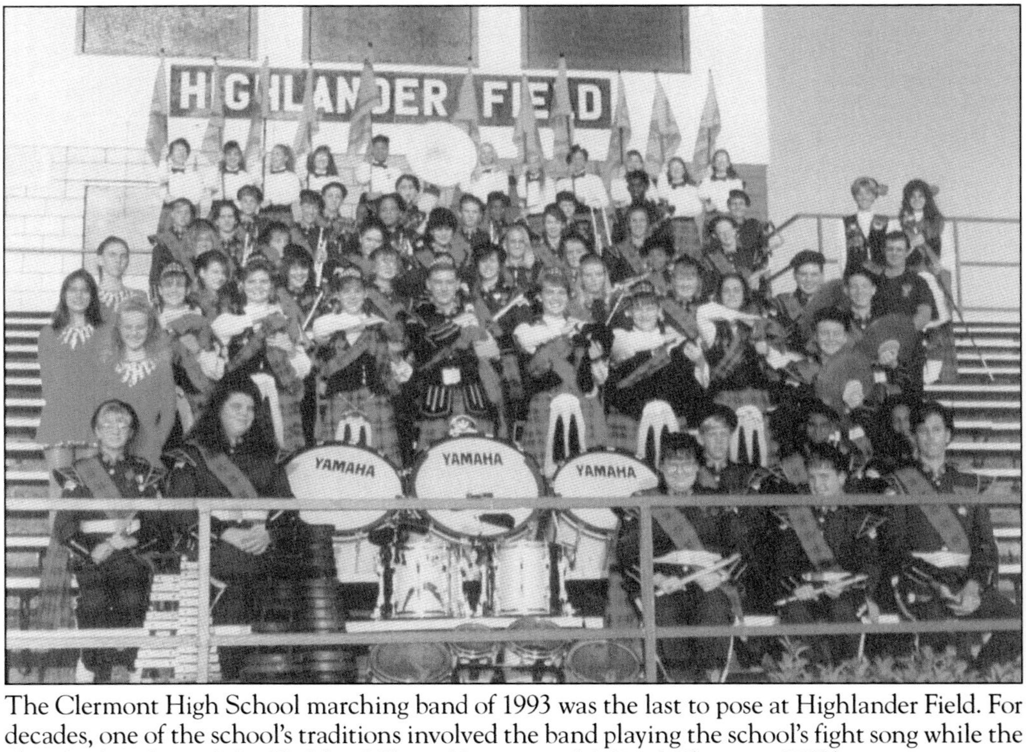


The Clermont High School marching band of 1993 was the last to pose at Highlander Field. For decades, one of the school's traditions involved the band playing the school's fight song while the cheerleaders danced the Highland Fling. (Courtesy of *A Final Glance at CHS.*)

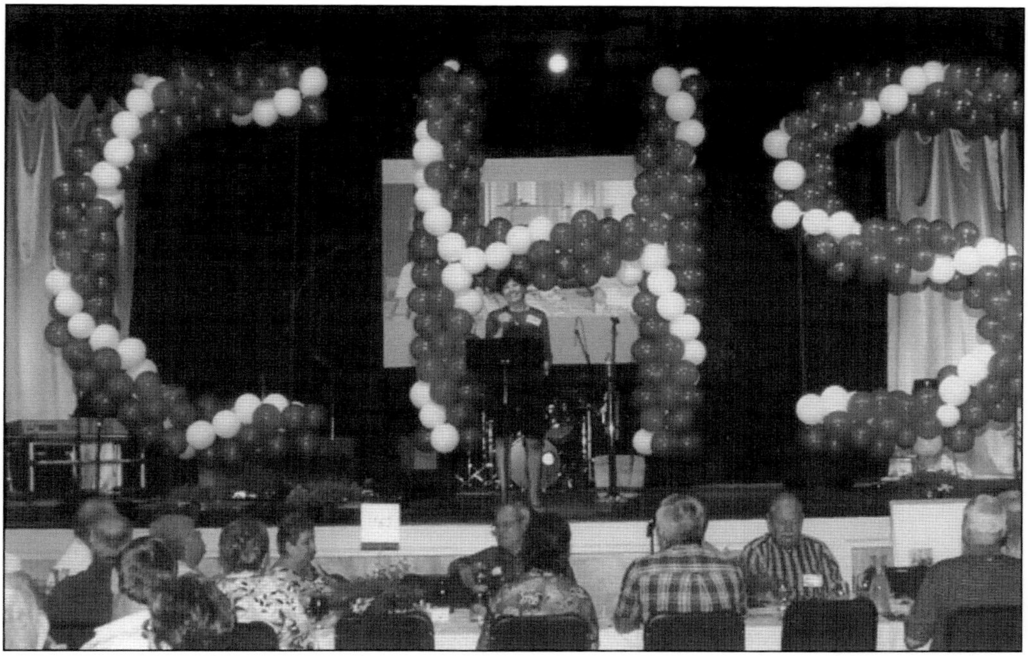

Clermont High School alumni from 1921 to 1993 have been meeting since the 1980s. The annual get-togethers for the Hilltoppers and Highlanders include a dinner, slide show, and lots of reminiscing, as the alma mater noted: "Telling of those times together, we all loved so well." (Courtesy of Karen Newman and Susan Schommer.)

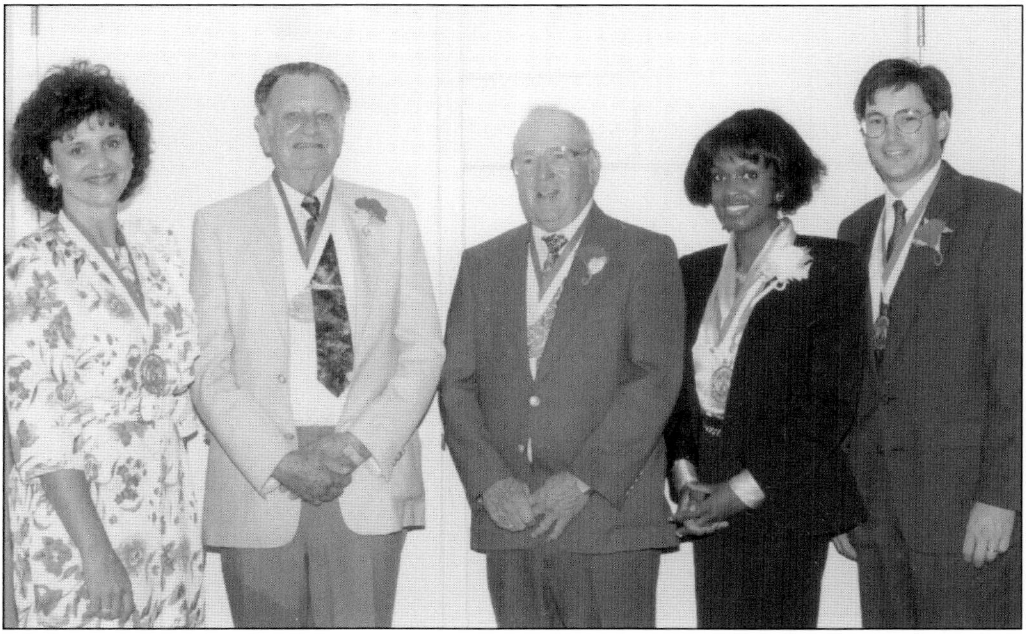

The last Clermont High School Hall of Famers were honored during graduation ceremonies in 1993. Seen here from left to right are Carmen Schoolcraft Arnold, longtime Lake County educator and administrator; E. T. Brantley, standing in for his son, inventor Thomas Brantley; Jack Gaines, former Clermont High School coach; Julia Johnson High, former public service commissioner; and Dean Saunders, former state representative. (Courtesy of Toni Bell.)

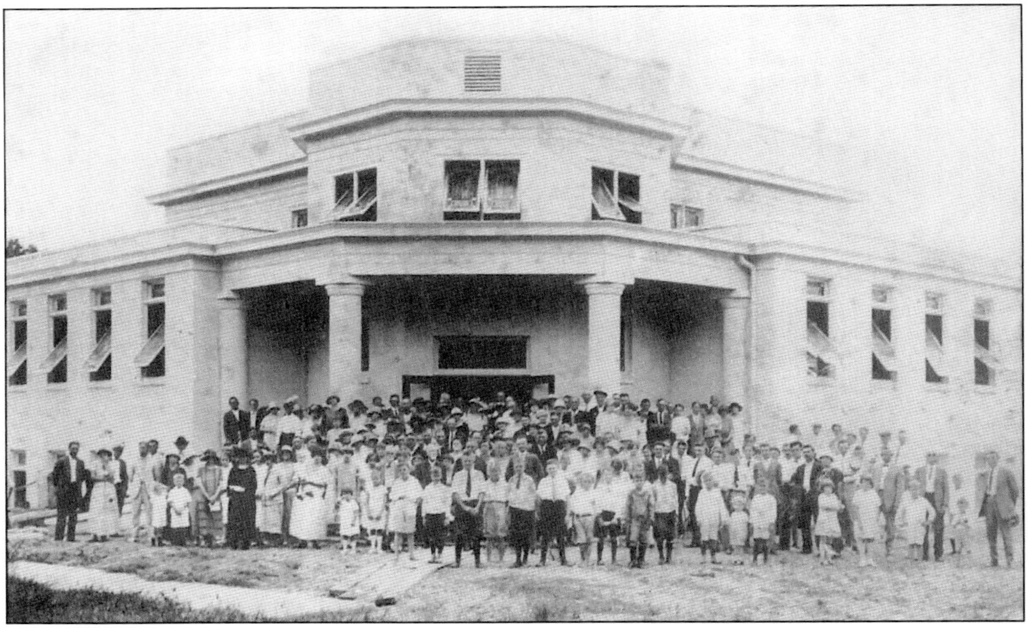

Early settlers of all denominations worshipped together each Sunday taking turns reading the Bible in a space above Wilson's General Store. In 1888, the Baptists organized with five members and built a frame church at the corner of Fifth and Montrose Streets. In 1924, members of Grace Baptist Church were photographed after the first service in their new, larger church (shown here) built at the same site. (Courtesy of Cooper Memorial Library Association.)

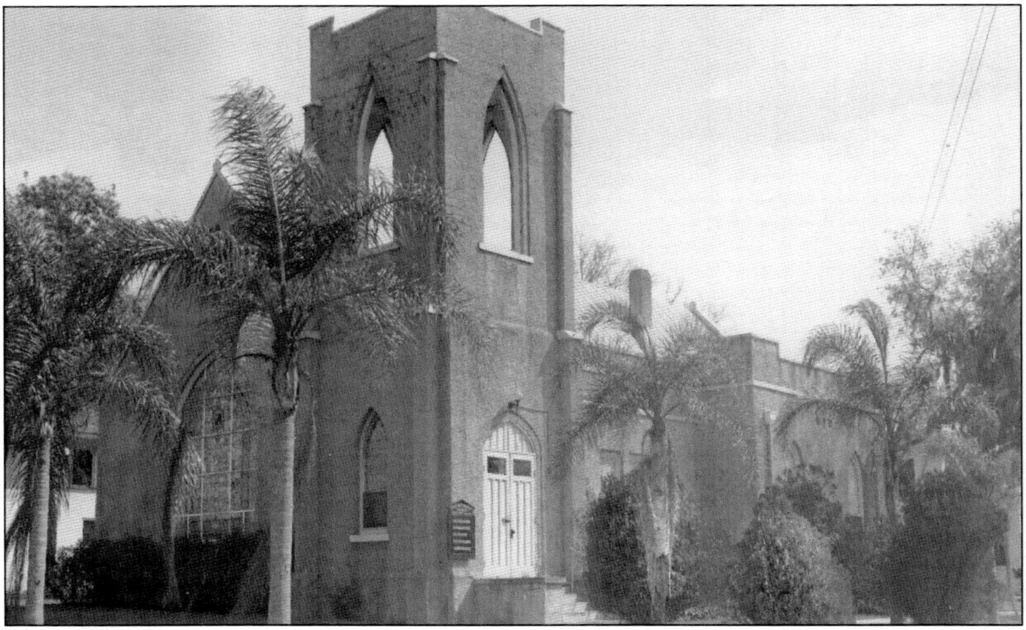

In 1866, a group of 10 Methodists led by Rev. John Hanner Jr. organized the First Methodist Church of Clermont. Five years later, the congregation built a small frame church. In 1921, church members remodeled the sanctuary, adding a bell tower and stuccoing the entire exterior, in addition to other improvements. The church was located on the southeast corner of Seventh and Broome Streets. (Courtesy of Cooper Memorial Library Association.)

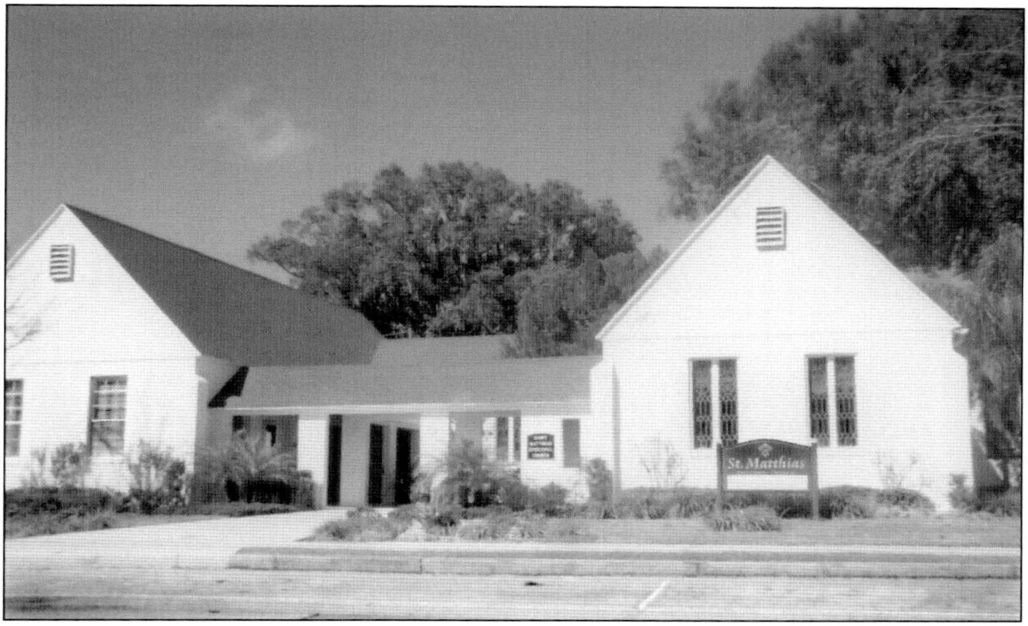


In 1943, Clermont's 13 Episcopalians were assigned a priest from Eustis, who held services every Sunday at 4:00 p.m. in the community house on Minneola Avenue. In 1945, a church member converted her garage into a chapel, and the congregation worshipped there until 1948, when land was donated for the construction of St. Matthias Episcopal Church, which still stands today. (Courtesy of Ann Dupee.)

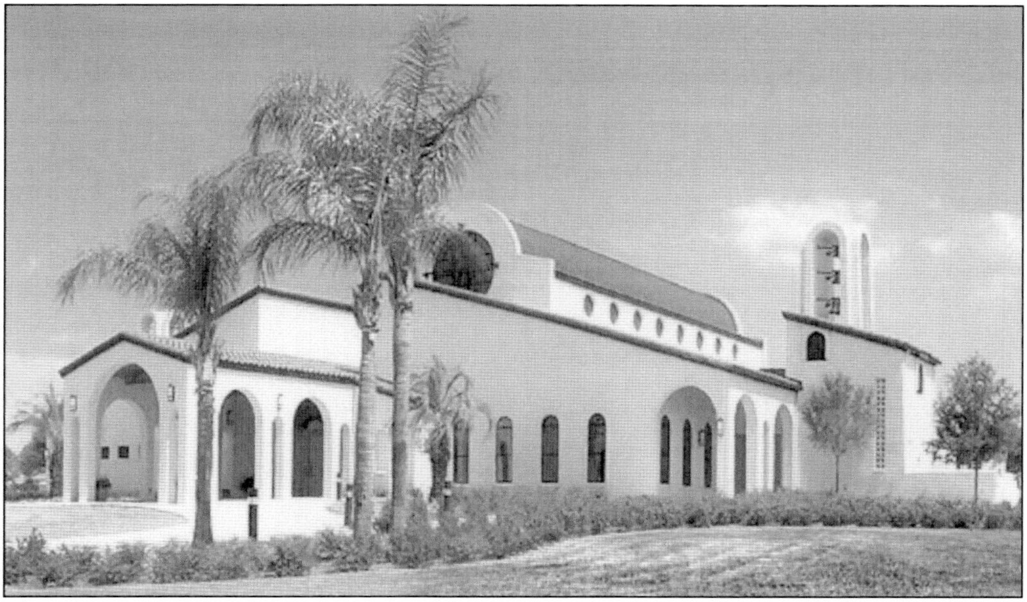

Catholic families began meeting in the homes of the Lynch, DyFrene, and Frisz families to celebrate Mass around 1910. The Pool family donated land on Lake Avenue, and a frame mission church was built there. Fifty local Catholic families celebrated their first Mass in the new church building on Christmas Day 1933. In 1961, Fr. Hugh Keane was assigned as the first pastor; two years later, the parish built a church on its current Twelfth Street property. (Photograph by Doris Bloodsworth.)

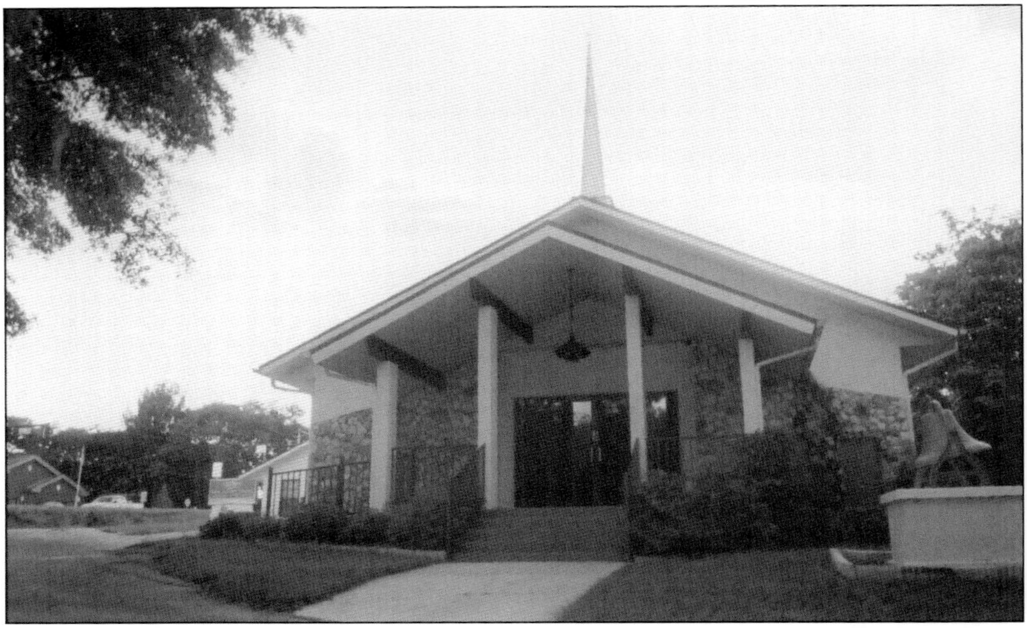

New Jacob's Chapel Missionary Baptist Church's congregation first met in a Chestnut Street home prior to building their first church on Highland Avenue in 1908. The church's early supporters included the Odum, Hilton, and Jones families. The church was dedicated on June 20, 1948. Rev. A. C. Crooms gave the dedication ceremony. The new church on Highway 50 was built in 1982. (Photograph by Doris Bloodsworth.)

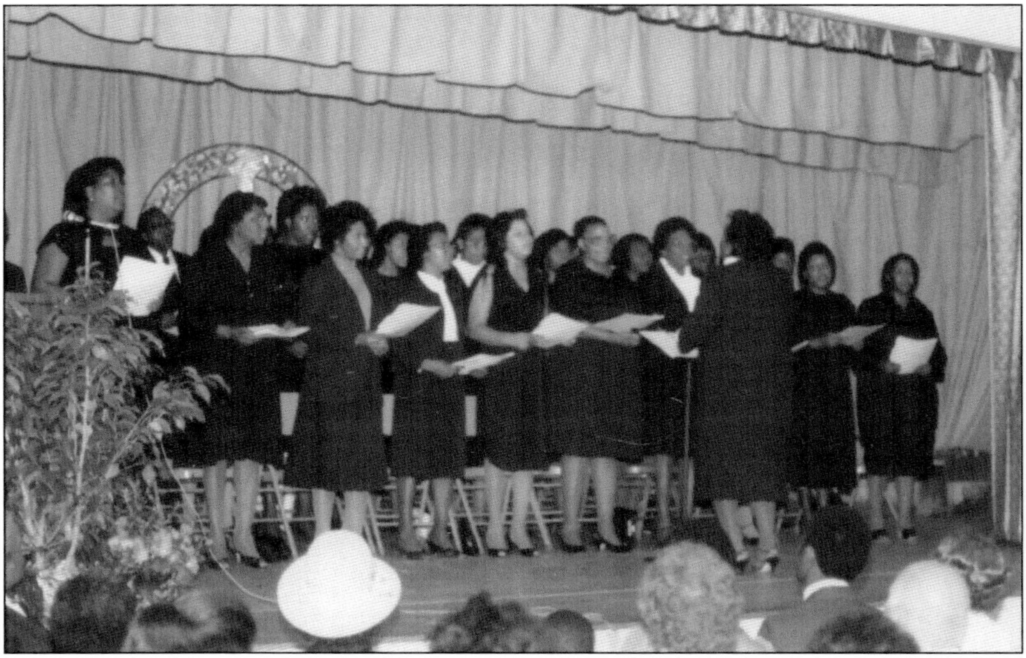

During the city's 100th anniversary celebration in 1984, church choirs combined to perform at the Clermont Centennial Soul Food Dinner. The event brought together some of the community's pioneer families such as Doc Jones and Sallie Benson, granddaughter of Clermont's first black settlers, James and Sallie Townsend. (Courtesy of Cooper Memorial Library Association.)

# *Seven*

# History Makers

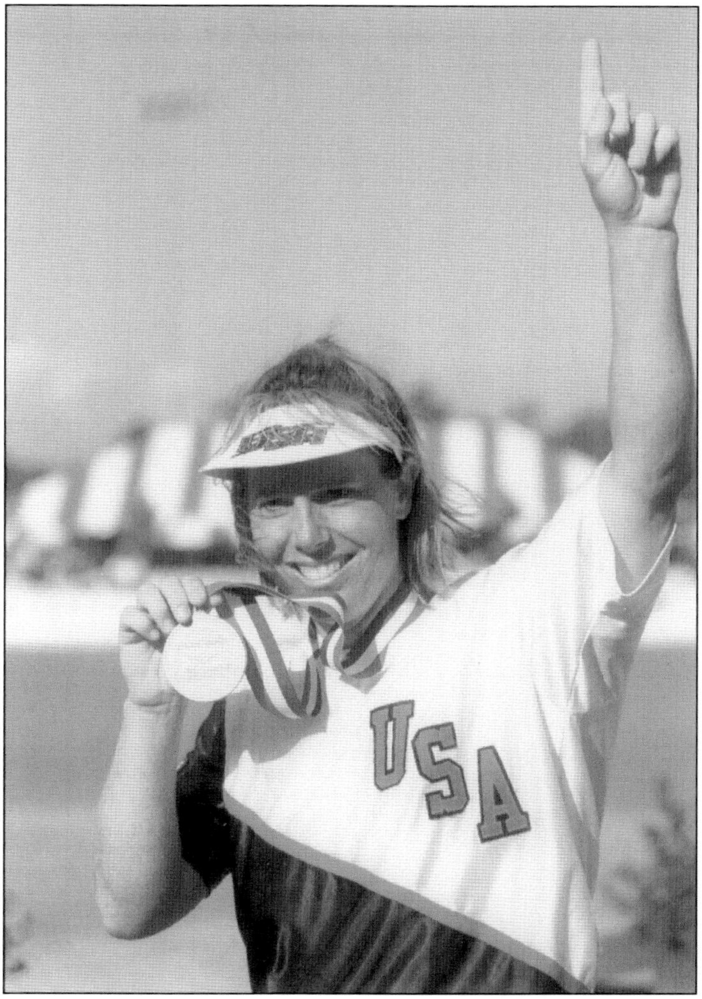

Clermont's natural beauty and lifestyle have attracted history makers such as Dr. Dot Richardson, who hit the winning home run in the 1996 Olympics. She won another gold medal in 2000. In the 1980s, she was named the NCAA's Player of the Decade. Today the softball champion and orthopedic surgeon is the medical director and head of Clermont's National Training Center. Dr. Richardson is seen here holding a gold medal from the 1999 U.S. Olympic Cup games. (Courtesy of PHOTOSPORT.)

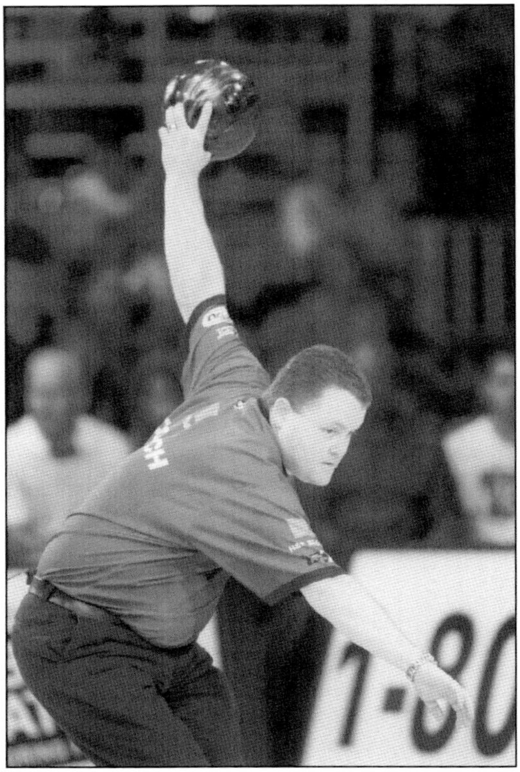

Jason Couch is the only person in history to win three back-to-back Professional Bowlers Association (PBA) Tournaments of Champions. Couch is a 15-time PBA National Tour Title Holder, was the 1992 PBA Rookie of the Year, and is ranked No. 24 on the list of the greatest players in PBA history. Clermont is also home to PBA champions Norm Duke and Randy Pedersen. (Courtesy of Jason Couch.)

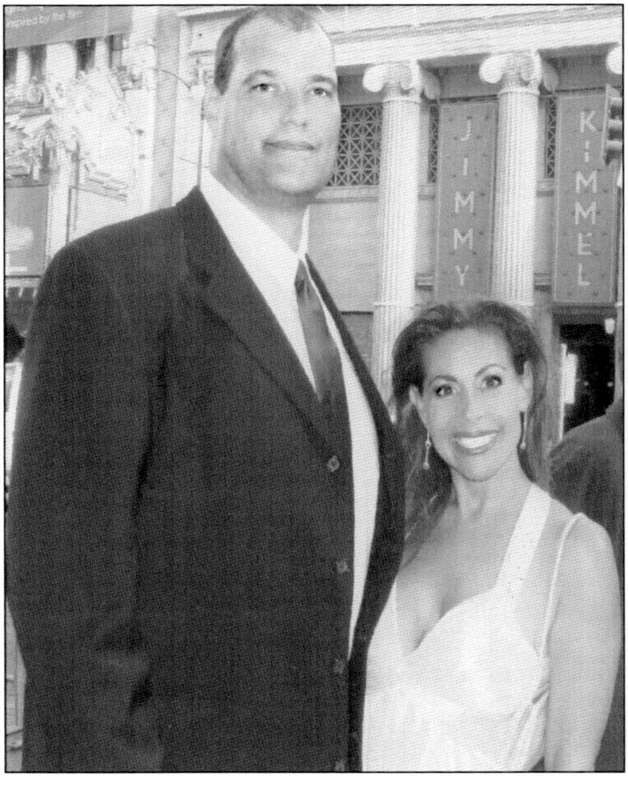


Jeff Chase, who was born Jeffrey Sniffen in New Jersey, has helped put Clermont on the map through his roles as an actor, stuntman, and football star. Chase played college football at West Virginia University and professionally in the Arena Football League before turning to acting. Chase has appeared in dozens of television programs and movies. He and his wife, Kimberly, are shown at the 2009 *Star Trek* premiere. As a stuntman, he was once stabbed accidentally during the filming of *Dexter.* (Courtesy of Jeff Chase.)

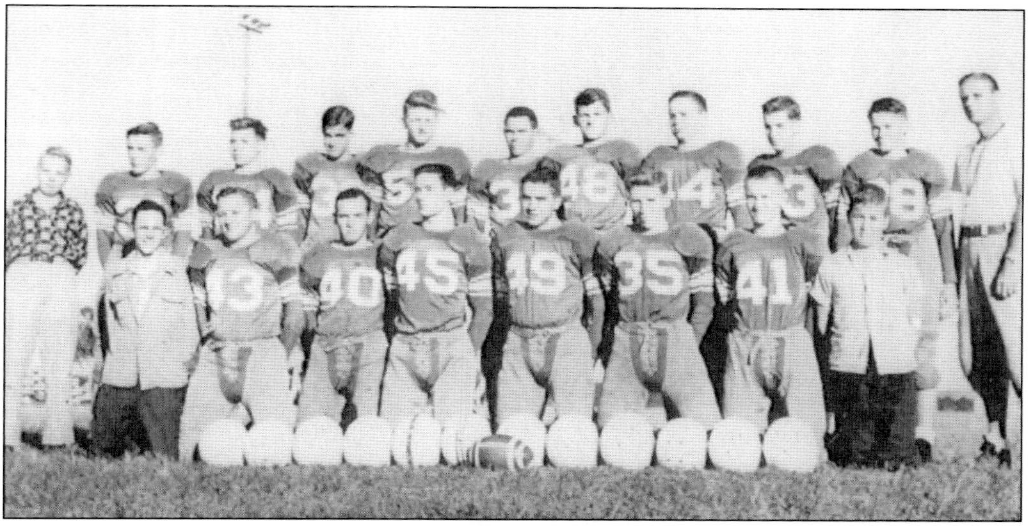

Clermont High School alumnus Harold Cummings, No. 49 (first row, fifth from left), holds the state record for the most touchdowns scored in a single high school football game. In 1953, he scored 12 touchdowns against St. James High School. Cummings played halfback on the Highlander squad and ran 100 yards in 9.9 seconds. He played football at Florida State University with Burt Reynolds and Lee Corso. (Courtesy of the *Highlander*.)

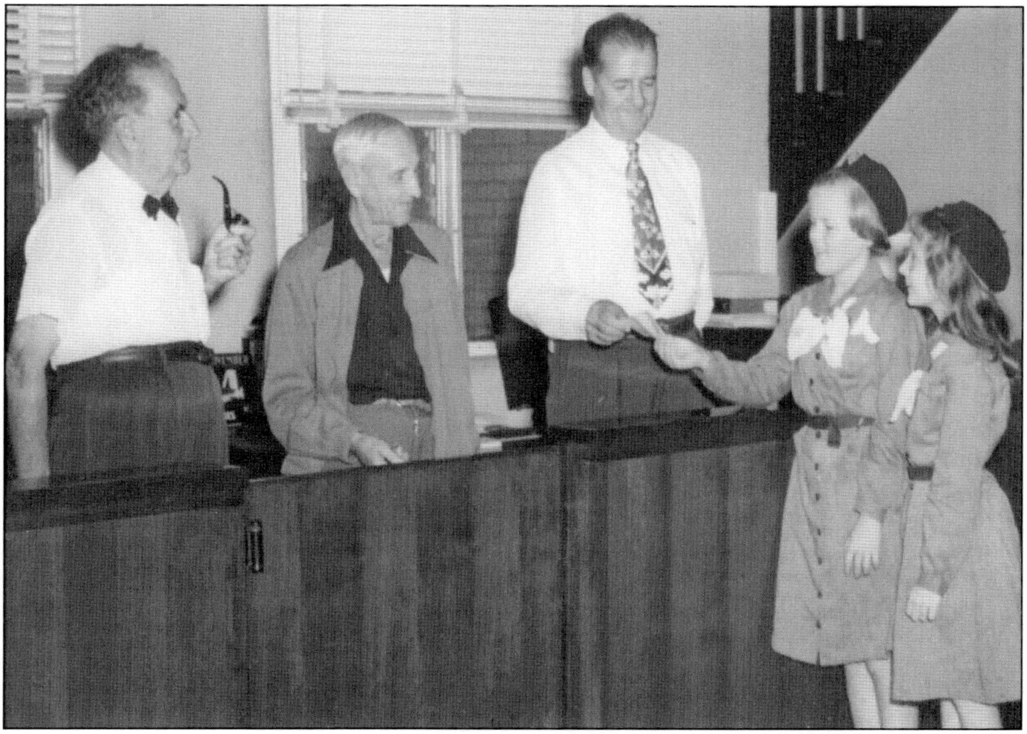

Charles Short (left), a retired General Motors researcher, held almost 400 patents. After retiring in 1929 to Clermont, he conducted the world's largest citrus experiments. He was president of the bank for 25 years and is pictured here with Harry Stokes (center) and an unidentified man (right) in 1955 presenting a check to Glenna Middleton (left) and Marty Fields to kick off the annual Girl Scout cookie sales. (Courtesy of Glenna Scaife.)

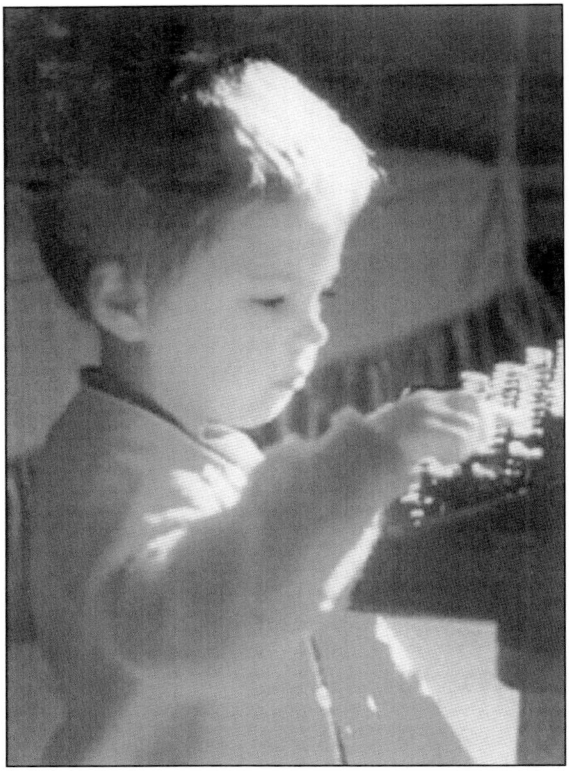

Kate DiCamillo was raised in Clermont and showed inclinations even as a child of loving to write. DiCamillo is the author of *Because of Winn-Dixie*, a Newberry Honor book, and *The Tale of Despereaux,* winner of the Newberry Medal. Both books were made into popular movies. DiCamillo currently lives in Minneapolis, Minnesota, but has family members still living in Clermont. (Courtesy of Winding Oak and Candlewick Press.)

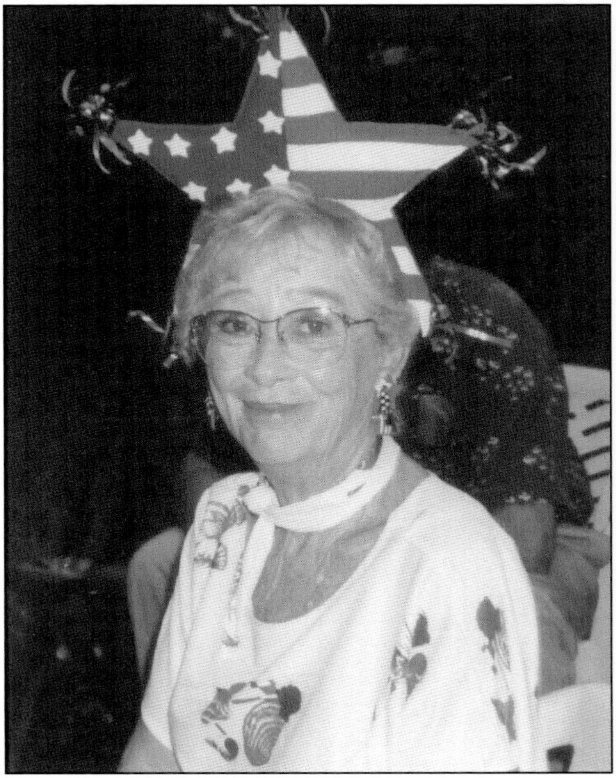

Ann Dupee and her husband, George, bought the *South Lake Press*, where she worked as editor and later publisher. Previously, she was the advance publicist for the Ice Capades. She was the first inductee to the Lake County Business Hall of Fame in addition to being inducted into the Lake County Women's Hall of Fame. She served on the Clermont City Council and library board as well as the county and state League of Cities and was president of the South Lake Kiwanis Club, South Lake Chamber of Commerce, and Beta Theta ESA. (Courtesy of Ann Dupee.)

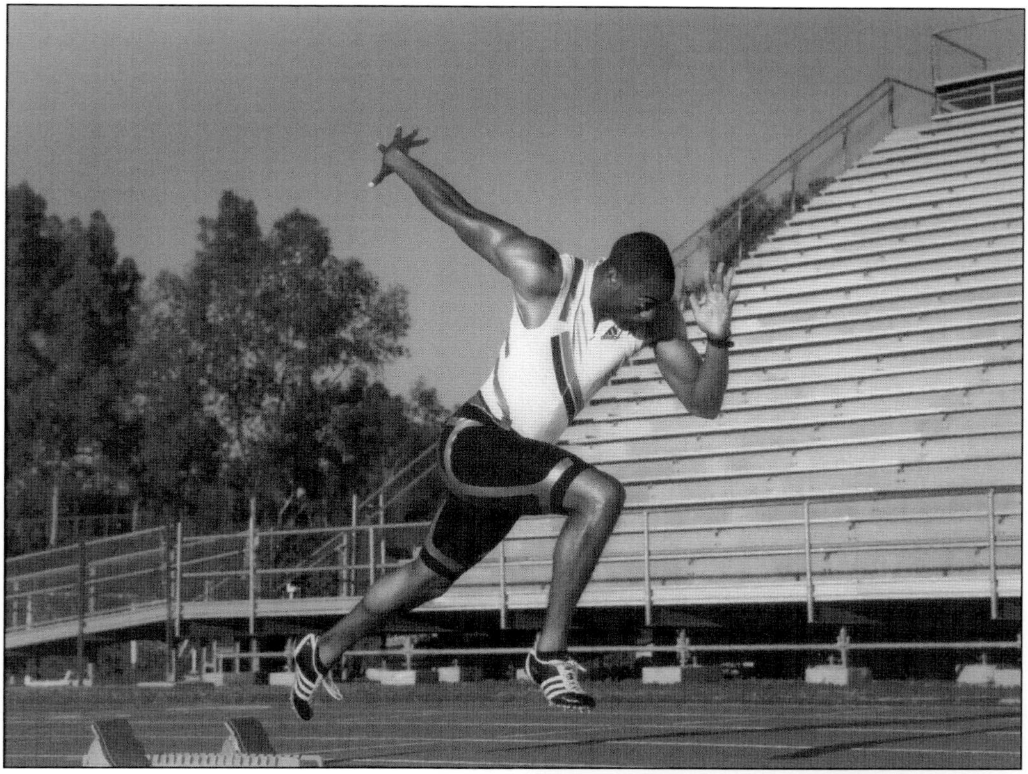

Clermont resident Tyson Gay is one of the fastest men on the planet, holding the American record for the 100-meter dash. His athletic achievements include a silver medal in the 2009 World Championships, a championship at the 2008 U.S. Olympic Trials, a world first-place ranking at the 100- and 200-meter events in 2007, and the title of 2007 International Association of Athletics Federations (IAAF) Male Athlete of the Year. (Courtesy of adidas.)

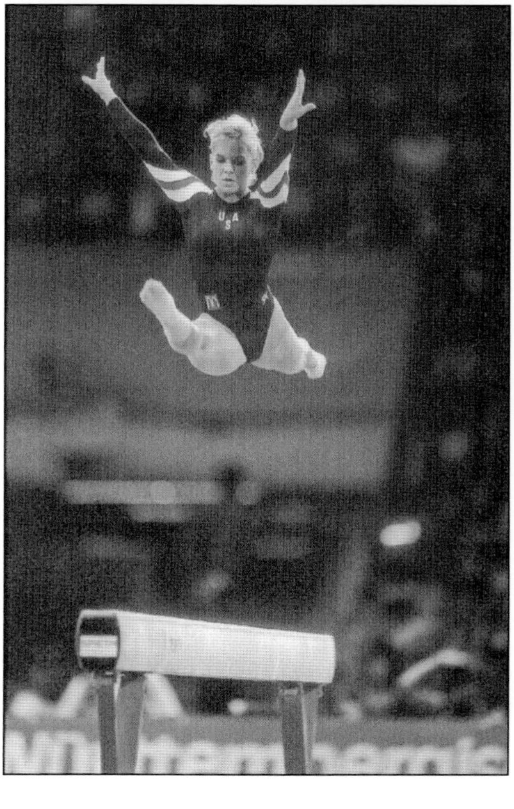

Brandy Johnson-Scharpf is an Olympic gymnast, gymnastics judge, stuntwoman, and owner of Brandy Johnson's Global Gymnastics in Clermont. In 2000, she was inducted into the USA Gymnastics Hall of Fame. At the 1988 Olympics, her 10th-place finish was the highest for an American gymnast. She worked as a stunt double in Hollywood before moving to Clermont. (Courtesy of USA Gymnastics.)

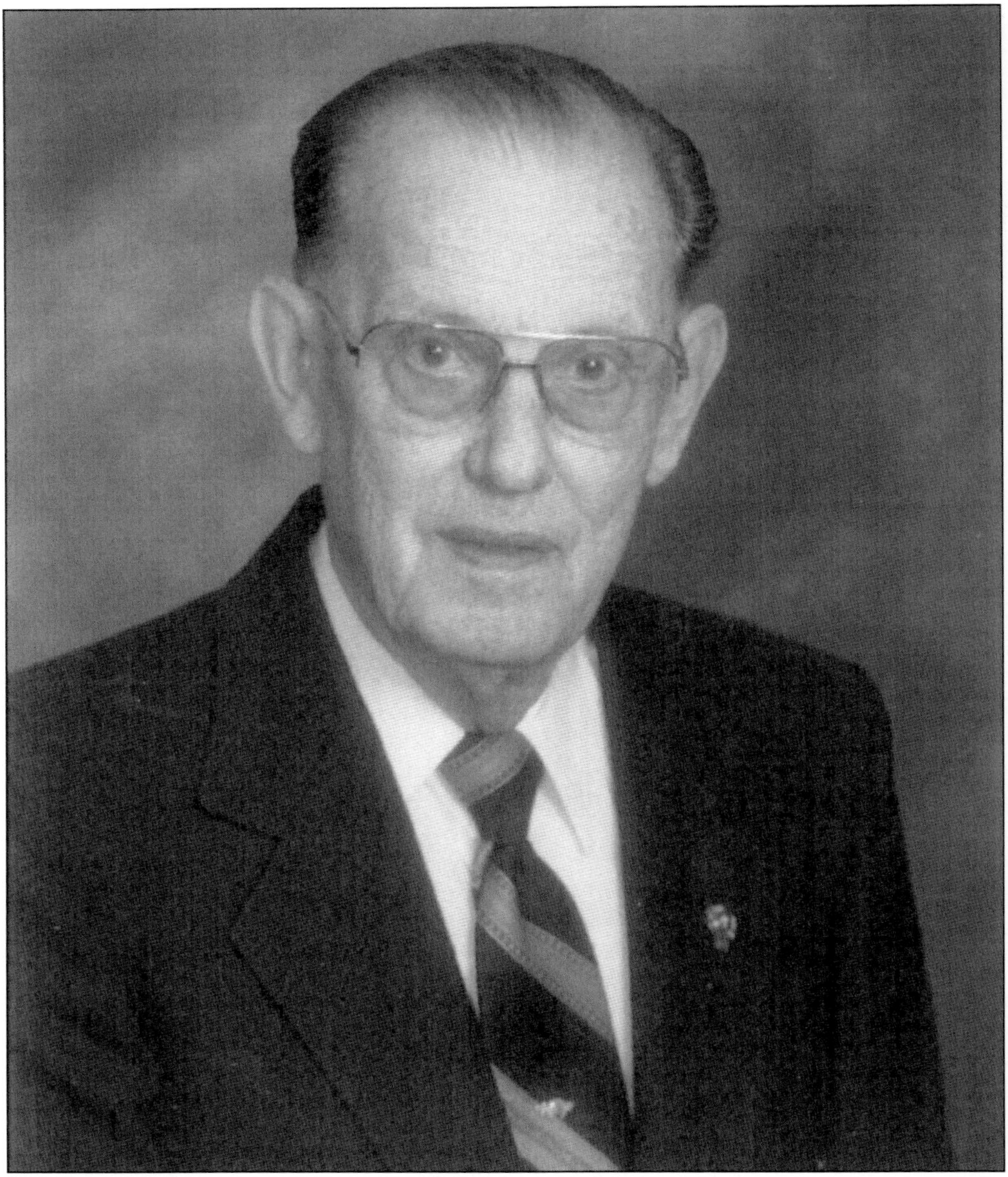

Robert "Oakley" Seaver was known as "Mr. Clermont." When he died in 2006, a friend observed, "I heard someone say that the measure of a man is what's in his heart; and based on that, Oakley was a giant of a man." Seaver was a descendant of the city's original settlers. He was a lifelong resident except when serving in World War II. He was Clermont's postmaster for 32 years and was named Florida's Postmaster of the Year. He was active in the Clermont Kiwanis Club where he had 59 years of perfect attendance and founded the Clermont Kiwanis Foundation. His other civic accomplishments include serving as president of the South Lake County Historical Society and founding Friends of Cooper Memorial Library and the South Lake Jaycees. He served on the South Lake Hospital Board for decades, was a charter member of the South Lake Chamber of Commerce, and was chosen to be the grand marshal in the city's centennial anniversary parade in 1984. Oakley Seaver Drive was named in his honor the year before he died. (Courtesy of the Oakley Seaver family.)

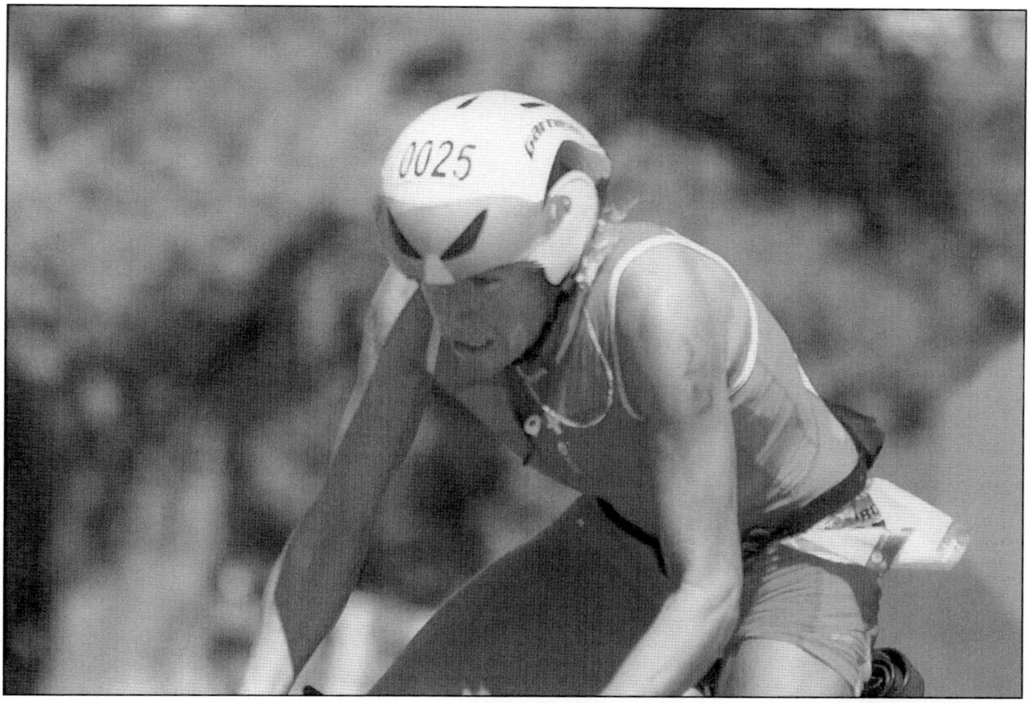


Clermont's designation as the "World's Triathlon Destination" has drawn many world-class athletes who now call the city their home. One of them is German-born Nina Kraft, seen here riding in the Ford Ironman Louisville Triathlon. She has won first place in at least 15 competitions, including the International France Championship, Ironman Brazil, Half-Ironman St. Croix, and Ironman South Africa. (Courtesy of Tom Briggs.)

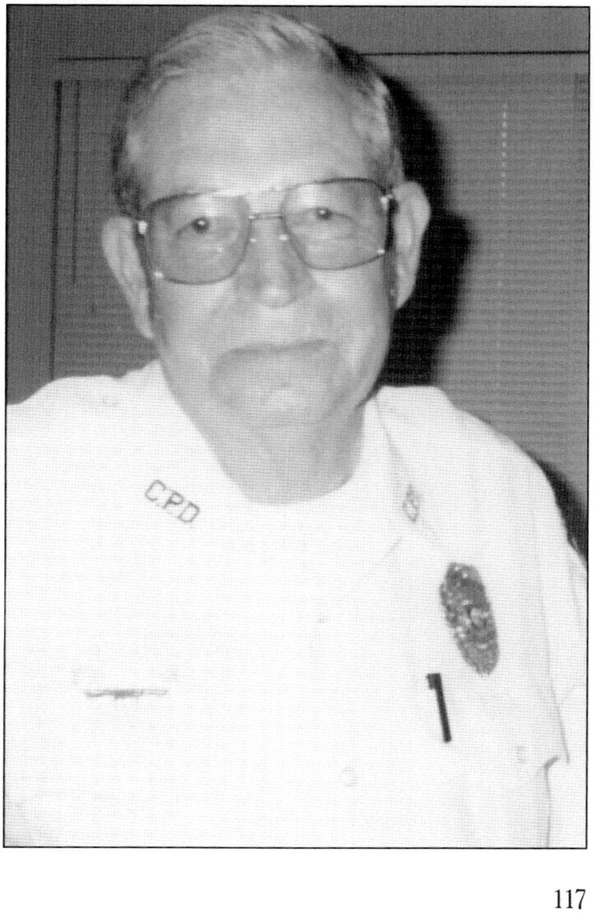


When Clermont police chief Prentice Tyndal retired in 1996 after 37 years as the city's top cop, he held the record as the longest-serving police chief in the nation. He received awards from Pres. Bill Clinton and Florida governor Lawton Chiles. The City of Clermont gave him the 1992 Crown Victoria police car he drove during his last four years of service. (Courtesy of Ann Dupee.)

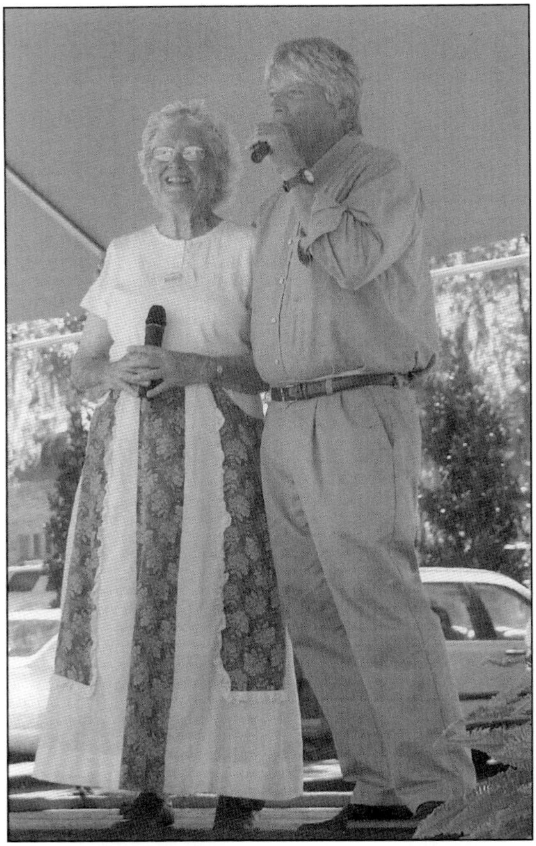

Mayor Hal Turville presented Dolores Gano Walker with a proclamation naming her the honorary historian of Clermont. Walker is a descendant of Archibald Gano, one of the city's earliest settlers and signer of Clermont's incorporation papers in 1891. She has been active in the South Lake County Historical Society, helping to coordinate the city's 125th anniversary celebrations and the restoration of buildings in Clermont's Historic Village. (Courtesy of Linda Charlton.)

U.S. Masters swimming champion Charles Weatherbee displays the All-American plaques he received while swimming competitively in 1952 and as a master swimmer 50 years later. Weatherbee has earned an international reputation, setting records and winning numerous gold medals around the world. In the World Police and Fire Games, he has never lost the 200-meter medley and broke the record for the 100-meter fly. During a local triathlon, he outswam an alligator that followed him across Lake Minneola. (Courtesy of Charles Weatherbee.)

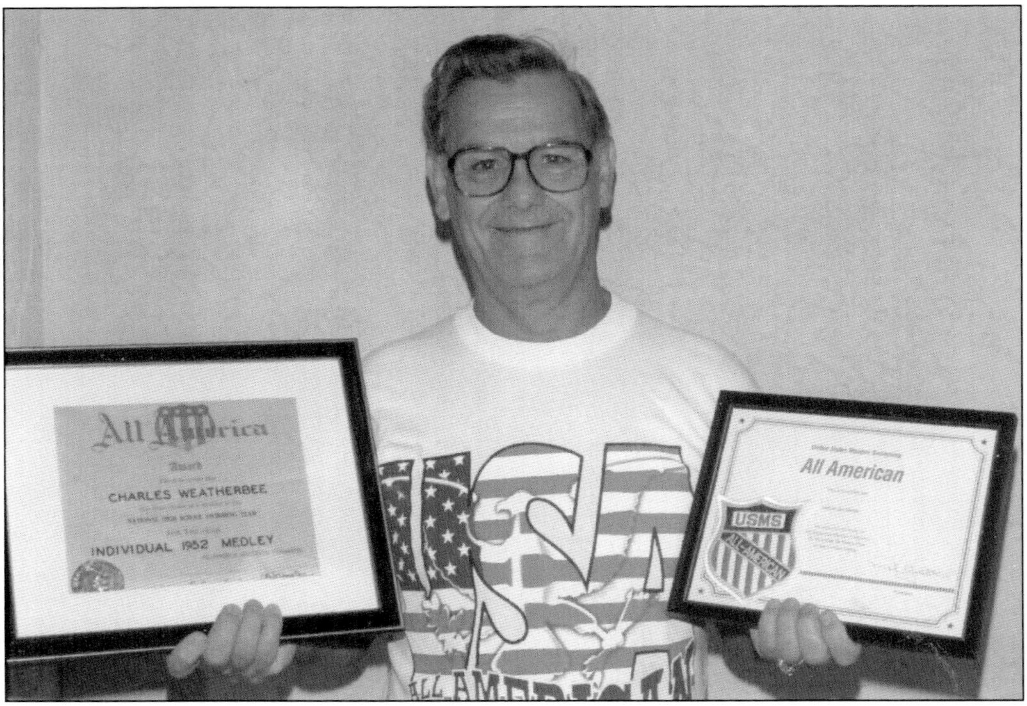

# *Eight*

# Milestone Celebrations

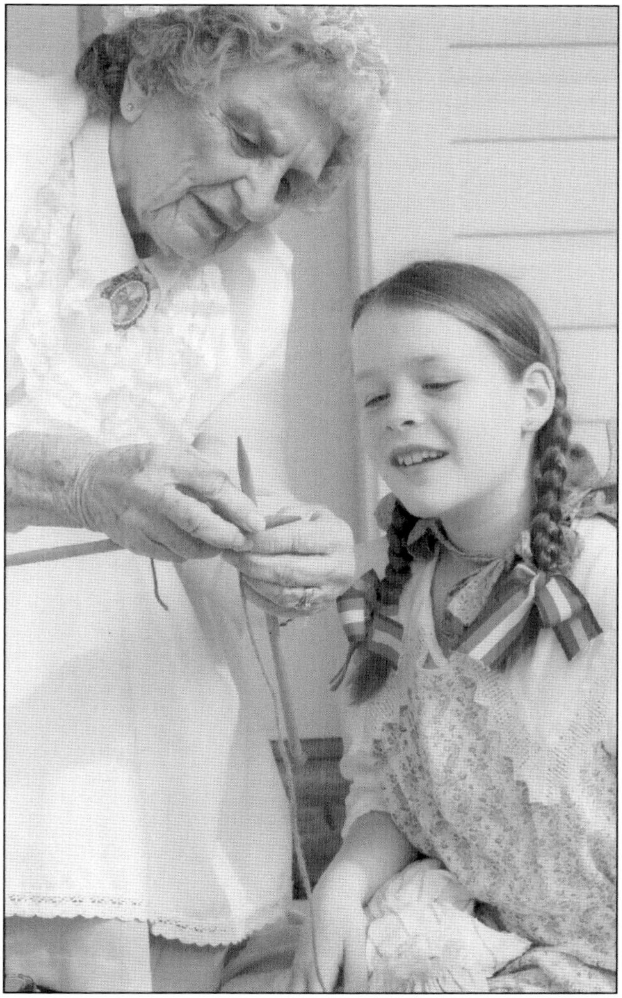

Proud of its heritage, Clermont residents held major celebrations in 1984 and 2009 when the city honored its 100th and 125th anniversaries. The 125th centennial in October 2009 featured a Pioneer Day with tours at Historic Village and folk craft demonstrations. Janet Thomas, a member of the South Lake County Historical Society, showed eight-year-old Mallory Spivey how to knit. (Courtesy of Bonnie Gearhart.)

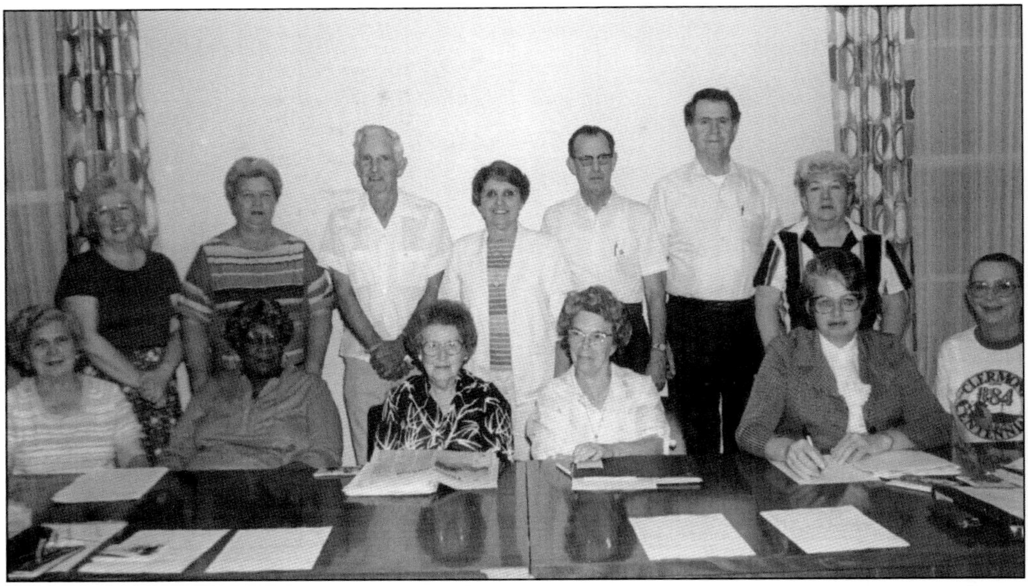

In 1984, centennial committee members worked many months to plan activities that celebrated Clermont's 100th anniversary. From left to right are (first row) Ella Mae Sheldon, Sallie Benson, Miriam Johnson, Frances Oswalt, Bonnie Ray, and Ann Dupee; (second row) Lily Nichols, Virginia Caughell, Dick Stokes, Dolores Vander Meer, Oakley Seaver, Elbert Richie, and Jean Winston. (Courtesy of Ann Dupee.)

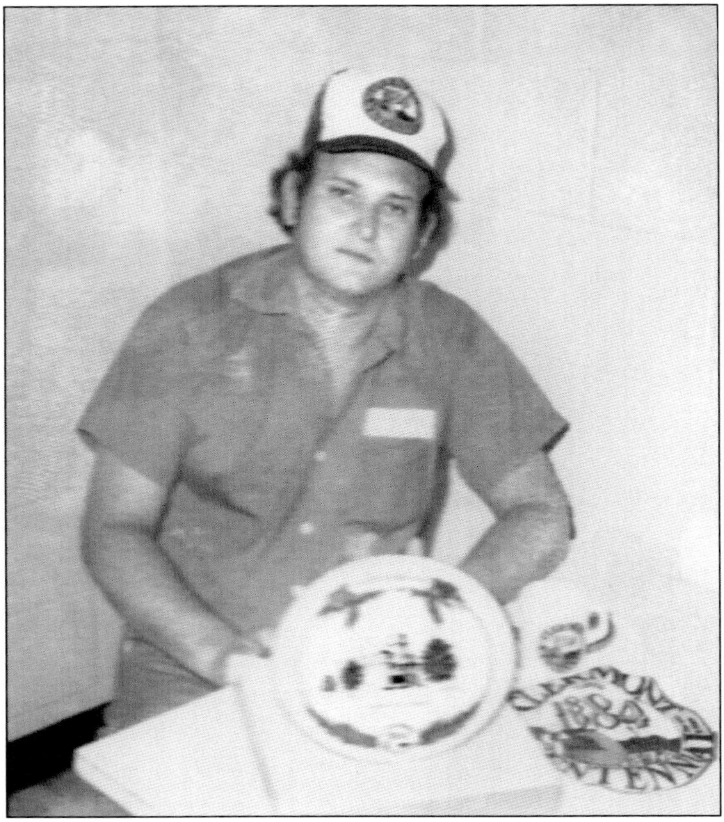

The centennial committee held a contest for the best logo creation. The result was a colorful design created by a veteran commercial artist. Ironically, artist Steve Monn had never seen Clermont and had drawn the design while behind bars for drug trafficking. He eventually settled in Clermont and successfully started *ACTIVE South Lake Magazine*. (Courtesy of Ann Dupee.)

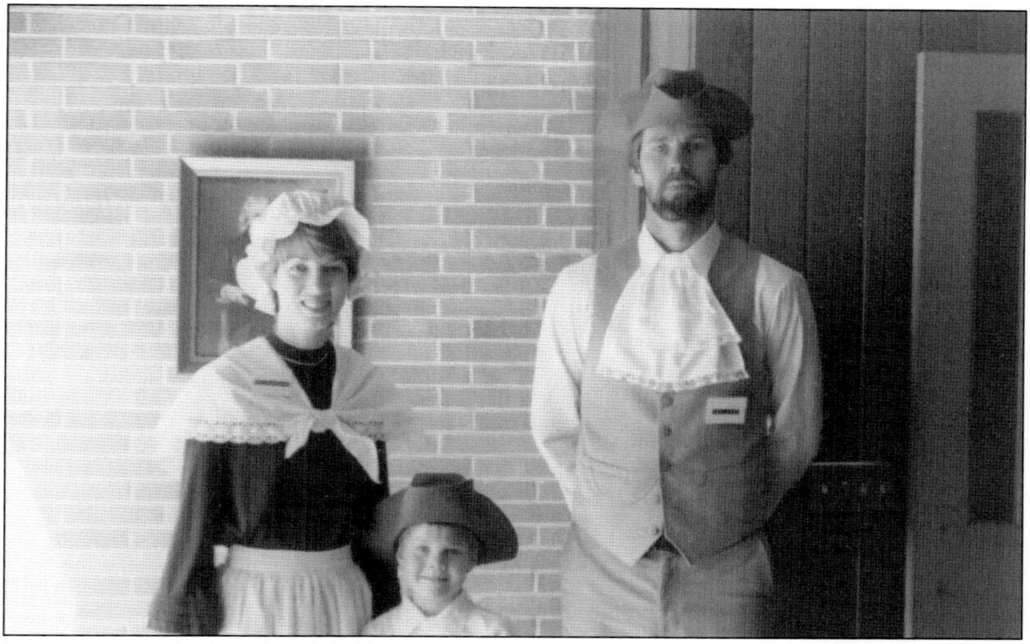

First United Methodist Church held Heritage Sunday to commemorate the city's 100th anniversary. The Bishop family dressed in patriotic clothing. Carle Bishop, the city's fire chief, is a sixth-generation descendant of the Bishop and Cooper families who were among Clermont's earliest settlers. His wife, Wendy, and son Nathaniel are also shown in their period attire. Some church members came in antique cars. (Courtesy of Cooper Memorial Library Association.)

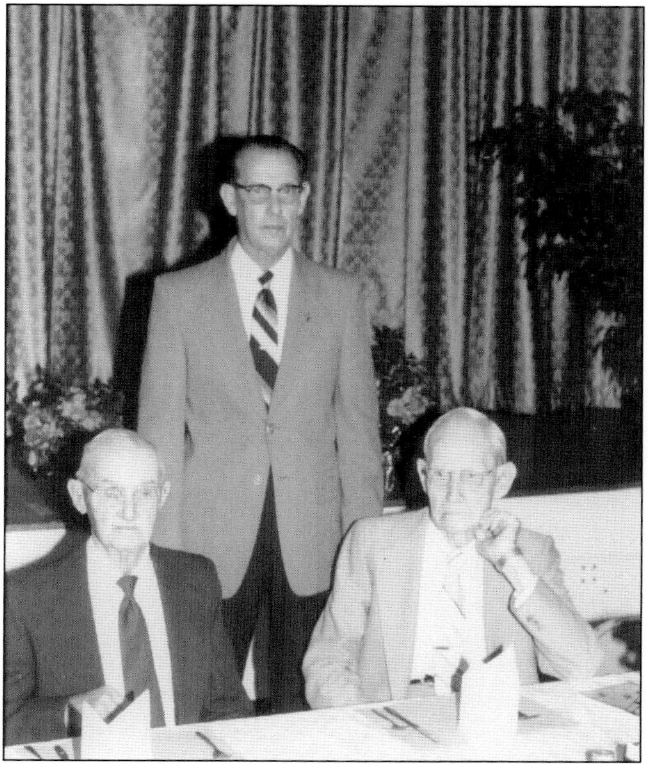

The chamber of commerce sponsored the Orange Blossom Breakfast to mark the city's 100th birthday party. Among the guests were (from left to right) Max Hooks, Oakley Seaver, and Percy Seaver—all of whom were related to the city's earliest pioneer, Herring Hooks. The breakfast featured *Clermont: Gem of the Hills* authors Miriam Johnson and Rosemary Young. (Courtesy of Cooper Memorial Library Association.)

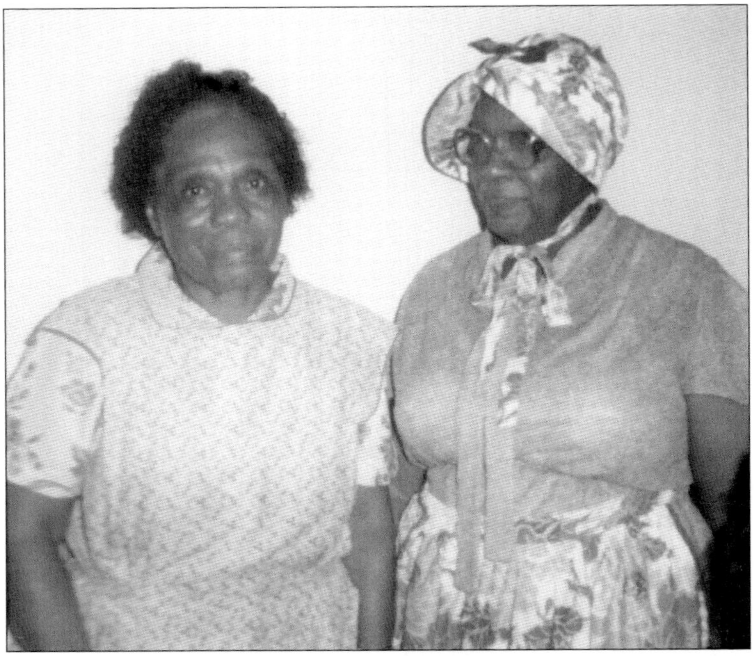

Clermont's African American community held a centennial Soul Food Dinner that included live choir music and a chance to dress in period costume. The dinner also recalled early African American settlers such as James and Sallie Townsend, the grandparents of Sallie Benson (right), and the family of Mattie Odum Jones (left). Benson taught at Lincoln Park High School prior to integration. (Courtesy of Cooper Memorial Library Association.)

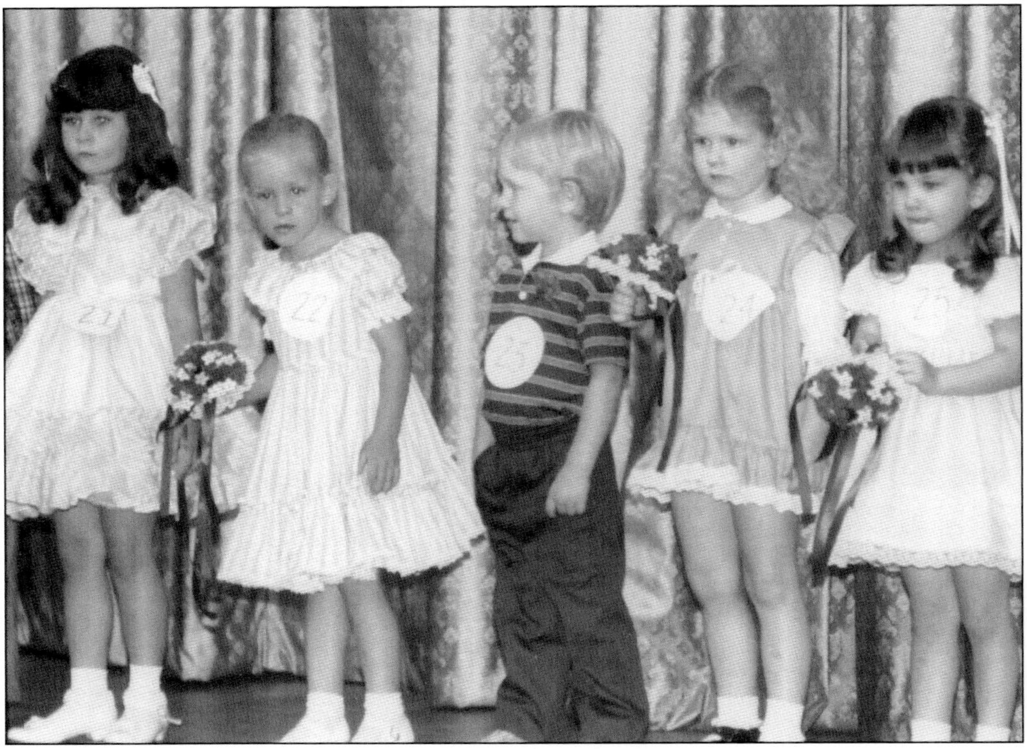

Children competed in the "Little Mr. and Miss Clermont" contest during the centennial. The winners got to ride in the big parade that served as the 100th anniversary celebration's grand finale. From left to right are Kelly Graham, Rachel Miller, Aaron Aycock, Carrie Breeden, and Tiffany Augustine. The event was held at the Jenkins Auditorium. (Courtesy of Cooper Memorial Library Association.)

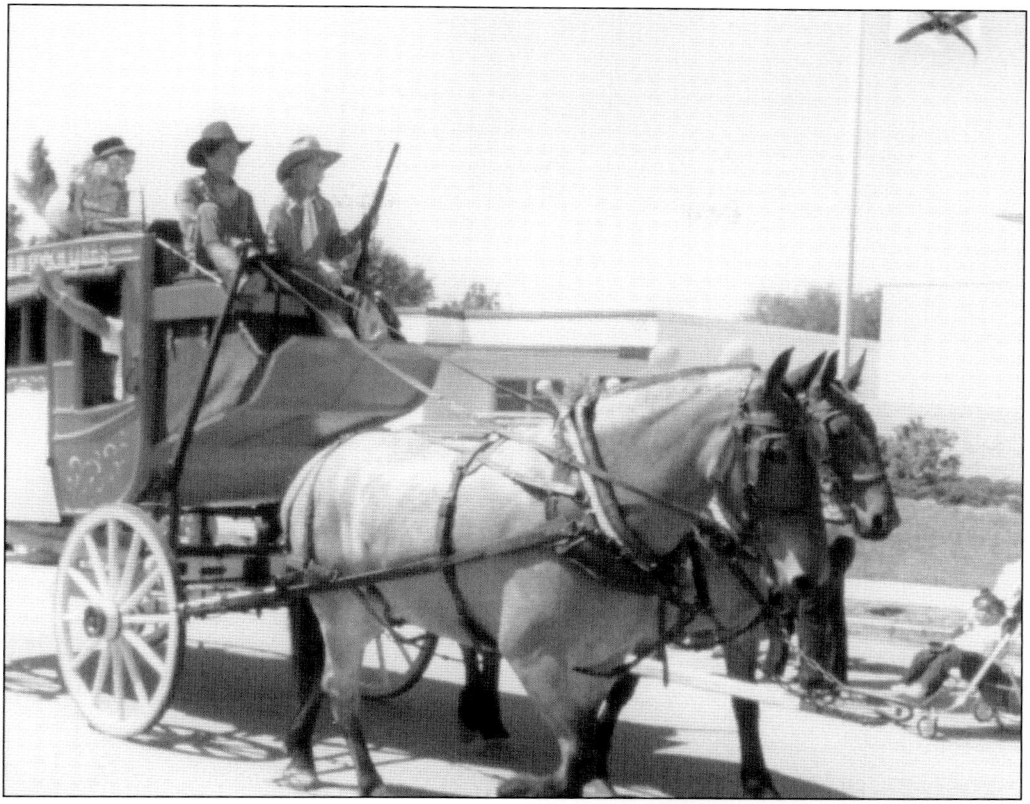

The giant centennial parade included a stagecoach (above), trolley, floats, fire truck, train, antique cars, and the Clermont High School Highlander Band. Several women dressed in historic costumes and carried signs that promoted women in various professions. (Courtesy of Cooper Memorial Library Association.)

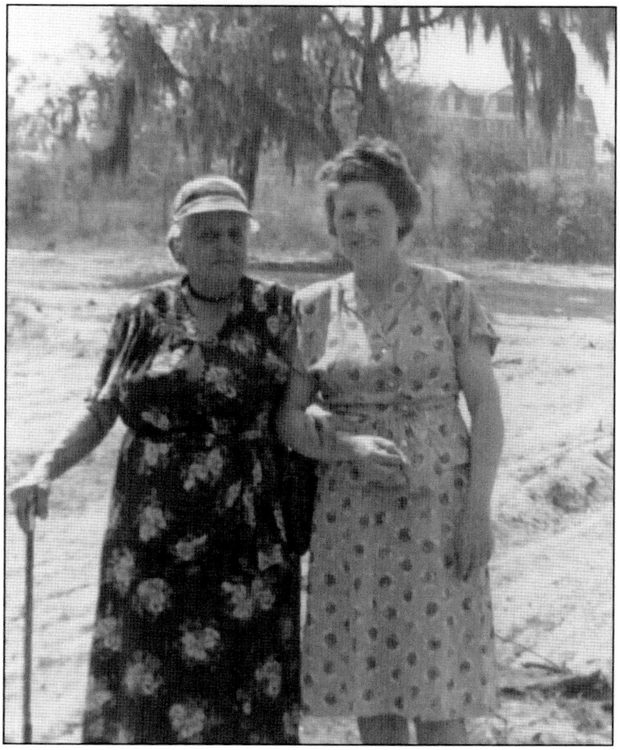

For the centennial, coauthors Miriam Johnson (right) and Rosemary Young (not pictured) wrote *Clermont: Gem of the Hills*. They interviewed more than a dozen longtime residents, such as Hattie Millholland, seen here walking with Johnson in south Clermont near the historic Log House. The exhaustively researched book detailed the city's first 100 years. (Courtesy of the Lake County Historical Society.)

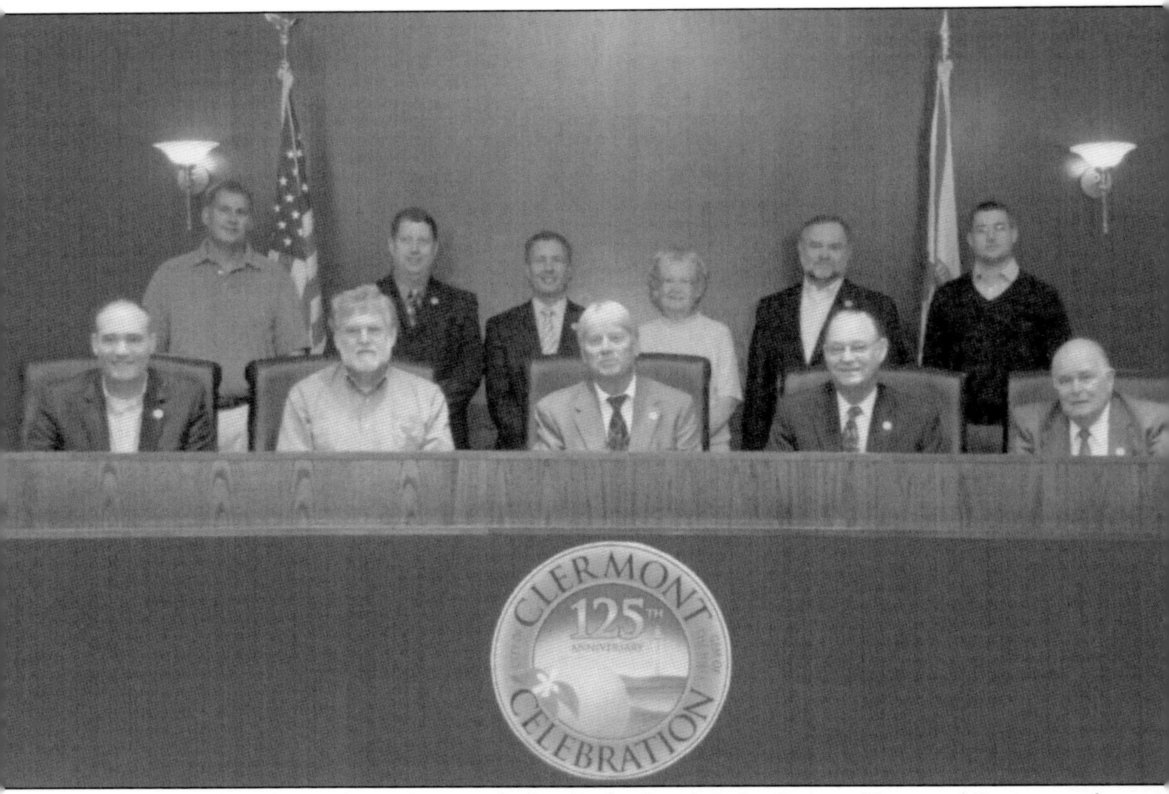


Clermont City Council members worked with the South Lake County Historical Society and a special committee to plan weeklong festivities in October 2009 celebrating the 125th anniversary of the city's founding. Pictured here with the logo from the event are, from left to right, (first row) council member Robert Thompson, council member Keith Mullins, Mayor Harold Turville, council member Ray Goodgame, and council member Jack Hogan; (second row) city staff member Dave Teske, anniversary committee chairman Mike Latham, assistant city manager Darren Gray, South Lake County Historical Society anniversary chair Dolores Gano Walker, city manager Wayne Saunders, and committee marketing chairman Bobby Wesley. Special events included Pioneer Day, the Great Florida Triathlon, an art show, the South Lake Kiwanis Wine Gala, a carnival, fireworks, and a street party with native-Florida rockers Molly Hatchet. Thousands attended the various programs that started on October 14 and culminated with the fireworks display on October 25. (Courtesy of Bonnie Gearhart.)

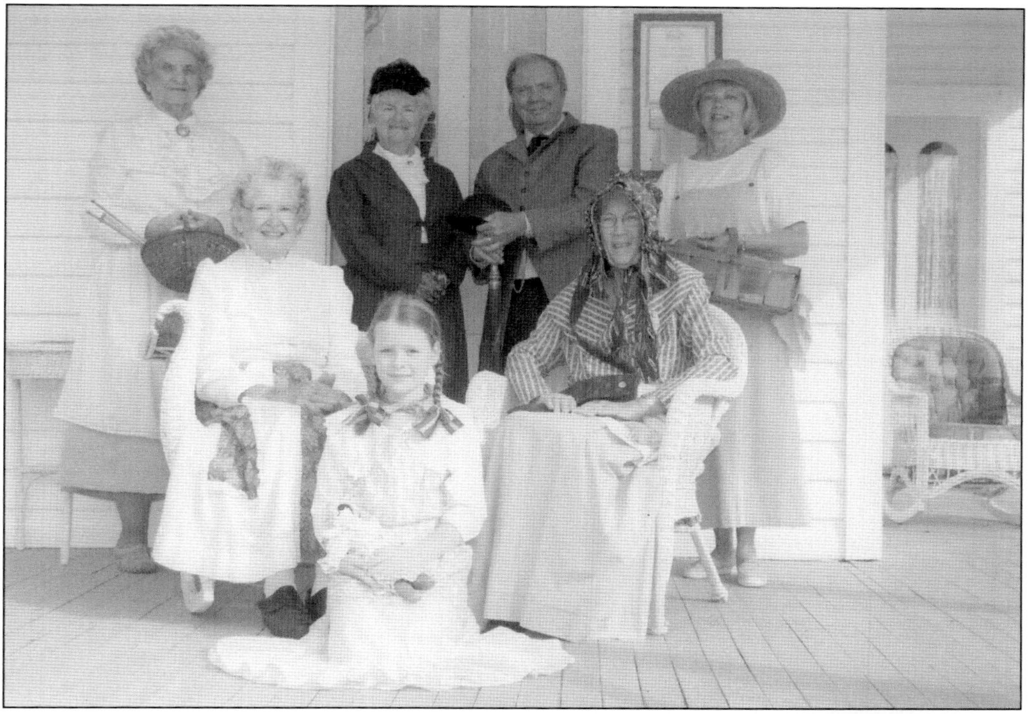

The Historic Village was the main venue for Pioneer Day, part of the 125th anniversary celebrations. Seen here at the restored Alexander Kern home is (first row) Mallory Spivey; (second row) Dolores Gano Walker and Eloise Pitts; (third row) Janet Thomas, Anne Bellehumeur, Tom Bellehumeur, and South Lake County Historical Society president Louise Stockton. The Bellehumeurs were dressed as the home's original owners, Alexander and Eleanor Kern. (Courtesy of Bonnie Gearhart.)

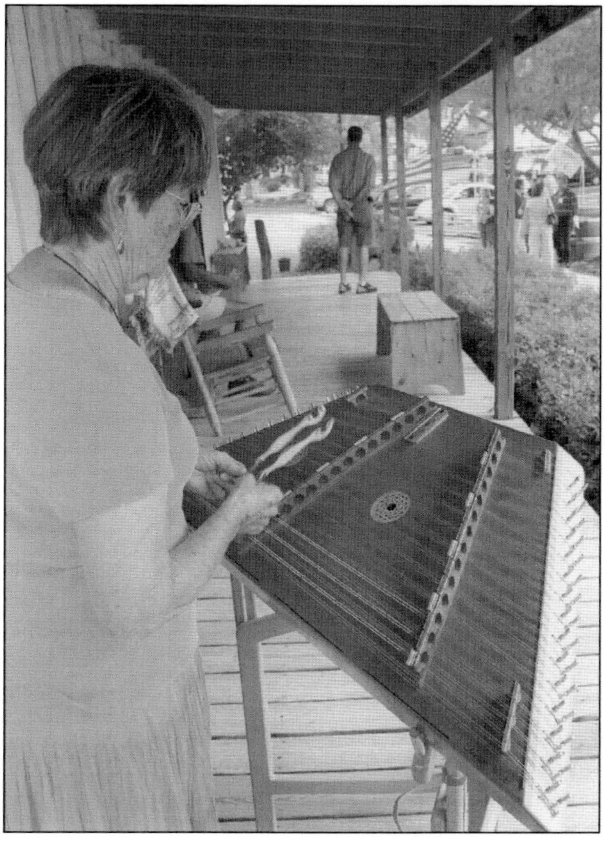

Judy Jackson played the hammered dulcimer as part of the Pioneer Day celebrations. She is seen here on the porch of the restored Townsend home. Other folk arts represented included whittling and weaving, among many others. Groups such as the Kings Ridge Singers sang old-fashioned favorites. (Courtesy of Linda Charlton.)

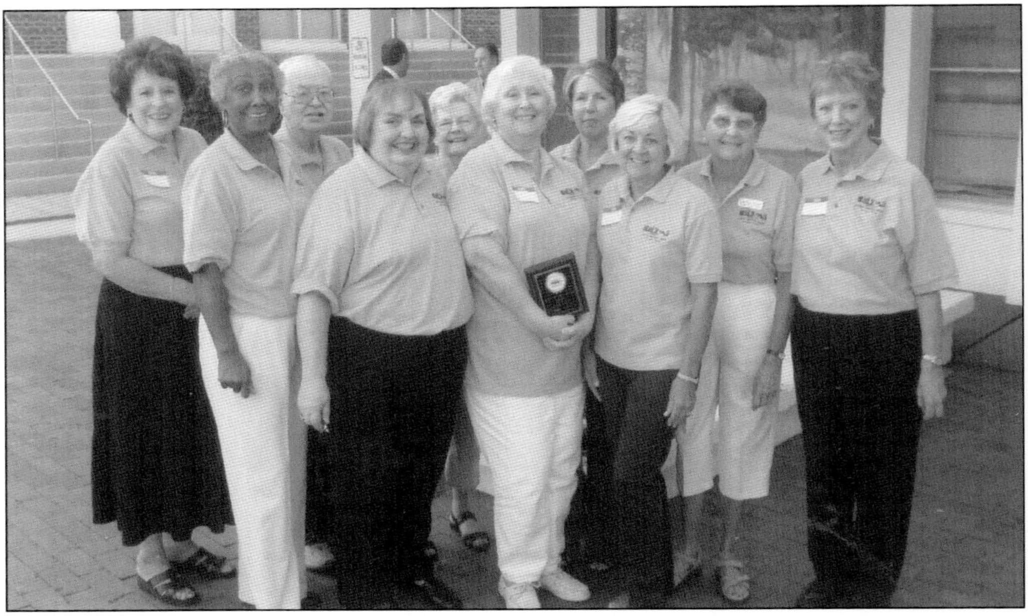

The Clermont Chamber of Commerce honored Friends of Cooper Memorial Library as the outstanding nonprofit organization for 2009. The organization created a calendar with historic photographs from Clermont's past to mark the city's 125th anniversary. From left to right are (first row) Gloria Pasteur, Joyce Neese, president Jody Close, and Kathy Weaver; (second row) Pat VandeVoorde, Richard Neese, Betty Kirby, Judy Beatty, Lucille Gross, and Martha Heinrich. (Courtesy of Friends of Cooper Memorial Library.)

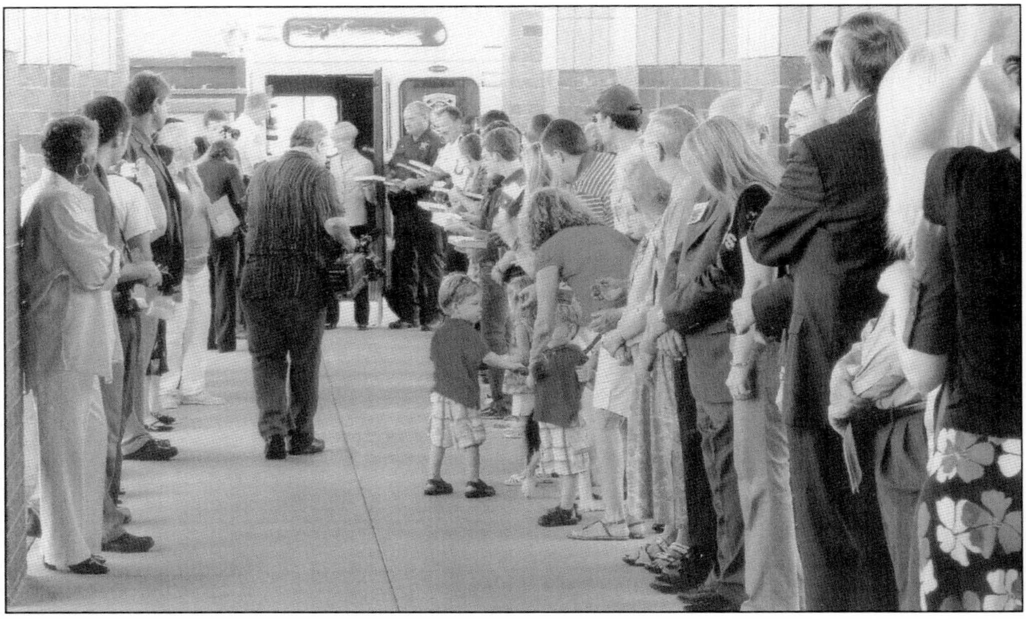

Dignitaries, library staff, and local residents recreated a book brigade as part of the grand opening ceremonies of the new Cooper Memorial Library in October 2009. The event recalled the book brigade of 1980 when residents passed books from person to person between the original library on DeSoto Street to the new location on Montrose Street until all the books were moved. (Courtesy of Lake-Sumter Community College.)

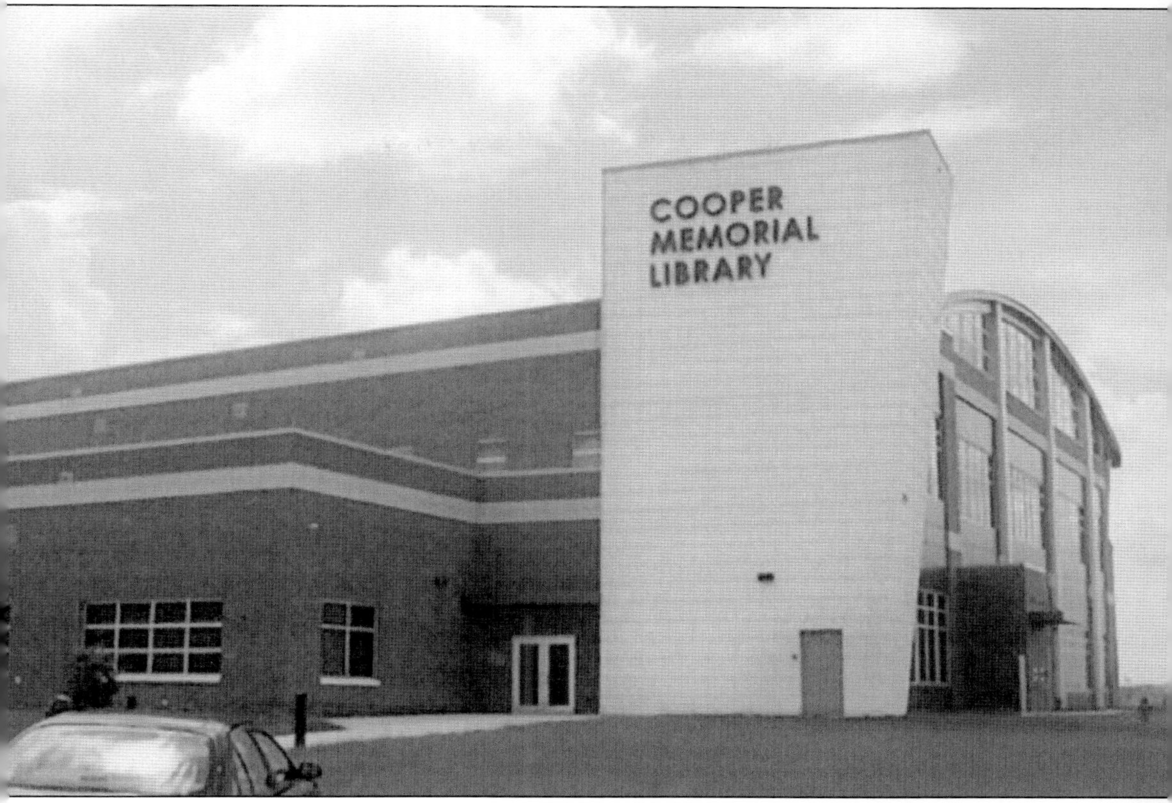


The gleaming new Cooper Memorial Library, the largest library in Lake County, sits atop one of the highest hills in Florida. The $12.7 million, 50,000-square-foot library is the result of a joint partnership between the county's library system, Lake-Sumter Community College, and the University of Central Florida. The library is supported by two volunteer organizations: the Cooper Memorial Library Association, headed by Terry Moherek, and Friends of the Cooper Memorial Library, led by president Jody Close. The author is sharing proceeds from sales of Images of America: *Clermont* with both support groups to honor the library where she got her first library card at age 10 and to continue the historic love of reading shared by Clermont residents. (Courtesy of the Lake County Library System.)

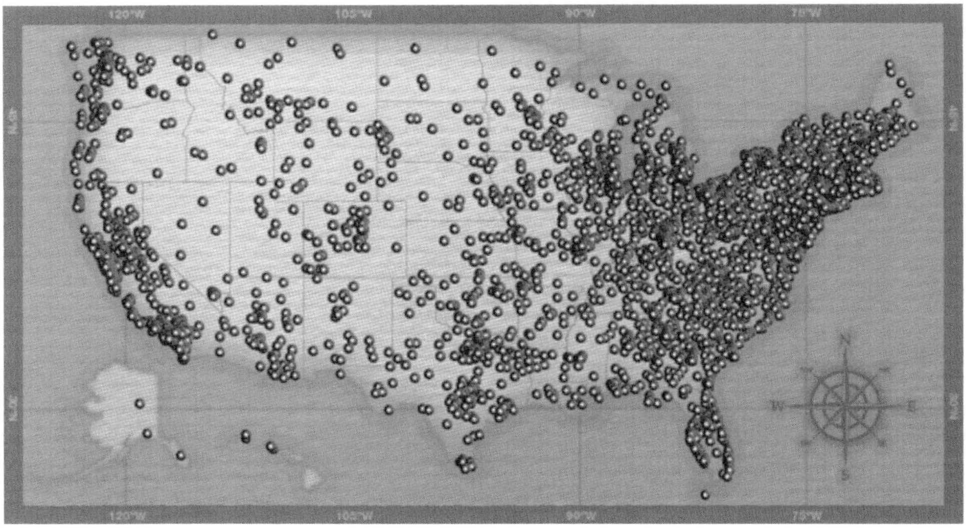